Time of Beauty, Time of Fear

Time of Beauty, Time of Fear

The Romantic Legacy in
the Literature of Childhood

EDITED BY JAMES HOLT MCGAVRAN, JR.

University of Iowa Press, Iowa City

University of Iowa Press, Iowa City 52242

Copyright © 2012 by the University of Iowa Press

www.uiowapress.org

Printed in the United States of America

Design by Ashley Muehlbauer

The University of Iowa Press is a member of Green Press Initiative and is committed to preserving natural resources. Printed on acid-free paper

Library of Congress Cataloging-in-Publication Data

Time of beauty, time of fear: the Romantic legacy in the literature of childhood / edited by James Holt McGavran, Jr.

　　p. cm.

Includes bibliographical references and index.

ISBN 978-1-60938-100-4, 1-60938-100-9 (pbk)

1. Children's literature, English—History and criticism.

2. Children's literature, American—History and criticism.

3. Romanticism. 4. Children in literature. I. McGavran, James Holt.

PR990.T56 2012

820.9′9282—dc23   2011042574

"Fair seed-time had my soul, and I grew up

Fostered alike by beauty and by fear"

—WILLIAM WORDSWORTH, *The Prelude* (1850) 1:301–02

Contents

Acknowledgments

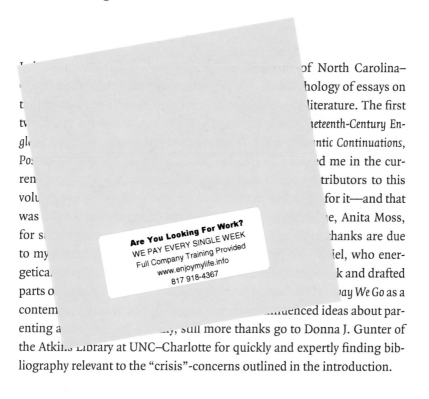

of North Carolina–
hology of essays on
literature. The first
teenth-Century En-
gl intic Continuations,
Po d me in the cur-
ren tributors to this
volu for it—and that
was e, Anita Moss,
for s hanks are due
to my iel, who ener-
getica k and drafted
parts o ay We Go as a
contem uenced ideas about par-
enting a ..y, still more thanks go to Donna J. Gunter of
the Atkins Library at UNC–Charlotte for quickly and expertly finding bibliography relevant to the "crisis"-concerns outlined in the introduction.

Introduction

JAMES HOLT MCGAVRAN, JR.,
AND JENNIFER SMITH DANIEL

As you watch Sam Mendes's 2009 sleeper hit film *Away We Go*, the Romantic poets, children's literature, and childhood studies are not likely to be the first source connections that you make. Burt and Verona (John Krasinski and Maya Rudolph), a thirty-something couple with a baby on the way, decide to visit old friends and relatives to see how they are raising their children. Their journey takes them from the Southwest to the Great Lakes, from Montreal to Miami. What they learn is that—staring down heredity, environment, and chance—they must determine for themselves as best they can what their parental roles should be. The couple might look to their own parents as examples, but in Burt and Verona's case, the role models have left the building: Burt's parents inanely decide to move to Belgium a month before the birth of their first grandchild, and Verona's parents died when she was twenty-two, possibly in a wreck—a terrible, aching loss she has not been able to confront fully after more than a decade. But early on, almost before we know what to make of it, British Romantic Big Daddy William Wordsworth makes an appearance, channeled through American Romantic Big Daddy Mark Twain.

Burt starts this process of discovery before they begin the journey. While speaking about their unborn daughter, Burt says, "I really want her to have an epic kind of childhood. I want her to run along streams and to know how to work a canoe, be able to entertain herself outside. I want her childhood to be Huck Finn-y. You know?" And Verona, in a first reticent allusion to her own girlhood, responds simply, "Yeah, I had that," which Burt reinforces with "Yeah, exactly" (*Away We Go* DVD). After Burt says this, the camera frames their car driving through a rugged, mountainous Colorado landscape complete with snow remnants and fog—perhaps an intentional contrast to the film's final scenes by Florida waters. At this early moment, the film gives us a visual metaphor for the kind of encounters Burt wants his daughter to have in nature and thus foreshadows that nature itself will become a key player in their lives. Not that such encounters are always joyful or even pleasant: like that of his creator, Huck's own childhood was anything but pleasant, and Wordsworth preceded Twain in recounting in *The Prelude* early memories that were "fostered alike by beauty and by fear" (1850 1:302). But it seems Burt would rather his daughter have a childhood free to explore, learn, and even suffer than to keep her cooped up in the superstructured spaces of contemporary society.

During their travels, the couple finds themselves confronted with a variety of families—all hurting in one way or another. The first visit, with Verona's former boss, Lily, in Phoenix, reveals a grotesquely dysfunctional group, literally and emotionally dehydrated in the burning Arizona sun. Lily and her husband, Lowell, take their preteenage children to the dog races—perhaps a metaphor for life as they live it—and alternate between ignoring and insulting them. Escaping, Burt and Verona pay a quick visit to Verona's younger and more extroverted sister, Grace, in Tucson, and there is a surprisingly moving scene in which the sisters visit a home remodeling center and Grace insists that Verona climb into a bathtub with her, as they did in their girlhood, and then begs her to tell stories of their parents: "You're the big sister. You remember more." Verona brushes her off because she is not yet ready to remember, let alone speak of it. The second family, in Madison, Wisconsin, are pretentious and judgmental academics whose New Age beliefs border on child abuse in the form of protracted breastfeeding and bundle bags since they abhor the idea of strollers that "push the child away from the parent." Finally, arriving in Montreal to visit old college friends, Burt and Verona find what seems to be a happily functioning family. In spite of a charming multiracial group of adopted children, however, there lingers the pain of infertility since the wife, after repeated miscarriages, still longs to give birth. The last family Burt and Verona visit is Burt's brother, Courtney, who calls unexpectedly from Miami while they are still in Canada. They immediately decide to fly south to help him deal with his wife's sudden desertion of him and their daughter, Annabelle.

Ultimately, Burt and Verona settle in her childhood home on a lake northwest of Orlando (the house in the film is located in Leesburg, Florida, according to the film voiceover) that could just as well be on the banks of Huck's Mississippi. Before they walk through the double doors of the elegant but rundown two-story house, Verona pauses on the porch, gathering her emotions and thoughts. Across the empty foyer is another set of double doors that overlooks the water. As Burt opens these, Verona begins to move into the house, walking through the foyer and stopping by Burt; then they sit in the back doorway framed by the house, with water, foliage, and Spanish moss showing through the opening. This view complements the previous shot of the Rockies, and while the Deep South setting is as far from Colorado as it is from the English Lake District, the Wordsworthian connections involving landscape, memory, and self-fashioning are clearly made. As Verona reenters her parental home, herself so visibly pregnant, she is reborn into her future from her past in a moving final frame for which she has prepared herself and Burt in Miami by suddenly telling him, for the first time, a beautiful memory of her early life with her parents and Grace, when the women of the family tied artificial fruits on the husband-father's stunted orange tree, making it a symbol of life and family love. Thus the movie ends as Verona reclaims her childhood, with Burt's loving sympathy and support, determined that from now on, to paraphrase and regender one of Wordsworth's best-known short lyrics, "The Child"—both her own child-self and the daughter she is carrying—will become "Mother of the Woman" (see Wordsworth's "My Heart Leaps Up," l. 7, *Oxford Wordsworth* 246). By choosing to move into the house, a symbol of both life (their unborn child) and death (her parents), they ground themselves in the future and the past in a way that Wordsworth, an orphan from the age of thirteen, would surely have understood.

It is now two and a half centuries since Jean-Jacques Rousseau first wrote so evocatively of the freedom of natural man in *Social Contract* (1762) and of experiential education in *Émile* (1762). His emphasis on the early years as a crucial part of life drove the Romantic reconceptualization of childhood articulated by Wordsworth, Coleridge, Blake, and others—the idea that children have special knowledge to teach their elders as well as the other way around. Wordsworth's assertion in the *Intimations Ode* (1807) that children come to earth "trailing clouds of glory" from God

(l. 64, *Oxford Wordsworth* 299) has continued to haunt Western literature and culture—too much, really, since posterity has not sufficiently recognized Wordsworth's concomitant awareness of the toils and dangers children—and their parents—have always had to face. This dual awareness guides, though in widely varying ways and degrees, the writers of the essays in this collection. In his magisterial *Children and Childhood in Western Society Since 1500* (2005), Hugh Cunningham summarizes: "Romanticism embedded in the European and American mind a sense of the importance of childhood, a belief that childhood should be happy, and a hope that the qualities of childhood, if they could be preserved in adulthood, might help redeem the adult world" (72). He also emphasizes that Romanticism "was much more influential as a body of ideas than as an active force in day-to-day child rearing" (72)—in other words, that Romantic ideas floated freely beyond as well as within the struggle to articulate what was good or bad about parenting or childhood in any particular generation. Later, in his conclusion, Cunningham writes: "The popularity of the ideas of . . . the Romantic poets . . . indicates the beginning of a period when children began to cease to be seen as the embodiment of souls in need of salvation, and became instead either like the young of some domestic pet in need of habit training or like a seed which should be allowed to grow naturally" (202). The same conflict between habit training and seed planting shows up with a different face in *The Making of the Modern Child*, Andrew O'Malley's materialist study of middle-class childhood and parenting in the Romantic Age. O'Malley forefronts Locke's tabula rasa and the rational knowledge late-eighteenth-century parents wanted for their children rather than the Rousseauvian child of nature (4–5), arguing too that the Wordsworthian escape into nature is an upper-class privilege unavailable to most children at that time or ours, "a nostalgic conservatism" (128); still, he acknowledges that "a new brand of imaginative, fantasy writing for children" began to appear in England by the turn of the nineteenth century (131) and reached its zenith in the Victorian Age (135). The habit training/seed planting controversy continues in the United States today in the clashes between "teaching for the test"—what children need to know to game their societies and get into a good college—and holistic, imagination-based teaching that opens inner and outer worlds to the young. Similarly, in *Huck's Raft: A History of American Childhood* (2004), Steven Mintz references Samuel

Clemens's own rugged early years in Hannibal, Missouri (2), to argue that there never was a purely golden age of childhood. Mintz emphasizes that childrearing has always been dominated by socioeconomic status, but also by whatever ideas were prominent in any given period—Puritan ideas of control of the child's sinful nature, Romantic-Victorian ideas of loving and protecting the child's innocence, contemporary ideas based on mass media and sociological-pedagogical research. He emphasizes the importance, from the nineteenth century forward, of the "Romantic vision, which viewed children as symbols of purity, spontaneity, and emotional expressiveness, who were free from adult inhibitions" (76) and sees Huck Finn's raft as a complex image of "peril and freedom," symbolic of the child's danger amid the currents of societal forces, and simultaneously, of "a carefree time of adventure." He concludes that children need the "odyssey of psychological self-discovery and growth" (5) that can only come with risking the currents as Huck did in his journey down the Mississippi with Jim. Which brings us back to Burt's wish, the driving force behind *Away We Go*, for that "Huck Finn-y childhood," his desire to set his daughter free on society's and nature's currents in hopes she can find and navigate her own direction in life.

Some recent scholars seem to want, from a variety of critical stances—Marxist, poststructuralist, psychoanalytic—to dismantle the Romantic concept that childhood is a special time, lamenting that childhood is dead or in crisis or positioning the Child as an Other sealed away both in time and within the brain of the adult. Few of them recognize how deeply the sense of crisis—of repeated threats to children and childhood across time, class, race, and gender—is embedded in the Romantic concept itself; to phrase it alternatively, carefree childhood is a myth, and not one promulgated by Wordsworth, at least not intentionally. As Mintz has stated it, "We cling to a fantasy that once upon a time childhood and youth were years of carefree adventure, despite the fact that for most young people in the past, growing up was anything but easy" (2). Momentum for the crisis-notion may partly originate in Marxist uber-critic Jerome McGann's powerful attacks on what he calls "the Romantic ideology," but cycles of crisis-angst seem rampant in all the multidisciplinary scholarly writers on children's issues—to the point that crisis seems more permanent than cyclical. Much investigated concerns today include the possibly deleterious role of technology, including television, video games, social media, and the internet (see for example Livingstone and Brake, Hu, Lee, Linn, Matyjas, Mesch, Wilson); the redefinition of parenting to include single parents, grandparents, and same-sex couples (DeHart and Altshuler, "Family Pediatrics Report," H. Demo, Hanson and Lynch, and Smith-Ruiz); the growing gap between rich and poor in America and much of the rest of the developed world (Boudway, Wax, "More or Less Equal?"); the childhood obesity epidemic (Brandes, Cecil-Karb and Grogan-Taylor, Chernin, Dozier et al., Jordan, and Zimmerman and Bell); and the debate about education versus training for the test spawned by the second Bush administration's passage of the No Child Left Behind Act of 2001 (Baker and Johnston, Murnane and Papay, Finkel, Amrein-Beardsley, Nichols and Berliner, Smyth, Darling-Hammond, Nichols et al., Altshuler and Schmautz). This same research, however, suggests that the Romantic-driven desire to see childhood as a special time of life and protect it still forms a strong current in our contemporary culture, perhaps even driving the researchers and crisis-prophets who hear the death rattles. Harvard researchers Richard J. Murnane and John P. Papay, summarizing teachers' reactions to "No Child," write passionately of the disconnect between the teachers' commitment to their students and the kind of instruction they have been required to provide:

> In our view, most people who enter the teaching profession do so because they want to improve the lives of children. . . . A significant number of teachers, particularly those working in under-resourced schools serving high concentrations of disadvantaged children, felt great conflict between what they were told to do to raise test scores and what they felt they should do to best serve children. (164–65)

Wanting to improve the lives of children may or may not have its roots in a Romantic-born feeling about the importance of childhood (I strongly believe it does), but for these teachers, "No Child" clearly has nothing to do with improving the lives of children. British pedagogue David Halpin has recently argued (2006, 2008) for the importance for teachers of keeping a view of childhood based on the Romantic imagination ("Why a Romantic," "Pedagogy"). And British sociologist Mary Jane Kehily (2010) examined "a range of cultural texts: media reports, policy documents, popular commentaries on childhood and pregnancy magazines" to conclude that the "childhood-in-crisis" idea grows in adults' minds as they themselves grow increasingly insecure in the extremely rapid pace of technological change in the twenty-first century. She sees the possible emergence of "a reconfigured approach to childrearing in late modernity that blends Romantic ideals with technological advances" (172, 183)—partly, no doubt, because it becomes more and more unimaginable to separate children or their parents from said technology.

Does childhood become an inaccessible or incommunicable Other for the adult? Jacqueline Rose's much referenced 1984 psychoanalytic study of *Peter Pan* and the "impossibility of children's fiction"—*so* much referenced that it was reissued with a new introduction by Rose eight years later—led to the "discovery" that the child could be viewed as an Other, so great was/ is the gap between the child and the adult. Just as Edward Saïd argued in *Orientalism* (1978), his early classic of postcolonial theory, about the West's controlling gaze at the East, Perry Nodelman argued in 1992, referencing Saïd, that adults create the gap between themselves and children as a way of dominating them—colonizing them, in effect. In 2000 Thomas Travisano added to this by invoking W. E. B. DuBois's argument from *The Souls of Black Folk* (1903) about the "two-ness" of the African-American experience, the inhabitant of the dark body relentlessly victimized and controlled by the white gaze. Although at first Nodelman thought Rose had gone too far, by 2010, in a special issue of the *Children's Literature Association Quarterly* commemorating a quarter-century of Rose's influence, he was ready to acknowledge how much his and others' ideas about the child as Other originated in one statement of hers: "If children's fiction builds an image of the child inside the book, it does so in order to secure the child who is outside the book, the one who does not come so easily within its grasp" (Rose 2, qtd. Nodelman "Former Editor's" 231). In the same issue of the *Quarterly*, David Rudd argues that a Bakhtinian reading of what Rose called the "space between" adult and child would allow travel through that space in a dialogic process, not an isolation of the child in the adult mind but a back-and-forth between older and younger selves ("Return to Rose" 294), thus interrogating Rose's Lacanian view of the young child caught in the mirror stage, separated from the mother's Imaginary but with nowhere to go but into the Symbolic adult male world of words and systems. Working outside the controversy stirred by Rose, influenced instead by the memory research of Harvard psychologist Daniel Schacter, Beth Lau (2002) challenges the Freudian concepts often used by literary critics, including earlier generations of Wordsworthians, who try to understand memory only in terms of repression and obsession. Lau shows how self-formation may rely on the shaping and reshaping of one's own memories to build and rebuild a unified self (682) and uses Wordsworthian texts that show memory to be far more fluid and changeable than earlier critics had assumed. What can surprise and delight the theory-jaded academician even today is the way Wordsworth himself articulates not only the adult longing for a lost childhood self but the very kind of dialogism and mental revaluation Rudd and Lau bring to the discussion. In a key passage from Book Two of *The Prelude*, Wordsworth speaks of navigating this gap between the adult and the child within the self, not to "secure the child" as Rose put it, because that is impossible, but to commit to building and rebuilding the bridge that is always de-/re-forming:

> A tranquillising spirit presses now
> On my corporeal frame, so wide appears
> The vacancy between me and those days
> Which yet have such self-presence in my mind,
> That musing on them, often do I seem
> Two consciousnesses, conscious of myself
> And of some other Being.
> (1850, 2:27–33 Norton *Prelude*)

The "tranquillising spirit" coexists in the poetry with the de-tranquillizing awareness of the "two consciousnesses." Here, differing from *Lyrical Ballads* like "We Are Seven" and "Anecdote for Fathers" where he juxtaposes child and adult voices, the sense of interior dialogue is rendered entirely in the voice of the mature speaker; but the sense of a Bakhtinian reciprocity in the mind still comes across clearly in the verse. He does it a little differently in another familiar passage, the "Boy of Windermere" (Book 5 [1850] 364–88), who called to the owls across the lake. The poet writes this "spot of time" atypically in third person, but we know from manuscript revisions that this experience was his (see Norton *Prelude* 492). Then, as if to deepen the gap between the "two consciousnesses," he has the boy die at the age of twelve, and continues:

Fair is the Spot, most beautiful the Vale
Where he was born: the grassy churchyard hangs
Upon a slope above the village school;
And through that churchyard when my way has led
On summer evenings, I believe that there
A long half-hour together I have stood
Mute, looking at the grave in which he lies!
(1850: 391–97)

If childhood ever becomes Other for the adult, Wordsworth seems to be saying as he narrates the boy's death and temporarily shuts poetry down into muteness, it is an alterity that can be regularly explored through memory-writing that traverses, articulates, and reconstructs the spaces between younger and older selves. He further suggests here, as he continues by fondly remembering his adventures with his schooltime friends, that children actually benefit from a sense of being Other to adult institutions and ideologies and that their explorations of the spaces of their lives, whether indoor or outdoor, are absolutely necessary to their growing into adults that have any control over themselves and their worlds. He describes the village church and churchyard where he says the boy is buried; then he exclaims:

May she [the church] long
Behold a race of young ones like to those
With whom I herded!
[. . .]
A race of real children; not too wise,
Too learned, or too good; but wanton, fresh,
And bandied up and down by love and hate;
Not unresentful where self-justified;
Fierce, moody, patient, venturous, modest, shy;
Mad at their sports like withered leaves in winds:
Though doing wrong and suffering, and full oft
Bending beneath our life's mysterious weight
Of pain, and doubt, and fear; yet yielding not
In happiness to the happiest upon earth.
(1850: 406–20)

In a wide-ranging article in *Social and Cultural Geography* (2005), Paul Cloke and Owain Jones of the University of Bristol could well be channeling this passage from *The Prelude*, as well as both Gaston Bachelard's *Poetics of Space* (1962) and Homi Bhabha's *Location of Culture* (1994), to argue that children's habitation of what Cloke and Jones call "disordered spaces" or "between-spaces" helps them finally to create the adults they eventually become: "Children's disordering of space, then, represents a transformative potential for children which is a far cry from the soft criminality which is often inferred from disruption of adult order" (316) and, I suggest, may lead to what Bachelard famously called "felicitous space."

The essays in this collection continue to trace the evolution of the Romantic child in spite of all the above-named menaces and more; they also display careful scholarship, sophisticated use of contemporary literary theory, and close readings of texts while recuperating and analyzing materials from over two centuries of British and other anglophone cultural history. They play off well against each other, both within three traditional historical periods—Romantic, Victorian, and Modern/Postmodern—and across these categories as well. My essay on "Michael" and "Christabel" contests overly glib assumptions about the Romantic child and his/her parents while tying intergenerational conflict to late-twentieth-century psychologists' investigations of kinship tensions and "good-enough" parenting. Malini Roy's essay on angry girls in two Wollstonecraft texts shows the author of the *Vindication of the Rights of Woman* in a Blakean use of multiple voices to urge young girls to challenge their societal subjugation in patriarchal culture. Andrew Smyth deconstructs two texts by Maria Edgeworth to find both commitment and uneasiness in her concern with the education of the lower classes. And Elizabeth Dolan's essay focuses on the complex depictions of slavery in Charlotte Smith's children's books; Smith deplored slavery and wanted to teach children that it was a moral wrong even as she worked hard to secure for her children the money from the sale of one of her father-in-law's slave plantations in Barbados.

In the Victorian Era essays, Elizabeth Gargano argues that the relatively loose structure, use of embedded narratives, and less didactic tone of Mrs. Molesworth's *The Tapestry Room* open up the novel to its child characters' explorations of alternative worlds while still leaving them trapped in the house of traditional British culture. Nicely related in its emphasis on multiple discourses is Dorothy H. McGavran's study of language, truth, and power for adolescent female characters in Elizabeth Gaskell's masterpiece *Wives and Daughters*. The other two essays in this section use painstaking archival research to examine religious, scientific, and other cultural issues in popular writings of the period. Thus Mary Ellis Gibson shows how nineteenth-century missionary literature for children served the interests of both church and empire, while Jochen Petzold studies changing views of the boyish practice of "bird-nesting" (the stealing of birds' nests)—from sin to adventure to science—to bring out Victorian reactions to the cultural upheavals brought on by Darwinian evolutionary theory.

The essays on more recent writers look seriously into the question of Romantic carryovers lurking in the children's literature and popular culture of our times. Richard Flynn takes a nostalgic but rigorous look at the neo-Romantic dreams promulgated and fostered by the folksinging voices of the 1960s and what has followed in their wake, both personally and politically, as our society struggles to find its way in the twenty-first century. Claudia Mills's essay reviews major elements of Jean-Jacques Rousseau's revisionary analyses of nature, freedom, and childhood while finding important Rousseauvian echoes and dissonances in recent children's books on homeschooling. Jan Susina studies the *Teletubbies* TV series he originally viewed with his young son and finds both Romantic echoes and a technological serpent lurking in the rural garden. Finally, Roderick McGillis argues against the deconstructionist, anti-Romantic approach of Jerome McGann and others to find, as does Susina, both neo-Romantic and anti-Romantic elements uneasily suspended in the text and illustrations of Alan Moore's *Promethea* graphic novels.

WORKS CITED

Altshuler, Sandra J., and Tresa Schmautz. "No Hispanic Student Left Behind: The Consequences of 'High Stakes' Testing." *Children and Schools* 28.1 (2006): 5. *MasterFILE Premier*. EBSCO. Web. 30 Jan. 2011.

Amrein-Beardsley, Audrey. "The Unintended, Pernicious Consequences of "Staying the Course" on the United States' No Child Left Behind Policy." *International*

Journal of Education Policy and Leadership 4.1–11 (2009): 1–13. Education Research Complete. EBSCO. Web. 30 Jan. 2011.

Away We Go. Directed by Sam Mendes. Focus Features, 2009.

Bachelard, Gaston. The Poetics of Space. Trans. Maria Jolas. Boston: Beacon, 1969.

Baker, Melissa, and Pattie Johnston. "The Impact of Socioeconomic Status on High Stakes Testing Reexamined." Journal of Instructional Psychology 37.3 (2010): 193. MasterFILE Premier. EBSCO. Web. 30 Jan. 2011.

Bhabha, Homi. The Location of Culture. London: Routledge, 1994.

Boudway, Ira. "The Rich Get Richer . . . and You Know the Rest." Bloomberg Businessweek 4198 (2010): 33–34. Business Source Premier. EBSCO. Web. 10 Mar. 2011.

Brandes, A. H. "Leisure Time Activities and Obesity in School-Based Inner City African American and Hispanic Children." Pediatric Nursing 33.2 (2007): 97. CINAHL Plus with Full Text. EBSCO. Web. 30 Jan. 2011.

Cecil-Karb, Rebecca, and Andrew Grogan-Kaylor. "Childhood Body Mass Index in Community Context: Neighborhood Safety, Television Viewing, and Growth Trajectories of BMI." Health and Social Work 34.3 (2009): 169–77. ERIC. EBSCO. Web. 30 Jan. 2011.

Chernin, Ariel. "Television Viewing and Childhood Overweight: Evidence and Explanations." Pediatrics for Parents 25.7/8 (2009): 29–31. Health Source—Consumer Edition. EBSCO. Web. 30 Jan. 2011.

Cloke, Paul, and Owain Jones. "'Unclaimed Territory': Childhood and Disordered Space(s)." Social and Cultural Geography 6.3 (2005): 311–33.

Cunningham, Hugh. Children and Childhood in Western Society Since 1500. Harlow, UK: Pearson Longman, 2005.

Darling-Hammond, Linda. "Race, Inequality and Educational Accountability: The Irony of 'No Child Left Behind.'" Race, Ethnicity and Education 10.3 (2007): 245–60. Academic Search Premier. EBSCO. Web. 30 Jan. 2011.

DeHart, Dana D., and Sandra J. Altshuler. "Violence Exposure among Children of Incarcerated Mothers." Child and Adolescent Social Work Journal 26 (2009): 467–79.

Dozier, D., et al. "Brand Name Logo Recognition of Fast Food and Healthy Food Among Children." Journal of Community Health 34.1 (2009): 73–78. Social Work Abstracts. EBSCO. Web. 20 Jan. 2011.

Du Bois, W. E. B. The Souls of Black Folk: Essays and Sketches. Electronic resource. Chapel Hill: U of North Carolina P, 2001.

"Family Pediatrics Report of the Task Force on the Family." Pediatrics 111.6 (2003): 1541. MasterFILE Premier. EBSCO. Web. 10 Mar. 2011.

Finkel, Ed. "Black Children Still Left Behind." *District Administration* 46.10 (2010): 26. *MasterFILE Premier*. EBSCO. Web. 30 Jan. 2011.

H. Demo, David. "Children's Experience of Family Diversity." *National Forum* 80.3 (2000): 16. *MasterFILE Premier*. EBSCO. Web. 10 Mar. 2011.

Halpin, David. "Pedagogy and the Romantic Imagination." *British Journal of Educational Studies* 65.1 (2008): 59–75.

———. "Why a Romantic Conception of Education Matters." *Oxford Review of Education* 32.3 (2006): 325–45.

Hanson, Marci J., and Eleanor W. Lynch. "Family Diversity: Implications for Policy and Practice." *Topics in Early Childhood Special Education* 12.3 (1992): 283. *MasterFILE Premier*. EBSCO. Web. 10 Mar. 2011.

Hu, Mu, and Daniel McDonald. "Social Internet Use, Trait Loneliness, and Mood Loneliness." *Conference Papers—International Communication Association* (2008): 1–47. *Communication and Mass Media Complete*. EBSCO. Web. 30 Jan. 2011.

Jordan, Amy B. "Heavy Television Viewing and Childhood Obesity." *Journal of Children and Media* 1.1 (2007): 45–54. *Communication and Mass Media Complete*. EBSCO. Web. 30 Jan. 2011.

Kehily, Mary Jane. "Childhood in Crisis? Tracing the Contours of 'Crisis' and Its Impact upon Contemporary Parenting Practices." *Media, Culture and Society* 32.2 (2010): 171–85.

Kirkorian, Heather L., Ellen A. Wartella, and Daniel R. Anderson. "Media and Young Children's Learning." *Future of Children* 18.1 (2008): 39–61. ERIC. EBSCO. Web. 30 Jan. 2011.

Lau, Beth. "Wordsworth and Current Memory Research." *Studies in English Literature, 1500–1900* 42.4 (2002): 675–92.

Lee, Sook Jung. "Online Communication and Adolescent Social Ties: Who Benefits More from Internet Use?" *Journal of Computer-Mediated Communication* 14.3 (2009): 509–31. *Communication and Mass Media Complete*. EBSCO. Web. 30 Jan. 2011.

Linn, Susan. "Too Much and Too Many: How Commercialism and Screen Technology Combine to Rob Children of Creative Play." *Exchange: The Early Childhood Leaders' Magazine Since 1978* 186 (2009): 45–48. ERIC. EBSCO. Web. 30 Jan. 2011.

Literature and the Child: Romantic Continuations, Postmodern Contestations. Ed. James Holt McGavran. Iowa City: U of Iowa P, 1999.

Livingstone, Sonia, and David R. Brake. "On the Rapid Rise of Social Networking Sites: New Findings and Policy Implications." *Children and Society* 24.1 (2010): 75–83. *Academic Search Premier*. EBSCO. Web. 30 Jan. 2011.

Matyjas, Bożena. "Cyberculture: Dangers for Childhood." *New Educational Review* 16.3/4 (2008): 195–208. *Education Research Complete*. EBSCO. Web. 30 Jan. 2011.

McGann, Jerome J. *The Romantic Ideology: A Critical Investigation*. Chicago: U of Chicago P, 1983.

Mesch, Gustavo S. "Family Characteristics and Intergenerational Conflicts over the Internet." *Information, Communication and Society* 9.4 (2006): 473–95. *Communication and Mass Media Complete*. EBSCO. Web. 30 Jan. 2011.

Mintz, Steven. *Huck's Raft: A History of American Childhood*. Cambridge, MA: Harvard UP, 2004.

"More or Less Equal?." *Economist* 390.8625 (2009): 11–13. *Academic Search Premier*. EBSCO. Web. 10 Mar. 2011.

Murnane, Richard J., and John P. Papay. "Teachers' Views on No Child Left Behind: Support for the Principles, Concerns about the Practices." *Journal of Economic Perspectives* 24.3 (2010): 151–66. *EconLit with Full Text*. EBSCO. Web. 30 Jan. 2011.

Nichols, Joe, et al. "Robbing Elementary Students of Their Childhood: The Perils of No Child Left Behind." *Education* 128.1 (2007): 56. *MasterFILE Premier*. EBSCO. Web. 30 Jan. 2011.

Nichols, Sharon L., and David C. Berliner. "Testing the Joy Out of Learning." *Educational Leadership* 65.6 (2008): 14. *MasterFILE Premier*. EBSCO. Web. 30 Jan. 2011.

Nodelman, Perry. "Former Editor's Comments: Or, the Possibility of Growing Wiser." *Children's Literature Association Quarterly* 35.3 (2010): 230–42.

———. "The Other: Orientalism, Colonialism, and Children's Literature." *Children's Literature Association Quarterly* 17 (1992): 29–35.

O'Malley, Andrew. *The Making of the Modern Child: Children's Literature and Childhood in the Late Eighteenth Century*. New York: Routledge, 2003.

Romanticism and Children's Literature in Nineteenth-Century England. Ed. James Holt McGavran, Jr. Athens: U of Georgia P, 2009.

Rose, Jacqueline. *The Case of Peter Pan, or the Impossibility of Children's Fiction*. Philadelphia: U of Pennsylvania P, 1992.

Rudd, David. "Children's Literature and the Return to Rose." *Children's Literature Association Quarterly* 35.3 (2010): 290–310.

Saïd, Edward W. *Orientalism*. New York: Pantheon, 1978.

Smith-Ruiz, Dorothy. "African-American Grandmothers Providing Extensive Care to Their Grandchildren: Socio-Demographic and Health Determinants of Life Satisfaction." *Journal of Sociology and Social Welfare* 35 (2008): 29–52.

Smyth, Theoni Soublis. "Who Is No Child Left Behind Leaving Behind?." *Clearing House* 81.3 (2008): 133. *MasterFILE Premier*. EBSCO. Web. 30 Jan. 2011.

Travisano, Thomas. "Of Dialectic and Divided Consciousnesses: Intersections Between Children's Literature and Childhood Studies." *Children's Literature* 28 (2000): 22–29.

Wax, Amy L. "Engines of Inequality: Class, Race, and Family Structure." *Family Law Quarterly* 41.3 (2007): 567–99. *Academic Search Premier*. EBSCO. Web. 10 Mar. 2011.

Wilson, Barbara J. "Media and Children's Aggression, Fear, and Altruism." *Future of Children* 18.1 (2008): 87–118. *Education Research Complete*. EBSCO. Web. 30 Jan. 2011.

Wordsworth, William. *The Prelude: 1799, 1805, 1850*. Ed. Jonathan Wordsworth, M. H. Abrams, and Stephen Gill. New York: Norton, 1979.

———. *Oxford Authors Wordsworth*. Ed. Stephen Gill. Oxford: Oxford UP, 1984.

Zimmerman, Frederick J., and Janice F. Bell. "Associations of Television Content Type and Obesity in Children." *American Journal of Public Health* 100.2 (2010): 334. *MasterFILE Premier*. EBSCO. Web. 30 Jan. 2011.

JAMES HOLT MCGAVRAN, JR.

Missing But Presumed Alive

Lost Children of Lost Parents in Two Major Romantic Poems, "Michael" and "Christabel"

William Wordsworth's "Ode: Intimations of Immortality from Recollections of Early Childhood," the Ur-text behind so much "classical" children's literature—and perhaps too much children's literature criticism—casts long, dark shadows in which stalk the monsters that always devour childhood innocence, simplicity, and spirituality. True, Wordsworth essentializes the child as a heavenly visitant, apostrophizing the newborn, "Mighty Prophet, Seer Blest!" But the "Ode" also prophesies the dangers that lie in wait for these angel-children, showing how parents and other adults, often but not always with the best intentions, drive the young to subterfuge or despair by forcing them to play all the parts their secular society requires, "as if . . . [their] whole vocation / were endless imitation," and thus setting them "blindly with . . . [their] blessedness at strife" (ll. 114, 106–07, 128 *Oxford Wordsworth* 300). In *Lyrical Ballads*, Wordsworth praises little children like the girl in "We Are Seven" and the boy in "Anecdote for Fathers" who subvert the attempts of bullying adults to teach them to think, speak, and act correctly, thus perhaps holding on if only temporarily to "the hour / Of splendor in the grass, of glory in the flower" that the poet himself so splendidly invokes in the "Ode" (ll. 180–81 *Oxford Wordsworth* 302). And critics Catherine Robson and Judith Plotz have reminded us that in the first two books of *The Prelude*, recreating his own boyhood self, he presents a sensitive, sometimes spiritual but sometimes lawbreaking good-bad boy (Robson 17–18; Plotz 45–47; see also McGavran, "Wordsworth, Lost Boys . . ." 131), almost a Lake District Huck Finn, who finds both sublimity and morality through his early experiences in nature that will guide him later when he is handed the various scripts society expects him to learn by heart: the university student, the city dweller, the political activist (see *Prelude* Books Three, Seven, and Nine through Eleven respectively).

But Luke and Christabel, children respectively of Wordsworth's sturdy old shepherd, Michael, and Samuel Taylor Coleridge's whiny old lord of the castle, Sir Leoline, neither act the acceptable parts nor have the strength to script alternative selves. Instead of trailing "clouds of glory / From God" (ll. 64–65 *Oxford Wordsworth* 299) like the child in the "Ode," by the end of their respective texts, "Michael" and "Christabel," they seem possessed by demons. Like conjoined twins with a shared heart of darkness, in spite of their differences of sex and class, they grow up seemingly snug and safe only to be lost to parents who must have thought—on a mountain, in a castle—to protect them from the evil of the world, to give them a childhood while they learned to be grownups. Beautiful, promising ingenues as their stories begin, they yield like Joseph Conrad's Kurtz a century later to both internal and external temptation, committing transgressions that alienate them from themselves and their parents, while the latter cannot rescue them and indeed share in the responsibility for their abrupt and terrifying declines. Cutting through the obvious surface differences between Wordsworth's wet, windy mountaintop naturalism and Coleridge's spooky Lenten gothicism, both texts, far from child-worship, destabilize any simplistic reading of Romantic childhood to call parenting and ultimately kinship itself into question, as Kenneth Johnston and David Collings have noted (Johnston 744; Collings 157–79 esp. 168–69). And metadramas abound, reinforcing these doubts with personal and interpersonal conflicts. Both poets, orphaned early, draw perhaps unconsciously on memories of their own sadly truncated childhoods as they write. Moreover, the intertwined textual history of these poems documents rifts in the intense friendship of their creators, reinscribing kinship tensions on interpersonal and textual levels: Coleridge, better known as a poet than his friend through most of the 1790s, lost poetic ground with the first publication of *Lyrical Ballads*, which contained far more of Words-worth's poems. And while the Wordsworths had praised the second part of Coleridge's poem when they first heard it in the fall of 1800, William worked obsessively afterward to finish "Michael" as a replacement for "Christabel" in the second edition of *Lyrical Ballads* (Gill 187; Johnston 743). Yet, as Collings has written, "Michael," written "to oust Coleridge's improper and extravagant text from his own apparently domesticated collection, becomes another version of it" (161; see also Johnston 745).

Like other familiar Romantic Era fathers—Jane Austen's Mr. Bennet and Mary Shelley's Victor Frankenstein to name two—Sir Leoline has retreated into himself and away from parental responsibility. Meaning well, perhaps, but by no means always doing good—or indeed doing anything at all—Leoline has somehow managed to teach his daughter, "whom her father loves so well" (I: 24 *Oxford Coleridge* 67) to think that he is on her side; thus Christabel brags to Geraldine early on about her father's authority and power: "O well, bright dame! may you command / The service of Sir Leoline" (I: 106–07 *Oxford Coleridge* 69). True enough, Geraldine does command the Baron by the end of Part II; but he is hardly to be regarded as a service-provider of any sort; his is "a world of death" (II: 333 *Oxford Coleridge* 75), a world of sleeplessness and bad health where he has been stuck ever since Christabel's mother died giving birth to her—although he mourns less in spousal grief than because he has been missing the best male friend of his youth, Lord Roland, all the years of Christabel's childhood. His neglected, lonely, bored, and sexually curious daughter becomes the plaything of Geraldine, monstrous but gorgeous, who appears like Blake's tiger "burning bright" in the moonlight, seduces and silences the besotted girl, but then drops her to go after Leoline (having already confronted and banished the spirit of Christabel's dead mother). But of course Christabel enables Geraldine, indeed almost wills her to appear, by leaving her father's castle at midnight, ostensibly to pray for her faraway boyfriend.

Michael and Isabelle, Luke's parents in William Wordsworth's equally tragic antipastoral, would not at first glance seem to belong in the same company with the Bennets, the Frankensteins, and Sir Leoline. Do they not provide an inspiration, a literal and figurative beacon of hardworking, clean-living goodness and love, not just for their son Luke but for their entire community? "The Evening Star," that's what the neighbors call the lamp in their window: "The Light was famous in its neighbourhood, / And was a public Symbol of the life, / The thrifty pair had liv'd" (ll. 146, 136–38 *Oxford Wordsworth* 228). Shining as bright as—Geraldine? Upon closer study, Michael and Isabelle appear not as the rurally pure, unstained contrary of Leoline and the others but rather as having much in common with them in their Burkean obsession with money, land, inheritance, and control and thus intensifying our final recognition, when we see Michael sitting and "never . . . [lifting] up a single stone" at the unfinished sheepfold (l. 475 *Oxford Wordsworth* 236), that they have lost their only child *and* their land because of their greed and hubris. For his part, Luke tearfully agrees—or at least submits—to his father's wish for a covenant between them but seems almost as eager as Christabel to escape the safety of home and seek his fortune in London, that ultimate Blakean forest of the night that leads to his and his family's undoing. The manifestly unfinished state of Coleridge's poem makes it impossible for us to know for sure whether Christabel and/or Langdale Hall will be lost to Leoline's posterity, but the future does not look good at the end of Part Two. Surrounded like her father by "whispering tongues that poison truth" (II: 409 *Oxford Coleridge* 77) speaking perhaps of same-sex unions, Christabel collapses on her father's floor, writhing like a serpent, after begging her father by her mother's soul to send her seducer away. Michael and Isabelle's Luke—an Isaac unspared by the Lord, a prodigal who can't or won't go home again—falls in London to some evil so irremediable, or so alluring, that he exiles himself far away across the seas where his heartbroken old parents cannot follow him and forgive him.

If first-time readers of "Christabel" are perplexed when the poem stops in mid-career after Part Two, they are thoroughly confused by Coleridge's addition, ostensibly as a "Conclusion to Part II," of a verse-letter he had written to Southey in 1801 that seems totally unrelated to the poem (II: 656–77 *Oxford Coleridge* 84; Griggs 2:398). In it Coleridge describes the complex, contrary feelings he experiences while watching his young son Hartley at play: "And pleasures flow in so thick and fast / Upon his heart, that he at last / Must needs express his love's excess / With words of unmeant bitterness"; continuing to the verge of sadomasochism, he writes, "Perhaps 'tis tender too and pretty / At each wild word to feel within / A sweet recoil of love and pity" (II: 662–65, 670–72 *Oxford Coleridge* 84). Cynics take this textual patchwork as a Coleridgean admission of defeat, proof in spite of his various recorded plans for finishing the poem[1] that he really had no clue how to finish it. Unlike Coleridge's other famous fragment, *Kubla Khan*, which has often been read as a complete poem on the tensions rife in both sexual and artistic creation, "Christabel" remains not only unfinished but disintegrating, collapsing like its eponymous heroine under the weight of its own indeterminacy: Is Geraldine good, evil, or beyond easy moral definition? Is her embrace of Christabel sexual, spiritual, psychological, political, or all—or none—of the above?[2] What is going to happen next? Will Christabel rise to life again? Or, struck by the tiger Geraldine, whose horror Christabel alone can see, is Sir Leoline's daughter, to use another Blakean analogy, a rose too sick ever to recover?

But perhaps Coleridge added the verse-letter about Hartley, drenched in the tone of the adoring but potentially abusive parent, because he wanted readers to see the gothic creepiness of "Christabel," its concern with both same-sex and opposite-sex relationships, its social-psychological-verbal collapse and paralysis in the larger context of intergenerational conflict within the nuclear family. Geraldine's putative disfigurement, then— "Behold her bosom and half her side!" (I: 252 *Oxford Coleridge* 73)—may thus inscribe faultlines that crack apart the supposedly solid, safe, and tranquil precincts of the bourgeois castle home—or the healthily windswept family farm—just as the verse-letter to Southey adds an initially dissonant voice to that of the ballad narrator in "Christabel." Over forty years ago, Gerald Enscoe integrated the "non-conclusion's" message of intergenerational conflict into his Eros-based reading of "Christabel" when he wrote that to save his child from the world a father must destroy its innocence (58), and thus that the parent's "words of unmeant bitterness" *are* in a way meant, and they are in any case necessary, customary if the child is to grow up knowing all its lines, all its scripts. But Anya Taylor counterargues that "the father's wounding words . . . can [and do] blight a child's growth" (9), permanently damaging her psyche; and she sees this monstrous mental trauma happening to Christabel.

However much their real estate both elevates and curses them, however much they even unconsciously send Luke to London to complete his education, Michael and Isabelle are no more solely responsible for the moral collapse Luke apparently experiences in London than Leoline is for his daughter's failure. Granted, as Guinn Batten has eloquently put it,

> "It is no coincidence that the era that produced . . . Wordsworth's 'Michael' invented our . . . ideal of the family as an intimate, private, and loving space where two heterosexual, married adults delay the child's fall into the world. Yet the family then as now . . . served as the site for the child's instruction in experience and for the interpellation of ideology as often as it offered the child its shelter." (6)

Luke, then, learned more from his parents' early experiment in the nuclear family than to love the land and to run a sheep farm; they instructed him in the commodity capitalism of his times, and thus he came to suffer from what Batten calls the orphaned imagination—and the dehumanization and melancholy that accompany this. Luke is not literally an orphan, but he "orphanizes" himself by cutting himself off from both the sheltering and teaching functions of his family. Wordsworth is intriguingly vague about the exact nature of Luke's downfall: the poet may have felt limited by the gaps in the real-life stories upon which the poem is based, one of a profligate son and one of a sheepfold-building shepherd (see Moorman 497); or he may have deliberately enhanced the mystery by omitting particulars; but he says enough to imply that Luke succumbs to some temptation to which he had never been exposed in the Lake District, something which neither he nor his parents could anticipate or prevent. Trying as hard as they can to integrate their traditional rural work ethic and love of their land with an up-to-date awareness of how English economic life was changing around them, Michael and Isabelle struggle to raise a good son, stepping surprisingly wide—as we shall see—around the class and gender stereotypes that shackled the Bennets and the Frankensteins, but manage instead, to produce an errant one. Moreover, unlike Christabel, Lydia Bennet, and Victor's patchwork son, prodigals who transgress and then long to return to their fathers' good graces, Luke crosses a border he is unable, but also perhaps unwilling, to recross—from "good" to "bad," from country to city, from seeming part of his family to internalizing a role as Michael's Other.

In his much quoted 1801 letter to Parliamentary Whig leader Charles James Fox, Wordsworth describes Michael as one of a dwindling group of "small independent *proprietors* of land here called statesmen, men of respectable education who daily labour on their own little properties" (*Letters: Early Years* 314). And in the poem Wordsworth idealizes Michael's attachment to his land: "These fields, these hills / Which were his living Being, even more / Than his own Blood—what could they less? had laid / Strong hold on his affections, were to him / A pleasurable feeling of blind love, / The pleasure which there is in life itself" (ll. 74–79 *Oxford Wordsworth* 226). Note, however, that Michael's love is "blind," missing something, deluded in some way. Michael and Isabelle try to act appropriately to secure Luke's inheritance, unlike Austen's Mr. Bennet, who looks far more the country bumpkin by contrast since he makes no attempt to offset the loss that the entailment of Longbourn will impose upon his wife and daughters when he dies. Reversing the impression Wordsworth himself gives in the letter to Fox, that Michael and Isabelle were among the very last of a dying breed of English small landowners, Alan Liu has argued that "we will do best to make the yeomanry . . . [that is, farmers like Michael] our norm of middle-class rural life" (241) of the late eighteenth century—that is, quite numerous in both life and literature. If we allow for the topographical differences, Michael and Isabelle are not far below the Musgroves in Austen's *Persuasion* and are quite the equals of the Martins in *Emma*, whom Emma herself sneeringly calls yeomanry (25). Michael's relatives in the city make their livings in the new market economy; in fact it is to one of them that they turn for financial help—"a prosperous man, / Thriving in trade" like the Bennet sisters' Uncle Gardiner—just as it is to another relative that Michael owes the forfeiture, a nephew "of an industrious life, and ample means" who yet has become a victim of "unforeseen misfortunes," amounting to "little less / Than half his substance" (ll. 259–60, 222–23, 226–27 *Oxford Wordsworth* 230–31).

Far more awake to the world than Leoline, Luke's parents are all too familiar with the vicissitudes of individual fortunes caused by unwise investments or market fluctuations. Moreover, we later learn that Michael himself came into only half of his inheritance as a young man, the rest having been mortgaged away, and "toil'd and toil'd" (l. 387 *Oxford Wordsworth* 234) until he was forty to buy back the rest of it. Critic Tracy Ware has called this "the most perplexing detail in the poem" (371) and has noted, as have many others, that rather than send him off to London, Michael and

Isabelle could simply have let Luke in his turn inherit half the land and, through careful management of his resources, earn enough to recoup the other half like his father before him (Ware 372; see also Lea 58).

How, and why, did this happen to Luke? And how much of it can be laid at the feet of his parents? At a historical moment when childhood, family life, and education were hot-button topics (Batten 6; Richardson 17), partly of course because of Wordsworth's and Coleridge's own writings, Michael and Isabelle seem to have homeschooled their only child to live a life like theirs—isolated but not intellectually barren or emotionally unawakened. Wordsworth agreed with Rousseau about the importance of experiential education, but as The Prelude and many other poems make clear, he disagreed with the manipulative structure of Émile's learning activities, preferring for children to learn through their own interactions with their world. Does he mean to imply here that Michael and Isabelle structured Luke's life too closely or completely, didn't give him enough breathing space? In fact, the text shows that both parents strive to integrate their lives of "endless industry" with talk and with play. In the evenings after dinner, while the bright lamp beams out across the valley, Isabelle gets her husband and son to sit with her and help her card the wool or repair various implements; Michael makes games out of Luke's first shepherding duties and takes the time to make him a shepherd's staff out of a sapling to encourage him to play at herding before he must do it for real. Gender becomes a complex issue in this poem. On the one hand, we are told that "to Michael's heart / The Son of his old age was yet more dear" than his wife; and clearly, the failed covenant at the sheepfold is strictly a guy thing. But Luke's parents also show some gratifyingly liberated tendencies with regard to gender roles. Not only does Michael do the "babe in arms" "female service"—changing diapers?—besides rocking "His cradle, as with a woman's gentle hand" (l. 97, ll. 107–11, 190–98, 149–50, 163, 164, 168 Oxford Wordsworth 227–28), but it is the more assertive and extroverted Isabelle whose recollection of Richard Bateman actually sets Luke's course toward London and disaster.

Bateman's reputation, alluring but deadly as a tiger, acts insinuatingly upon Luke and his family much as Geraldine's actual presence acts upon Christabel. A poor boy, Bateman lived on the parish dole until the community decided to set him up as a traveling peddler. But instead,

> the Lad
> Went up to London, found a Master there,
> Who out of many chose the trusty Boy
> To go and overlook his merchandise
> Beyond the seas, where he grew wond'rous rich,
> And left estates and monies to the poor,
> And at his birth-place, built a Chapel, floored
> With Marble, which he sent from foreign lands.
> (ll. 273–80 Oxford Wordsworth 231)

This of course is capitalism with a vengeance, right down to the expensive, suspiciously showy acts of charity that will forever commemorate Bateman's wealth to the neighborhood. Of course the elephant in the room here, as we ponder the corrupt state of Bateman's orphaned imagination, is slavery, great driver of the British economy at this time. I reference not just the Africans who both themselves *were* and *produced* "merchandise / Beyond the seas," but the equally ominous implication that Richard himself has been enslaved by his "Master" and the mercenary mindset he has acquired. Moorman notes that during the troubled composition of "Michael" the great British abolitionist Thomas Clarkson stopped overnight with the Wordsworths (498). Kenneth Johnston has sensibly suggested that "given the story's circumstances," Luke's shame must "have something to do with money" (746). And I would not suggest that other sorts of enslavement—involving sex and/or substance abuse for instance—may be hinted at here, in the relations between Richard and his "Master" or other denizens of London, except that the language Wordsworth uses for Luke's subsequent decline seems to suggest moral collapse as much as, if not more than, simple criminality: "He in the dissolute city gave himself / To evil courses: ignominy and shame / Fell on him." Further, Luke's banishment, if not altogether self-imposed, was apparently self-executed: "he was driven at last / To seek a hiding-place beyond the seas" (ll. 453–56 Oxford Wordsworth 235–36); that is, he was *not* transported to Australia as were many British criminals at this time. Granted, as Johnston reminds us, young people have always tended to leave remote rural homes to seek their fortunes in cities (746), but it seems that something else comes into play with Luke that makes homecoming unthinkable. Johnston notes at one point that Luke, like Christabel, is "lost to 'dissipation'" (745); could he have submitted to a homosexual overture as she seems to have done?[3]

Coleridge certainly was no stranger to intergenerational conflict and disintegrating relationships within his own family. He lost his father at the age of nine and was banished from his native Devonshire to boarding school at Christ's Hospital in London, and his sometimes mercurial mother seems to have been inconsistent afterward in welcoming visits from her youngest child (see Holmes 23–24, 122, 289–90); before beginning "Christabel," he had already written of his own early homesickness in another poem addressed to Hartley, "Frost at Midnight." A young father in an already unhappy marriage when he began "Christabel" in the spring of 1798, and not much older when he wrote about Hartley in the 1801 verse-letter, Coleridge knew something of the turbulence of conflicting emotions involved in parenting and the accompanying fears of failure. And he was beginning to use, if not yet completely to depend on, laudanum. Further, by the time he finally published "Christabel" in 1816 with the letter at the end, he had seen enough of the adolescence of young Hartley to realize how much he was like himself and thus what a problem he would continue to be (Holmes 2:451–52, 463 *et passim*).

There is another parent-child relation in "Michael" too, one that may trump the pastoral narrative and ultimately lie behind Luke's deviation—and it is a double relation. I refer to Wordsworth's feelings toward his own parents, both of whom he lost early, his mother when he was eight and his father when he was thirteen, leaving him and his siblings as financially disadvantaged orphans; but noteworthy also is the paternal voice he seems to assume at the beginning of the text with regard to the "youthful Poets, who among these Hills / Will be my second self when I am gone" (ll. 38–39 *Oxford Wordsworth* 225). Johnston notes that like Luke, Wordsworth and his younger brother John were both sent out into the world by their uncle, Richard Wordsworth, with a guilt-loaded sense of obligation (746) in hopes of recouping the family's fortunes after their father's early death and the nonpayment of the debt Lord Lowther owed the family; further, while William hung back, John, like Richard Bateman, entered directly into the market economy by becoming captain of an Indiaman (a commercial ship traveling to the East Indies: 746–47). Wordsworth's grief at his mother's early death finds indirect expression in *The Prelude* through descriptions of his boyhood wanderings in remote rural areas of the Lakes and through painfully beautiful reminiscences of his mother, the "centre of the circle which" included him and his siblings (1805 *Prelude* 5:252) like a hen surrounded by her chicks. He reveals more complicated feelings of dependence and fear toward his father, Lord Lowther's workaholic henchman (Blank 55–58), whose presence may lie behind those "huge and mighty forms that do not live / Like living men" (1799 *Prelude* 1:127–28) and that stalk the boy after he "borrows" a rowboat and goes for a joyride on the lake. If Wordsworth imagined himself either an Isaac or a prodigal with regard to his own parents and their death-extinguished hopes for his life and career, then he may have felt he must dispose of Luke in order symbolically to lay to rest his own excesses or failings. Or perhaps his main concern in the metanarrative lies rather with other poets and issues of prodigality and sacrifice involving himself and them. He calls this text "a pastoral poem" but turns the genre inside out, creating not idealized rural intellectuals in isolated discussion but all-too-real people whose discussions bring them straight to financial and moral ruin. Is he a good literary son of great earlier British writers like Shakespeare and Milton, or a prodigal wasteful of his talents, even a self-made monster? That, as Johnston points out, would suggest a parallel not only with Luke but with Michael himself: Michael's inability to finish the sheepfold may parallel Wordsworth's inability to get on with the task Coleridge kept at him about, the writing of *The Recluse* (749)—or, for that matter, to make anyone pay attention to "Michael" itself. Charles J. Rzepka has pointed out that the sheepfold is not said in the poem to be heart shaped, as Dorothy Wordsworth described it in her journal, but is most likely circular, a placeholder, a zero ("Sacrificial" 210). And what of his readers? What use will they make of his advice, his modeling of a poetic life, when he is gone? Stephen Gill notes that Wordsworth was very anxious about "Michael" in the weeks leading up to its initial publication, demanding several last-minute typographical changes (185–86) that must have annoyed the printer. This indicates at the very least that Wordsworth cared about it. Surely the more logical place for Wordsworth's expression of concern for the fate of his story would be at the *end*, not the beginning, of the narrative. To voice these concerns, however circumspectly, at the start leaves all the text's interrogation of family, gender, and capitalist ideologies hanging over the reader throughout in a way that tends to destabilize any opinion we might attempt to form. Thus in its own way the text of "Michael" can seem nearly as polyvocal, and thus as indeterminate, as that of unfinished "Christabel" with its problematic letter-ending.[4]

There is still another way that "family matters" here: the substitute family, based on warm friendship and shared respect for each other's literary abilities and accomplishments, created by William and Dorothy Wordsworth and Coleridge in their early years of living and writing together. For both of the men (and for Dorothy, too, in her journals), it was an exhilarating time of poetic dialogue and even collaboration: it was Wordsworth's idea, based on a book he had read, for Coleridge to build "The Ancient Mariner" around a story of a seaman who had shot a bird; and Coleridge helped Wordsworth with lines in "We Are Seven" and other *Lyrical Ballads*. But there was competition, too, a sort of sibling rivalry that became a fight for space on the page and in the British mind, which along with Coleridge's increasing drug problem pulled the two friends further and further apart. Coleridge wrote the first part of "Christabel," with its hints of lesbian seduction, in the spring of 1798 perhaps partly in response to the homoerotic undertones in Wordsworth's "Discharged Soldier" poem (see McGavran "Defusing" 149–50), written earlier that same spring, which begins with the young Wordsworth walking alone at midnight, rather like Christabel, and whose main character seems a response to Coleridge's "Ancient Mariner." Thus Wordsworth, at this time not yet married to Mary Hutchinson and father only to his illegitimate French daughter, Anne-Caroline, reacted in "Michael" to disruptions in that Burkean line of intergenerational succession that also haunted his professional ambition to gain ground (not least over Coleridge) and possess the poetic landscape both of them, in their partly opposed ways, explored so well.

This leads me to a conclusion that many will not find especially conclusive—but it is based on many years of both reading and parenting, and I think it is the one to which Wordsworth and Coleridge themselves point us. And that is simply that raising children is neither an art nor a science but a muddle—involving genetics, environment, and choices, some of course better than others. Childhood and family life themselves, so often idealized then and now in a transhistorical, unthinking way, present to us in reality a tense and often grotesque dance of opposites—of love and manipulation, of support and obligation—that few can navigate without being emotionally damaged; indeed the family as an institution cannot always survive the demands it puts upon itself. Still, if some literary children are lost to various temptations, or because like Conrad's Kurtz they are hollow at the core, we can think of other protagonists who end up leading, or about to lead, happy lives and revitalizing or recreating kinship relations, in spite of weak, dissolute, or absent parents: not only Austen's older Bennet sisters in *Pride* but Anne Elliot in *Persuasion* come immediately to mind.

What difference then does it make whether parents are attentive like Michael and Isabelle or neglectful like Leoline, assertive or passive or both in warning them of the dangers of the world, living or dead—especially if their children will insist on making up the lives they want to live even when that leads to their destruction? Wordsworth and Coleridge don't answer the question here, but "Michael" and "Christabel" surely raise it, in all its complexity, as do the other Romantic Era texts I have referenced here. And of course the conflict over education, including the role of parents in the family, continues unabated into our own times. Readers today may well wonder or argue about, as did developmental psychologists in the early 1990s, whether it makes any real difference, short of overt abuse or neglect, what kind of parenting goes on.[5] Finally, both Lake poets know and speak to the heartbreaking truth Norman Maclean states at the end of his very Wordsworthian late-twentieth-century memoir, *A River Runs through It*, which chronicles the alcohol-and-gambling-driven decline and death of Maclean's younger brother Paul in the beautiful Big Blackfoot River country of Montana: "It is those we live with and love and should know who elude us" (113). What Maclean doesn't state but knows is that all too often we—parents, siblings, friends—elude them too, especially when they need us the most.

NOTES

1. His recorded comments suggest that he was conflicted between a Christian, moralizing conclusion, the song of Christabel's desolation, and one, confided to his physician, James Gillman, that is earthy and pagan, ending with Geraldine

banished and Christabel happily married to her returning boyfriend (Beer 198–99). Still, many of his earliest reviewers, including the influential William Hazlitt, lamented the poem's obscenity (Swann 543), and I find even today that students get squeamish when I try to discuss the seduction scene; like Hazlitt and countless others, they want to fall back on good old sin and expiation and straight-arm (so to speak) the gay theme. What astonishes me more is that excepting Julie Carlson and Anya Taylor, readers from Hazlitt to Benjamin Grossberg insist that the passage describing Leoline's youthful relationship with Geraldine's putative father, Lord Roland de Vaux of Tryermaine, presents a clear, unambiguous example of safe, healthy, non-homoerotic manly friendship (Grossberg 158–60; Swann 544):

> Alas! They had been friends in youth;
> But whispering tongues can poison truth;
> And constancy lives in realms above;
> And life is thorny; and youth is vain;
> And to be wroth with one we love
> Doth work like madness in the brain.
> And thus it chanced, as I divine,
> With Roland and Sir Leoline.
> Each spake words of high disdain
> And insult to his heart's best brother:
> They parted—ne'er to meet again!
> But never either found another
> To free the hollow heart from paining—
> (II, 408–20)

Are we marching to Tryermaine over Brokeback Mountain? Given the passion that overflows these lines, and the clear inference that Leoline loved Roland more than his wife ("never either found another"), it seems equally odd that no one even bats an eye at the relationship, also suggestive in this context, between Leoline's court poet, Bard Bracy, and the youth whom he "lov'st best" (II, 487). In this poem powerful same-sex relationships, whether sexually active or not, easily dominate the broken ties between Leoline and his long-lost wife, the back-burner ties between Christabel and her absent boyfriend, and the yet-to-be-formed ties—if indeed there will be any—between Leoline and Geraldine.

2. Critics of the poem almost always focus on Geraldine's role as a disturbance labeled as psychosexual or gender based (Enscoe, Spatz, Paglia, Rzepka [Self],

Koestenbaum, Carlson, Greenberg), textual or poststructuralist (Rand, Wheeler, May, Eilenberg, La Cassagnère, Channick), Marxist (Henderson), old or new historicist (Mulvihill, Fulford), or all of the above (Watkins): "the assertion of the [female] body occurs both within the gaps opened up by a weakening aristocratic authority and upon the energies generated out of an emergent bourgeois worldview" (Watkins 83).

3. Historians of male homosexuality in England know that there were the equivalent of gay bars and drag bars ("molly-houses") in eighteenth-century London as well as cruising grounds near barracks and parks (Bray 81–85; Norton 47, 49, 52, 84). If Luke were to stumble upon such a place, he would surely have attracted prurient attention for his youth and healthy country-boy appearance. What if he discovered he liked it? Or alcohol? Or both?

4. To use the words of children's literature critic David Rudd, influenced by Bakhtin's theories of polyvocality, both poems "draw attention to their origins in conflicting and competing discourses" to which we as readers contribute with our own readings and reactions ("Return to Rose" 302).

5. The Society for Research in Child Development, an organization of academic psychologists, was disturbed in 1992 when in her presidential address to the group Sandra Scarr put forward her controversial concept of "Good Enough Parenting." Basing her remarks on evidence she and others had gathered, which suggests that "children create their own experiences from the environments they encounter," regardless of the intensity of the parents' efforts to influence their development, she concludes, "The associations between a child's characteristics, those of the parents, and the rearing environment they provide are neither accidental nor a likely source of fruitful intervention, unless the child's opportunities for normal development are quite limited" (17). She also states:

> Good enough, ordinary parents probably have the same effects on their children's development as culturally defined super-parents. This comforting idea gives parents a lot more freedom to care for their children in ways they find comfortable for them, and it gives them more freedom from guilt when they deviate (within the normal range) from culturally prescribed norms about parenting. (15)

She was immediately attacked by colleagues such as Diana Baumrind, who decried Scarr's reliance on heritability analyses, and Jacquelyne Faye Jackson, who objected to how Scarr's opinions would impact upon African American families. Mainly, of course, the developmental psychologists did not want to be told that their decades of study were of limited value to parents. The problem remains, however, for parents and children as well as writers and readers of Romantic Era texts.

BIBLIOGRAPHY

Austen, Jane. *Emma*. Ed. James Kinsley. Introd. Terry Castle. Oxford: Oxford UP, 1995.

Batten, Guinn. *The Orphaned Imagination: Melancholy and Commodity Culture in English Romanticism*. Durham, NC: Duke UP, 1998.

Baumrind, Diana. "The Average Expectable Environment Is Not Good Enough: A Response to Scarr." *Child Development* 64 (1993): 1299–1317.

Beer, J. B. *Coleridge the Visionary*. New York: Collier, 1962.

Bennett, Paula. "Family Plots: *Pride and Prejudice* as a Novel about Parenting." In *Approaches to Teaching Austen's "Pride and Prejudice."* Ed. Marcia McClintock Folsom. New York: MLA, 1993.

Blank, G. Kim. *Wordsworth and Feeling: The Poetry of an Adult Child*. Madison, NJ: Fairleigh Dickinson UP, 1995.

Bray, Alan. *Homosexuality in Renaissance England*. London: Gay Men's Press, 1982.

Brown, Julia Prewitt. *Jane Austen's Novels: Social Change and Literary Form*. Cambridge: Harvard UP, 1979.

Carlson, Julie. "Gender." In *Cambridge Companion to Coleridge*. Ed. Lucy Newlyn. Cambridge: Cambridge UP, 2002. 203–16.

Channick, Debra. "'A Logic of Its Own': Repetition in Coleridge's 'Christabel.'" *Romanticism and Victorianism on the Net* (May 2008): 50; 27 parags.

Coleridge, Samuel Taylor. *Collected Letters*. Ed. Earl Leslie Griggs. 6 vols. Oxford: Clarendon, 1956–1971.

———. *Major Works*. Ed. H. L. Jackson. Oxford: Oxford UP, 1985.

Collings, David. *Wordsworthian Errancies: The Poetics of Cultural Dismemberment*. Baltimore: Johns Hopkins UP, 1994.

Eilenberg, Susan. *Strange Power of Speech: Wordsworth, Coleridge, and Literary Possession*. New York: Oxford UP, 1992.

Enscoe, Gerald E. *Eros and the Romantics: Sexual Love as a Theme in Coleridge, Shelley and Keats*. The Hague: Mouton, 1968.

Fulford, Tim. *Romanticism and Masculinity: Gender, Politics and Poetics in the Writings of Burke, Coleridge, Cobbett, Wordsworth, De Quincey and Hazlitt*. Handmills, Basingstoke, Hampshire: Macmillan, 1999.

Gill, Stephen. *William Wordsworth: A Life*. Oxford: Clarendon, 1989.

Grossberg, Benjamin Scott. "Making Christabel: Sexual Transgression and Its Implications in Coleridge's 'Christabel.'" *Journal of Homosexuality* 41 (2001): 145–65.

Henderson, Andrea. "Revolution, Response, and 'Christabel.'" *ELH* 57 (1990): 881–900.

Holmes, Richard. *Coleridge: Early Visions*. New York: Viking, 1990.

Jackson, Jacquelyne Faye. "Human Behavioral Genetics, Scarr's Theory, and Her Views on Interventions: A Critical Review and Commentary on Their Implications for African American Children." *Child Development* 64 (1993): 1318–32.

Johnston, Kenneth R. *The Hidden Wordsworth: Poet, Lover, Rebel, Spy*. New York: Norton, 1998.

Koestenbaum, Wayne. *Double Talk: The Erotics of Male Literary Collaboration*. New York: Routledge, 1989.

La Cassagnère, Christian. "The Strangeness of *Christabel*." *Wordsworth Circle* 32 (2001): 84–88.

Lea, Sydney. "Wordsworth and His 'Michael': The Pastor Passes." *ELH* 45 (1978): 60; qtd. Ware 372.

The Letters of William and Dorothy Wordsworth, The Early Years 1787–1805. Oxford: Clarendon, 1967.

Levinson, Marjorie. *Wordsworth's Great Period Poems: Four Essays*. Cambridge: Cambridge UP, 1986.

Liu, Alan. *Wordsworth: The Sense of History*. Stanford, CA: Stanford UP, 1989.

Maclean, Norman. *"A River Runs through It" and Other Stories*. New York: Pocket, 1992.

May, Claire B. "'Christabel' and Abjection: Coleridge's Narrative in Procession Trial." *SEL* 37 (1997): 699–721.

McGavran, James Holt, Jr. "Defusing the Discharged Soldier: Wordsworth, Coleridge, and Homosexual Panic." *Papers in Language and Literature* 32 (1996): 147–65.

———. "Wordsworth, Lost Boys, and Romantic Hom(e)ophobia." In *Literature and the Child: Romantic Continuations, Postmodern Contestations*. Ed. McGavran. Iowa City: U of Iowa P, 1999. 130–52.

Mellor, Anne K. *Mary Shelley: Her Life, Her Fictions, Her Monsters*. New York: Routledge, 1988.

Moorman, Mary. *William Wordsworth: A Biography. The Early Years 1770–1803*. 1957. London: Oxford UP, 1968.

Mulvihill. James. "'Like a Lady of a Far Countree': Coleridge's 'Christabel' and Fear of Invasion." *Papers on Language and Literature* 44:3 (2008): 250–75.

Norton, Rictor. *Mother Clap's Molly House: The Gay Subculture in England 1700–1830*. London: Gay Men's Press, 1992.

Paglia, Camille. *Sexual Personae: Art and Decadence from Nefertiti to Emily Dickinson*. New Haven: Yale UP, 1990.

Peterfreund, Stuart. "Wordsworth on Covenants, 'Heart Conditions,' Primogeniture, Remains, and the Ties That Bind in 'Michael' and Elsewhere." *Criticism* 40 (1998).

Plotz, Judith. *Romanticism and the Vocation of Childhood*. New York: Palgrave, 2001.

Rand, Richard A. "Geraldine." In *Unifying the Text: A Post-Structuralist Reader*. Ed. Robert Young. Boston: Routledge and Kegan Paul, 1981. 280–315.

Richardson, Alan. *Literature, Education, and Romanticism: Reading as Social Practice 1780–1832*. Cambridge: Cambridge UP, 1994.

Robson, Catherine. *Men in Wonderland: The Lost Girlhood of the Victorian Gentleman*. Princeton: Princeton UP, 2001.

Rudd, David. "Children's Literature and the Return to Rose." *Children's Literature Association Quarterly* 35 (2010): 290–310.

Rzepka, Charles J. "Sacrificial Sites, Place-Keeping, and 'Pre-History' in Wordsworth's 'Michael.'" *European Romantic Review* 15 (2004): 205–13.

———. *The Self as Mind: Vision and Identity in Wordsworth, Coleridge, and Keats*. Cambridge, MA: Harvard UP, 1986.

Scarr, Sandra. "Developmental Theories for the 1990s: Development and Individual Differences." *Child Development* 63 (1992): 1–19.

Spatz, Jonas. "The Mystery of Eros: Sexual Initiation in Coleridge's 'Christabel.'" *PMLA* 90 (1975): 107–16.

Swann, Karen. "'Christabel': The Wandering Mother and the Enigma of Form." *SiR* 23 (1984): 533–53.

Taylor, Anya. "Coleridge's 'Christabel' and the Phantom Soul." *SEL* 42 (2002): 707–30.

Ware, Tracy. "Historicism Along and Against the Grain: The Case of Wordsworth's 'Michael.'" *Nineteenth-Century Literature* 49 (1994): 360–74.

Watkins, Daniel P. *Sexual Power in British Romantic Poetry*. Gainesville: UP of Florida, 1996.

Wheeler, Kathleen M. "Disruption and Displacement in Coleridge's 'Christabel.'" *Wordsworth Circle* 20 (Spring 1989): 85–90.

Wordsworth, William. *The Oxford Authors William Wordsworth*. Ed. Stephen Gill. Oxford: Oxford UP, 1984.

———. *The Prelude: 1799, 1805, 1850*. Ed. Jonathan Wordsworth, M. H. Abrams, and Stephen Gill. New York: Norton, 1979.

MALINI ROY

→ Mary Wollstonecraft's Childish Resentment

The Angry Girl, the Wrongs and the Rights of Woman

[W]hat should induce me to be the champion for suffering humanity?—Who ever risked any thing for me?—Who ever acknowledged me to be a fellow-creature?

> "How many are you, then," said I,
>   "If they two are in heaven?"
> Quick was the little Maid's reply,
>   "O Master! we are seven."
>
> "But they are dead; those two are dead!
>   Their spirits are in heaven!"
> 'Twas throwing words away; for still
> The little Maid would have her will,
>   And said, "Nay, we are seven!"
>   (61–69)

Literary scholars of Romantic childhood are likely to be more familiar with the second of the two passages above, from William Wordsworth's "We Are Seven." In the poem, an adult I-narrator struggles fruitlessly to convince a "little Maid" of the stark reality that if two of her originally seven siblings have passed away, then five are now left alive (Wordsworth, *William Wordsworth* 83–85). The poem, originally published in Wordsworth and Coleridge's *Lyrical Ballads* in 1798, has long been a watershed text of English literary history. Owing to recent Romantic scholarship, however, which has dislodged the old dispensation in the prismatic project of deconstructing the canon, many readers may recognize the first passage, from Mary Wollstonecraft's unfinished novel *The Wrongs of Woman, or Maria* (published in 1798, the same year as *Lyrical Ballads*) (Wollstonecraft, "Maria," *Works* 1: 119). The lines are spoken by the character Jemima, an attendant at the madhouse where the novel's protagonist, Maria, is imprisoned. The lower-class Jemima recounts the many troubles of her orphaned and impoverished childhood and youth to the middle-class Maria and her fellow inmate and lover, Darnford. Her story educates them laterally into an awareness of their own socioeconomic privilege with respect to the lives of the others such as Jemima. Wollstonecraft captures her discontent eloquently in a cycliad of searing, furious, and unanswerable questions.

However, in studies of Romantic childhood, while Wordsworth's poem remains central to scholarly discussion, Wollstonecraft's take on the topic has yet to make a stage debut from a similar critical perspective. This essay addresses the oversight of Wollstonecraft's contribution to the literature of Romantic childhood, enquiring into its causes and implications, and aims to usher her work into the forefront of this growing scholarly field.

Wordsworth's poem has remained influential in critical receptions of the Romantic child as a spontaneous figure gifted with otherworldly knowledge, qualities that appear commensurate with those of the poem's source text *Lyrical Ballads*, where Wordsworth, in the preface, famously aired his (and Coleridge's) new poetics of "spontaneous overflow of powerful feelings." Indeed, Wordsworth's revisionary democratic agenda of using the "language really used by Men" is manifest in the colloquial rhythms in which the adult narrator converses with the "little Maid" (Wordsworth, *Norton Anthology* 262–72). The child's intuitive, quasi-mystical belief system resists the "meddling intellect" of the (slightly pompous) adult narrator's numeracy skills in insisting that her dead siblings, buried in the graveyard, still count among the final numbers (McGavran, Jr., *Romanticism* 54–71).[1]

Wollstonecraft's portrait of Jemima is much less well mapped in critical studies of Romantic childhood, and remains to be charted for its full importance. Jemima's childhood memories are voiced in words that might be music for any fan of the Romantic outsider. Her remembrance of her childhood is virulent, bitter, and world weary, expressing nothing of the reconciliatory, empathetic "still, sad music of humanity" that the adult Wordsworth claims to feel in his poem "Tintern Abbey" (Wordsworth, Lyrical Ballads 118). Jemima takes an unapologetic, confrontational attitude to the middle-class Maria, who remains a silent auditor of her rhetorical questions. Jemima's declamatory slew of interrogative pronouns, interweaved in the hypnotic, cyclical rhythm of "what" and "who," effectively shame denial from Maria or from society at large. Wollstonecraft's and Wordsworth's passages, in their different ways, voice the resistance of the child-speaker (present in Wordsworth's case; remembered in Wollstonecraft's) to codes of behavior expected of the girl child. Yet, there are differences between Wollstonecraft and Wordsworth. The child-speaker in "We Are Seven," unlike Jemima, invites the reader's protective fondness with her charming, pastoral "rustic, woodland air." She rebuts the relatively well-off, patronizing narrator gently with the submissive appellation of "Master," and is rather cute in her stolid insistence upon her opinion, to regurgitate the language of contemporary cliché (Wordsworth, William Wordsworth 83–85). Her ideological resistance (although she is, interestingly, female in contrast to the poetic persona of the male narrator), does not appear to dislodge the powerful adult's assumptions. By contrast, Jemima's recounting of her childhood trials points to a program of unself-fashioning within social convention. Her tale bears out Wollstonecraft's professed aims in Wrongs of Woman. According to the prefatorial notes to Wrongs, arranged by Wollstonecraft's husband, William Godwin, the text voices a politics of protest against the "misery and oppression, peculiar to women, that arise out of the partial laws and customs of society." This includes "the wrongs of different classes of women, equally oppressive" (Wollstonecraft, "Maria," Works 83–84). [2] Feminist scholars have shed valuable critical light on Wrongs as a merciless indictment of patriarchal oppression, focusing upon the violence in the lives of Maria and Jemima (Tauchert 103–16; Sapiro, A Vindication of Political Virtue 42–43; Taylor 233–45). The present study foregrounds their position as girls rather than incipient women, with a view toward Jemima's caustic response to society's "wrongs."

Jemima's looking back in anger, however, is not the only bitter glance at girlhood in *Wrongs*: indeed, Jemima's attitude is shared by that of the protagonist Maria. The phrase "childish resentment" (invoked in the title of this essay) is used by Maria's tyrannical husband in his characterization of her resistance to his patriarchal dominance. His pejorative term devalues and invalidates the concerns of his wife as an autonomous adult, earning him the disfavor of the author of the *Vindication of the Rights of Woman*. Wollstonecraft's disapproval of Venables is evinced through his invalidation of the concerns of the generic child in the diminutive suffix "-ish." Within the narrative of *Wrongs*, Wollstonecraft's siding with the "resentment" of the "childish" Maria remains an expression of the radical politics of the novel, aiming at the "improvement of the age." Maria reacts to *wrongs* perpetrated on both her gender and her ideational childhood; this study argues that both these disempowered categories are condensed and endorsed authorially by Wollstonecraft within portraits of unhappy, rebellious, and worldly-wise girls that pervade *Wrongs*, echoing her other works in theme. Wollstonecraft's "childish resentment," voiced through Jemima's anger, remains her largely underacknowledged contribution to Romantic childhood. Conceived within a narrative frame of social realism, such angry girls are not quite the ambivalent Romantic feral children in the mold of the young boat-stealing Wordsworth in *The Prelude* (Wordsworth, *Thirteen-Book Prelude* 22–25). Wollstonecraft's girls simmer in "resentment" at their lived experiences within the divisive gender politics of their society, signifying an aspect of Romantic childhood overlooked in the critically popular emphasis on the otherworldly child.[3]

These angry girls in *Wrongs* can be considered a fictive continuation and development of the ills of the female condition that Wollstonecraft had discussed through her career in texts from her early career, through her representations of the girl child. Wollstonecraft's self-named protagonist of the novel *Mary, a Fiction* (1788), published a decade earlier than *Wrongs*, is subjected to neglect as a child. Within her family, adults mock her by laughing at her secrets, but she, "left to reflect on her own feelings," creates and escapes into her alternative fantasy world, composing music and singing to angels in the woods. Unlike Wordsworth's feral youthful self in *The Prelude*, nurtured by a deified Nature, Wollstonecraft's Mary is not inherently solipsistic: had her parents loved her, the omniscient narrator states, she would not have sought out "a new world" at this early age (Wordsworth, *Prelude* 22–25; Wollstonecraft, "Mary," *Works* 1: 10–12; Kelly, *Revolutionary Feminism* 48).[4]

Wollstonecraft's portrait of Maria's childhood is a vivid and persuasive portrait of how the girl child is systemically disempowered within the inheritance laws of patriarchy. Maria's eldest brother, the "heir apparent," is unduly privileged by primogeniture: from an early age, he becomes a "despot" over his siblings, especially "his sisters" (Wollstonecraft, "Maria," *Works* 1: 124; Perry 111–31).[5] Maria's childhood home is a textbook case of patriarchal dictatorship, where the father keeps the family in a thrall of "passive obedience." Godwin's gloss on the autobiographical basis of Wollstonecraft's representation in his *Memoirs of the Author of A Vindication of the Rights of Woman* is worth revisiting in the present instance to mark how this aspect of Maria's childhood is produced by Wollstonecraft's authorial self-projection:

> When, in the Wrongs of Woman, Mary speaks of 'the petty cares which obscured the morning of her heroine's life; continual restraint in the most trivial matters; unconditional submission to orders, which, as a mere child, she soon discovered to be unreasonable, because inconsistent and contradictory; and the being [sic] often obliged to sit, in the presence of her parents, for three or four hours together, without daring to utter a word'; she is, I believe, to be considered as copying the outline of the first period of her own existence.

The context makes it highly probable that Wollstonecraft invests truth-value in Maria's remembrance of the draconian and arbitrary exercise of adult authority endemic to certain parenting methods, linguistically placing the child's experience in a juridical framework that creates a counter-discourse to vested dismissals of "childish resentment" (Wollstonecraft, "Maria," *Works* 1: 124). Maria is a probable imaginative self-representation of Wollstonecraft, a claim enforced by the character's nearly cognate first name. As a child, Wollstonecraft had resented her father's tyranny over her family: she was "not formed to be the contented and unresisting subject of a despot," as Godwin recounted in his *Memoirs* (Godwin 88–89).

The inequitable property rights imply that well into adulthood, Maria must depend on the goodwill of her generous and fortunately rich uncle to protect all the girls she is close to. She persuades him to settle a thousand pounds on each of her young sisters after her marriage. His will leaves the major share of his fortune to Maria's baby daughter, to prevent its appropriation by Maria's greedy husband, Venables (Wollstonecraft, "Maria," *Works* 1: 137, 166). Maria's uncle is a caring and benevolent adult mentor: he is a fantasy surrogate parent in contrast to her ineffectual biological parents. In schooling her into thinking and acting as a free agent, he "inculcated" in her "self-respect, and a lofty consciousness of acting right, independent of the censure or applause of the world; nay, he almost taught me to brave, and even despise its censure, when convinced of the rectitude of my own intentions." The ideology of resistance that Maria learns in childhood persists into adulthood as a refusal to accept her husband's tyrannical dictates blindly (Wollstonecraft, "Maria," *Works* 1: 126, 162). Furthermore, insofar as the character Maria stands in for Wollstonecraft's own political grouses, the remembered child functions as an internal muse. Worth considering here is a persuasive case put forth by Wollstonecraft scholar Gary Kelly, claiming that "the dominant discursive mode" of the post-French Revolutionary public discourse was "autobiographical." For Kelly, Wollstonecraft's writing exemplifies this "rhetorical strategy" for political ends, which underscores her "polemical works," including the epistolary work *Letters Written During a Short Residence in Sweden, Norway and Denmark* as well as *Wrongs*. Kelly surmises that these works, immersed in the contemporary literary culture of sensibility, served the important role of articulating female subjectivity to remap the political realm of public discourse (Kelly, *Mary Wollstonecraft and Mary Shelley* 19–32).

Another counterpoint to the patriarchal dictatorship of Maria's childhood home is the safety valve offered on those felicitous occasions when the young Maria and her siblings bound amidst flowers and meadows, revelling in moments of "open air and freedom" (Wollstonecraft, "Maria," *Works* 1: 124). Maria's spells of play amidst Nature appropriate, for the girl child, the physical freedom that Rousseau had advocated for the male Émile in figuring him as a normative human being (and, in one of his gender-emancipated moments, had also underlined as a guiding principle for women's clothes while rejecting the contemporary European fashion for corsets) (Rousseau 330). Maria's independence works as a liberatory fantasy for Wollstonecraft's traumatized memories of her own oppressed childhood. Godwin's *Memoirs* offers an appropriate gloss here (Godwin 91). "Dolls and the other amusements usually appropriated to female children, she held in contempt; and felt a much greater propensity to join in the active and hardy sports of her brothers, than to confine herself to those of her own sex." The character Maria's embrace of Nature's recuperative powers, in the company of her siblings, antedates the fraternity relished by the "little Maid" within the arcadian graveyard of Wordsworth's "We Are Seven." But Wollstonecraft's glorification of athletic girlhood yodels a political demand for female agency as well, on a note far more strident than Wordsworth's.[6] Wollstonecraft's borrowing of autobiographical material for her fictive girls, as a projection of her adult memories and desires, can be compared with philosopher Gaston Bachelard's thoughts in *The Poetics of Childhood*. Bachelard reads childhood memory as a lasting creative fount through an individual's adult life: "when reverie works on our history, the childhood which is within us brings us its benefits" (Bachelard 21). For Wollstonecraft the programmatic invocation, politically motivated, of childhood oppression, serves the rhetorical strategy of highlighting the gender-specific problems faced by a girl child, even as they illumine the importance of these monikers to Wollstonecraft's authorial identity.

If Maria is the character who wins narrative primacy in *Wrongs*, no less compelling is Wollstonecraft's portrait of Jemima, whose underprivileged background makes her even more vulnerable to exploitation than the middle-class Maria. Relating her childhood experiences to Maria and Darnford, Jemima tells how poverty and orphanhood conspired to make her a social outcast, "an egg dropped on the sand; a pauper by nature, hunted from family to family, who belonged to nobody—and nobody cared for me." Jemima attributes her ontological status as an outsider largely to her illegitimate birth to a servant girl who died shortly afterward. It is never self-evident to Jemima that an accident of birth should justify the social opprobrium heaped upon her: "ever called a bastard, a bastard appeared to me an object of the greatest compassion in creation" (Wollstonecraft, "Maria," *Works* 1: 110). Josephine McDonagh, in an important study of the phenomenon of child murder as a pervasive trope in the era within literary and cultural texts, has observed that the bastard was a particularly incendiary figure in the 1790s post-Revolution scene. New French legislation in 1793 passed marriage laws that gave equal rights of inheritance to legitimate and illegitimate children, horrifying politically conservative statesmen, including Edmund Burke, whom Wollstonecraft had pilloried in her early work *Vindication of the Rights of Men* (Wollstonecraft, *A Vindication of the Rights of Men* 35–47; McDonagh 80–88). In *Wrongs*, Wollstonecraft, in a provocative spirit, treats a figure of revolutionary disorder sympathetically, using Jemima's pained awareness to attack social injustice toward the disempowered.

Jemima, however, is no passive victim. She "continued to exist" despite adult "neglect." She survives her tribulations by an almost unearthly vitality that resists and transcends class and gender oppression, and this quality finds expression in her peripatetic, transgressive nature (Wollstonecraft, "Maria," *Works* 1: 107–08). Jemima relates that when she used to be sent outdoors on errands as a young servant girl, she often "followed a ballad-singer, to hear the sequel of a dismal story, though sure of being severely punished for delaying to return." Her wanderings, in defiance of the dictates of authority, persist into her adulthood as a taste for the "polish of civilization," that is, the refinements of art and culture. As a kept mistress, Jemima passes her time in leisure reading "to gratify an inquisitive, active mind" and in literary debates—intellectual activities that Wollstonecraft prized as markers of an advanced state of civilization (Wollstonecraft, "Maria," *Works* 1: 113; Wollstonecraft, *Short Residence* 70). Jemima's scholastic tastes correspond with those of Jane Austen's totemic heroine Elizabeth Bennet in *Pride and Prejudice* (written roughly contemporaneously with *Wrongs*, through 1796–1797). When Elizabeth browses through books rather than joining an evening company's sociable card game, she is paid the backhanded and tart compliment of being "a great reader" by a rival for Mr. Darcy's affections (Austen xxxiii, 27).[7] Moreover, through the portrait of the wandering Jemima, Wollstonecraft's politics reject the ethic of benevolent philanthropy advocated by the middle-class and evangelically inclined Sarah Trimmer, whom she had supported in her early career (Franklin 39). As the historian Hugh Cunningham has demonstrated in *The Children of the Poor* (1991), Trimmer's and other evangelicals' philanthropy can be construed as a means of exercising adult, middle-class authority over the children of the poor by regulating them into habits of work or education (Cunningham 47). Wollstonecraft, by contrast, indicates that the child Jemima's wandering habits are potentially redemptive in their interrogation of social expectations. In passing, one may remark upon Wollstonecraft's literary craftsmanship in her vivid portrait of Jemima, a lower-class figure who, unlike Maria, was a child the middle-class Wollstonecraft herself had never been.[8] Drawing attention to Jemima constitutes, for Wollstonecraft, an empathetic move that gesturing at what Percy Bysshe Shelley would later famously call "a going out of our own nature," in his characterization of "love" as an ethical force in The Defense of Poetry (Percy Bysshe Shelley, Shelley's Prose 275–97).

Wollstonecraft celebrates Jemima's peripatetic freedom in the vein that literary scholars are likely to recognize from familiar cultural tropes such as the Romantic wanderer (anticipating the figure of the flaneur famously celebrated by Walter Benjamin later on in the Arcades Project, 1927–40). However, there is a cautionary note to Wollstonecraft's eulogy: Jemima's transgressive nature lasts into her adulthood as an ominous "selfish independence." Wollstonecraft does not presume, or invite the reader, to judge Jemima: the quality eventually lets her help the middle-class Maria escape her confinement in the asylum (Wollstonecraft, "Maria," Works 1: 91, 174–75). Nevertheless, Wollstonecraft remains wary of Jemima's potential for runaway individualism: the transgressive quality of Jemima's childhood is shown not as a sentimental ideal to be striven for, but simply as a need-based means of resisting oppression. Lest the reader mistakenly idolize Jemima, Wollstonecraft inserts uglier aspects to her "selfish independence" as she wages a Hobbesian struggle for survival with other underprivileged women. A maidservant froze to death in winter as a result of Jemima's machinations, but the latter only "thought of her own" troubles. She justifies herself by claiming that she has simply repeated the oppression that was practiced upon herself throughout her childhood, asking Maria and Darnford the unanswerable rhetorical questions discussed in the opening to this essay (Wollstonecraft, "Maria," Works 1: 117–19). In counterpoint to the narrative of masculine individuation for the young wanderer in the early books of Wordsworth's Prelude, Wollstonecraft's Maria and Jemima translate their "childish resentment" into joint political action in their relatively empowered adulthood, enacting a feminist politics elevating social relations above the individual (Chodorow, The

Reproduction of Mothering 11–34; Benjamin, *The Bonds of Love* 19–20). Maria and Jemima's common anger against patriarchal oppression finds a focal point for redemptive hope in the shape of Maria's baby daughter, who is abducted by her father, Venables, when the disheartened Maria attempts to escape with her to Italy. The child provides ethical validation for Maria's attempt to escape from the madhouse in order "to fly to the succour of her child, and to baffle the selfish schemes of her tyrant—her husband" (Wollstonecraft, "Maria," *Works* 1: 169, 175).

Throughout the narrative, the baby is, like the elusive Godot, talked about rather than seen, except for a guest appearance at the very end (Wollstonecraft, "Maria," *Works* 1: 183–84). But her symbolic presence is instrumental in triggering storytelling exchanges between Jemima and Maria. When Jemima witnesses Maria's grief at the loss of her baby in the asylum, her curiosity and sympathy are awakened, and she determines to "alleviate all in her power." She tells Maria her own history: thus, the two women perceive the common social roots of their apparently dissimilar personal angst. Jemima's narration makes Maria realize that despite her baby's middle-class security, in the absence of maternal nurture her daughter may well be subjected to Jemima's sufferings in a patriarchal society: "Thinking of Jemima's peculiar fate and her own, she was led to consider the oppressed state of woman, and to lament that she had given birth to a daughter." Subsequently, Maria enlists Jemima's support to retrieve and protect her daughter, promising Jemima that she shall be the child's "second mother" (Wollstonecraft, *Works* 1: 120). The child's power for revolutionary change lies in her ability to dissolve class barriers between Maria and Jemima, and unite them in a plan for collaborative political action within a newly constituted feminist subculture.

The revolutionary politics that Wollstonecraft associates with Maria's struggles on behalf of this daughter find formal expression in the memoirs that Maria writes for the benefit of the latter. Repudiating the ethos of parental dictatorship that she faced in her own childhood, Maria writes the story of her life for her daughter as an alternative narrative to those constructed by patriarchy (Kelly, *Revolutionary Feminism* 213). In the memoirs, Maria professes that she does not wish to "influence" her daughter: her memoirs do not tell her daughter authoritatively how she must act. Rather, Maria hopes to "exercise" her daughter's autonomous "mind" through "counsel": her memoirs open up a conversation with her child. Maria offers her daughter the choice to act upon her mother's narrative, and to figure out her own solutions to the injustices of patriarchy, that is, the "aggravated ills of life that her sex rendered almost inevitable" (Wollstonecraft, *Works* 1: 123, 85). Virginia Sapiro's studies of Wollstonecraft's political theory have argued that in *Maria*, Wollstonecraft, like her protagonist in her memoirs, does not play the role of "authoritative reasoner" but asks her female readers to share their mutual histories, so they can find social solutions to their seemingly individual problems. Sapiro's interpretation helps contextualize how Maria's daughter facilitates the inception of a radical political process of storytelling and action (Sapiro, *A Vindication* 43; Sapiro, *Feminist Interpretations* 33–45).

Toward the close of the novel the baby is restored to Maria in a melodramatic reversal of misfortune, but this is no fairytale ending. The recovery of her daughter leads Maria to a theatrical declaration: "The conflict is over! I will live for my child!" (Wollstonecraft, *Works* 1: 184). But one never gets to know whether the child will live for her mother. She is described ambiguously as the "little creature, that, with tottering footsteps, approached the bed," in the part of the text that appears to conclude this unfinished novel. The reader knows nothing of the child's early experiences in life, and is left to guess whether the child totters because she is "little," or ill, or has been abused physically. Rather ominously, the narrator states that Maria placed the child "gently on the bed, as if afraid of killing it" (Wollstonecraft, *Works* 1: 183–84). This description of the baby's extreme vulnerability suggests that the child may be barely recovering from a state of trauma. Wollstonecraft's untimely demise makes it impossible to know how the baby negotiates her early experiences of suffering, and whether she turns into another angry girl remains elusive in this fragmentary work. But the figure of the angry girl certainly passes on as a legacy to the next generation of major writers in the family, that is, the Shelley couple who, among other acts of devotion to Wollstonecraft's works, read *Short Residence* together during their legendary elopement from the household of Mary Shelley's father, Godwin (Brekke and Mee, "Introduction," *Short Residence* ix–xxviii).

Perhaps the most memorable girl child in Percy Bysshe Shelley with a significant debt to Wollstonecraft is Cythna in *The Revolt of Islam* (1818), frequently apprehended in criticism as a Wollstonecraftian figure of the emancipated woman, equal in revolutionary fervor to her male coprotagonist, Laon (Duffy 123–48). Less frequently remarked upon, however, is Shelley's representation of the young Cythna as an anticipation of her adult self, much like Maria.

> What wert thou then? A child most infantine,
> Yet wandering beyond that innocent age
> In all but its sweet looks and mien divine;
> Even then, methought, with the world's tyrant rage
> A patient warfare thy young heart did wage
> (856–60)

Laon, remembering his lover Cythna as a "child," celebrates the young Cythna's looks as "innocent," "sweet," and "divine," in the vein of Wordsworth's elfin "little Maid" in "We Are Seven." However, at the same time, Laon feels that Cythna was "wandering beyond" the conventionally expected passive behavior of a girl. She resists the violent "rage" of the "world's" oppressors in a "patient" manner, encoding Shelley's own adherence to the politics of nonviolent resistance (Percy Bysshe Shelley, *Poems* 101; Young 7–33). But her steady "warfare" also recalls Maria's and Jemima's rebellious and uncompromising natures. Cythna's outsider status, while echoing Shelley's male Romantic wanderer, Alastor (or indeed the I-narrator of Wordsworth's *Prelude*), also recalls the young, unmoored Jemima. Shelley's Cythna is an imaginative appropriation of Wollstonecraft's unsettling of gender expectations. The hermaphroditic plenitude of Shelley's works has been explored in recent scholarly investigations, most vividly perhaps in Teddi Chichester Bonca's (psychoanalytically-oriented) study of the fluidity of gendered identities in *Shelley's Mirrors of Love*. In the present instance, Bonca's insight into such fluidity helps earmark how the young Cythna indexes a major woman writer's anticipation of the work of a canonical male poet, within the labile processes of Romantic literary creation.

Wollstonecraft's angry girls remain equally influential on her daughter Mary Shelley's work, and the latter's thematic improvisation on her mother's precedent is visible in the character Perdita, a Shakespearean orphan in Shelley's dystopian science fiction novel *The Last Man* (1826). Shelley's Perdita appears "cold and repulsive," and is subject to "visionary moods," much like Wordsworth's spiritually elect I-narrator in *The Prelude*. Perdita's characterization, however, also offers a logical continuation of Wollstonecraft's critique of social injustice toward an "unloved and neglected" girl (Mary Shelley, *Novels and Selected Works* 4: 15–16). The facet of the child adds an important angle to the significant body of feminist scholarship that has identified and explored literary genealogies and textual conversations between Wollstonecraft and Mary Shelley, most notably in the essay anthology *Mary Wollstonecraft and Mary Shelley: Writing Lives* (2001).

The afterlives of Wollstonecraft's angry girls thus uncover patterns of allusion, transmission, reception, and transformation, revealing that concepts of childhood in Wordsworth and later male writers, familiar to many readers as quintessentially Romantic, were not only created by a pioneering woman writer, but also appropriated and interrogated as intertexts within the girls represented by Wollstonecraft's inheritors.

It may be worth recapitulating the critical gains in locating and reinstating the angry girls of Wollstonecraft (and her descendants) within the critical narratives of Romantic childhood. Maria and Jemima are girls who do not merely suffer but seethe against unfair authority, and they articulate their experiences of childhood deprivation in their relatively empowered adulthood, as Wollstonecraft accords the (remembered) child a sharp sense of agency. The characters' first-person narratives remain imbued with the circumstantial and historical moment of the telling of the story, in the sense later exalted by Walter Benjamin in his essay about such mythic community figures, *The Storyteller* (Benjamin, *Illuminations* 83–109). Rather than relate their troubles to the reader in omniscient narrative, Wollstonecraft's speakers invite the reader to interpret and respond emotionally to their stories, in a sleight of persuasive strategy more familiar in critical accounts of Romantic childhood from the voluble child-speaker of Wordsworth's "We Are Seven," or even William Blake's *Songs of Innocence and Experience* (1794). Simultaneously, the angry girls in the novel *Maria* mark a generic departure from her formerly discursive works such as *Vindication* (1792), and signal a generic return to her earliest works such as *Mary: A Fiction* (1788). Through her articulate, angry girls, Wollstonecraft moves away from telling the ills of the girl child directly (as in her discursive works) to showing them indirectly within the novel's diegetic narrative, in a rhetorical move that is perhaps more subtle and effective (Genette 212–60; Rajan xi–xxv, 174–213).

This essay, while respectfully acknowledging the body of scholarship that has foregrounded women writers' contributions to the literature of childhood, accents Wollstonecraft's importance in this field by calling for a shift of critical emphasis toward a relatively theoretical understanding of her negotiations with childhood through literary representation, by drawing attention to a text unfamiliar in childhood studies as yet.[9] In identifying Wollstonecraft's representations of angry girlhood, and in the continuation and imaginative appropriation of this figure by the Shelleys, this study locates an alternative "tradition" within Romantic childhood. Side-by-side, this account historicizes the trendsetting nature of Wollstonecraft's contribution, by noting that she had died by the time *Lyrical Ballads* was published, a text that has kept Wordsworth and Coleridge at the focus of scholarly discussion about Romantic childhood. By contrast, Wollstonecraft's girls reveal ideological formations that foretell later thinking on childhood as a political category, including twentieth-century formulations of children's rights.[10] Wollstonecraft's near-contemporary Hannah More famously dismissed the Jacobin radicals for supporting the rights of men (denouncing Thomas Paine's fabular work, in the main), and women (censuring Wollstonecraft), and feared that "grave descants" would ensue on the rights of "youth," "children," and "babies" (More 147). More's fears were well founded, for Wollstonecraft had already written these "descants" in literary girls with a different name.

NOTES

1. See also Ross Woodman, "The Idiot Boy as Healer," *Romanticism and Children's Literature* 72–95, print; Marilyn Gaull, "Wordsworth and the Six Arts of Childhood," *1800: The New Lyrical Ballads*, eds. Nicola Trott and Seamus Perry (Basingstoke: Palgrave, 2001) 74–94, print; Judith Plotz, *Romanticism and the Vocation of Childhood* (New York: Palgrave, 2001) xii–85, print.

2. *Wrongs* was one of the texts left incomplete owing to Wollstonecraft's untimely death in 1797. These texts, collected and edited by her husband, William Godwin, were published in 1798 as *Posthumous Works of the Author of A Vindication of the Rights of Woman*.

3. See n.1.

4. Gary Kelly identifies Mary's "alienation" that produces "resistance to the hegemonic order."

5. Perry has argued that from the middle of the eighteenth century onward, British property laws worked systematically to "concentrate wealth in the male line" in the family, depriving women of financial independence.

6. See pp. 2–3.

7. See "Note on the text" by Fiona Stafford. A revised text was finally published in 1813.

8. Cf. Taylor 173. Taylor has made a convincing case for Wollstonecraft's growing sympathy toward the working classes in the latter part of her career, as a forerunner of the "socialist movement that emerged in Britain in the 1820s."

9. The importance of children's literature by Wollstonecraft was foregrounded by Mitzi Myers in studies that reclaimed and validated previously neglected late-eighteenth-century children's literature by women writers as worthy of scholarly enquiry. Myers threw the critical spotlight on the works of Wollstonecraft, Anna Barbauld, Maria Edgeworth, and Sarah Trimmer, who had once been dismissed by Charles Lamb as the "cursed Barbauld crew" of didactic writers who did not share Wordsworth, Coleridge, and Lamb's famous advocacy of imaginative fairytales for the child's reading (Lamb 81–82; Clarke 91–103). Since Myers's work, there have been valuable studies of Romantic Era children's literature, including the essay anthology *Opening the Nursery Door* (1997), as well as projects of historical recovery by scholar Matthew Grenby. Such studies have reclaimed intellectual seriousness for women writers' works for children, and concurrently, undone the former masculinist bias of the Romantic canon.

10. Cf. the landmark international legislation of the UNICEF Convention on the Rights of the Child (1989) to ensure that children are entitled to basic human rights all over the world.

Alexander, Meena. *Women in Romanticism: Mary Wollstonecraft, Dorothy Wordsworth and Mary Shelley.* Basingstoke: Macmillan, 1989. Print.

Austen, Jane. *Pride and Prejudice.* Ed. James Kinsley, introd. and annotated by Fiona Stafford, Oxford: Oxford UP, 2004.

Austin, Linda M. "Children of Childhood: Nostalgia and the Romantic Legacy." *Studies in Romanticism* 42 (2003): 75–98. Print.

Bachelard, Gaston. *The Poetics of Reverie: Childhood, Language and the Cosmos.* Trans. Daniel Russell. Boston: Beacon, 1971. Print.

Benjamin, Walter. *The Arcades Project.* Ed. Rolf Tiedemann. Trans. Howard Eiland and Kevin McLaughlin. Cambridge, MA: Belknap-Harvard UP, 1999. Print.

———. "The Storyteller: Reflections on the Works of Nikolai Leskov." *Illuminations: Essays and Reflections.* Ed. and introd. Hannah Arendt. New York: Schocken, 1968. 83–109. Print.

Blake, William. *Blake: The Complete Poems.* Ed. W. H. Stevenson. Longman: London and New York, 1989.

Bonca, Teddi Chichester. *Shelley's Mirrors of Love: Narcissism, Sacrifice, and Sorority.* Albany, NY: SUNY P, 1999. Print.

Braithwaite, Helen. *Romanticism, Publishing and Dissent: Joseph Johnson and the Cause of Liberty.* Basingstoke: Palgrave Macmillan, 2003. Print.

Carlson, Julie A. *England's First Family of Writers: Mary Wollstonecraft, William Godwin, Mary Shelley.* Baltimore: Johns Hopkins UP, 2007. Print.

Clarke, Norma. "'The Cursed Barbauld Crew': Women Writers and Writing for Children in the Late Eighteenth Century." *Opening the Nursery Door: Reading, Writing, and Childhood 1600–1900.* Ed. Mary Hilton, Morag Styles, and Victor Watson. London: Routledge, 1997. 91–103. Print.

Cunningham, Hugh. *The Children of the Poor: Representations of Childhood since the Seventeenth Century.* Oxford: Blackwell, 1991. Print.

Curran, Stuart. *Poetic Form and British Romanticism.* New York and Oxford: Oxford UP, 1986. Print.

De Man, Paul. *The Rhetoric of Romanticism.* New York: Columbia UP, 1984. Print.

Duff, David. *Romanticism and the Uses of Genre.* Oxford: Oxford UP, 2009. Print.

Duffy, Cian. *Shelley and the Revolutionary Sublime.* Cambridge: Cambridge UP, 2005. Print.

Faubert, Michelle. "A Gendered Affliction: Women, Writing, Madness." *Cultural Constructions of Madness in Eighteenth-Century Writing: Representing the Insane*. Ed. Allan Ingram and Michelle Faubert. Basingstoke: Palgrave Macmillan, 2005. 136–69. Print.

Franklin, Caroline. *Mary Wollstonecraft: A Literary Life*. Basingstoke: Palgrave Macmillan, 2004. Print.

Gaull, Marilyn. "Wordsworth and the Six Arts of Childhood." *1800: The New Lyrical Ballads*. Ed. Nicola Trott and Seamus Perry. Basingstoke: Palgrave, 2001. 74–94. Print.

Genette, Gerard. *Narrative Discourse: An Essay in Method*. Trans. Jane E. Lewin. Oxford: Basil Blackwell, 1980. Print.

Gilbert, Sandra, and Susan Gubar. *The Madwoman in the Attic: The Woman Writer and the Nineteenth-Century Literary Imagination*. New Haven and London: Yale UP, 2000.

Glaser, Brigitte. "Gendered Childhoods: On the Discursive Formation of Young Females in the Eighteenth Century." *Fashioning Childhood in the Eighteenth Century: Age and Identity*. Ed. and introd. Anja Müller. Aldershot: Ashgate, 2006. 189–98. Print.

Godwin, William. *Collected Novels and Memoirs of William Godwin*. Ed. Mark Philp. Introd. Marilyn Butler and Mark Philp. 8 vols. London: William Pickering, 1992. Print.

Grenby, Matthew. "Politicizing the Nursery: British Children's Literature and the French Revolution." *The Lion and the Unicorn* 27.1 (2003): 1–26. Print.

Hall, Stuart. "The Work of Representation." *Representation: Cultural Representations and Signifying Practices*. Ed. Stuart Hall. London: Sage, 1997. 13–62. Print.

Henderson, Andrea K. *Romantic Identities: Varieties of Subjectivity 1774–1830*. Cambridge: Cambridge UP, 1996. Print.

Jordanova, Ludmilla J. "Conceptualizing Childhood in the Eighteenth Century: The Problem of Child Labour." *British Journal for Eighteenth-Century Studies* 10 (1987): 189–99.

Kelly, Gary. "The Politics of Autobiography in Mary Wollstonecraft and Mary Shelley." *Mary Wollstonecraft and Mary Shelley: Writing Lives*. Ed. Helen M. Buss, D. L. Macdonald, and Anne McWhir. Waterloo, Canada: Wilfrid Laurier UP, 2001. 19–32. Print.

———. *Revolutionary Feminism: The Mind and Career of Mary Wollstonecraft*. Basingstoke: Macmillan, 1992.

Lamb, Charles, and Mary Lamb. *The Letters of Charles and Mary Anne Lamb.* Ed. Edwin W. Marrs. Vol. II. Ithaca: Cornell UP, 1976. Print.

Lau, Beth. *Fellow Romantics: Male and Female British Writers 1790–1835.* Farnham: Ashgate, 2009. Print.

McDonagh, Josephine. *Child Murder and British Culture 1720–1900.* Cambridge: Cambridge UP, 2003. Print.

McGavran, Jr., James. "Catechist and Visionary: Watts and Wordsworth in "We Are Seven" and the "Anecdote for Fathers," *Romanticism and Children's Literature in Nineteenth-Century England.* Ed. James McGavran, Jr. Athens: U of Georgia P, 1991. 54–71. Print.

Mellor, Anne. *Mothers of the Nation: Women's Political Writing in England, 1780–1830.* Bloomington: Indiana UP, 2000. Print.

More, Hannah. *Strictures on the Modern System of Female Education, with a View of the Principles and Conduct Prevalent among Women of Rank and Fortune.* London: T. Cadell Jun. and W. Davies. 2 vols, Vol. 1, 1799. Print.

Müller, Anja. "Fashioning Age and Identity: Childhood and the Stages of Life in Eighteenth-Century English Periodicals." *Fashioning Childhood in the Eighteenth Century: Age and Identity.* Ed. and introd. Anja Müller. Aldershot: Ashgate, 2006. 91–100. Print.

Myers, Mitzi. "Impeccable Governesses, Rational Dames, and Moral Mothers: Mary Wollstonecraft and the Female Tradition in Georgian Children's Books." *Children's Literature 14.* Ed. Margaret Higgonet and Barbara Rosen (1986): 31–59. Print.

———. "De-Romanticizing the Subject: Maria Edgeworth's 'The Bracelets,' Mythologies of Origin, and the Daughter's Coming to Writing." *Romantic Women Writers: Voices and Countervoices.* Ed. Paula R. Feldman and Theresa M. Kelley. Hanover, NH: UP of New England, 1995. 88–110. Print.

———. "Romancing the Moral Tale: Maria Edgeworth and the Problematics of Pedagogy." *Romanticism and Children's Literature in Nineteenth-Century England.* Ed. James Holt McGavran, Jr. Athens: U of Georgia P, 1991. 96–128. Print.

———. "Reading Children and Homeopathic Romanticism: Paradigm Lost, Revisionary Gleam, or 'Plus Ça Change, Plus C'Est La Même Chose?'" *Literature and the Child: Romantic Continuations, Postmodern Contestations.* Ed. James Holt McGavran, Jr. Iowa City: U of Iowa P, 1999. Print.

O'Malley, Andrew. *The Making of the Modern Child: Children's Literature and Childhood in the Late Eighteenth Century.* New York: Routledge, 2003.

Perry, Ruth. "Women in Families: The Great Disinheritance." *Women and Literature in Britain 1700–1800*. Ed. Vivien Jones. Cambridge: Cambridge UP, 2000. Print.

Pickering, Jr., Samuel F. *John Locke and Children's Books in Eighteenth-Century England*. Knoxville: U of Tennessee P, 1981. Print.

Plotz, Judith. *Romanticism and the Vocation of Childhood*. New York: Palgrave, 2001. Print.

Poovey, Mary. *The Proper Lady and the Woman Writer: Ideology as Style in the Works of Mary Wollstonecraft, Mary Shelley and Jane Austen*. Chicago: U of Chicago P, 1984. Print.

Rajan, Tilottama. *Romantic Narrative: Shelley, Hays, Godwin, Wollstonecraft*. Baltimore: Johns Hopkins UP, 2010. Print.

Rajan, Tilottama and Julia M. Wright, eds. *Romanticism, History and the Possibilities of Genre*. Cambridge: Cambridge UP, 1998. Print.

Reimer, Elizabeth. "Her favorite Playmate": Pleasure and Interdependence in Dorothy Wordsworth's "Mary Jones and her Pet-tart." *Children's Literature* 37 (2009): 33–60. Print.

Richardson, Alan. *Literature, Education and Romanticism: Reading as Social Practice 1780–1832*. Cambridge: Cambridge UP, 1994. Print.

Rousseau, Jean-Jacques. *Émile, or Education*. Trans. Barbara Foxley. Introd. P. D. Jimack. London: Dent; New York: Dutton, 1974. Print.

Sapiro, Virginia. "A Vindication of Political Virtue: The Political Theory of Mary Wollstonecraft," *Feminist Interpretations of Mary Wollstonecraft*. Ed. Maria J. Falco. University Park, PA: Pennsylvania State UP, 1996. 33–45. Print.

———. *A Vindication of Political Virtue: The Political Theory of Mary Wollstonecraft*. Chicago: U of Chicago P, 1992. Print.

Shelley, Mary. *The Novels and Selected Works of Mary Shelley*. Gen. eds. Nora Crook and Pamela Clemit. Introd. Betty T. Bennett. 8 vols. London: William Pickering, 1996. Print.

Shelley, Percy Bysshe. *Shelley's Prose; or, The Trumpet of a Prophecy*. Ed. David Lee Clark. Rev. ed. Albuquerque: U of New Mexico P, 1954. Print.

St. Clair, William. *The Reading Nation in the Romantic Period*. Cambridge: Cambridge UP, 2004. Print.

Steedman, Carolyn. *Strange Dislocations: Childhood and the Idea of Human Interiority, 1780–1930*. London: Virago, 1995. Print.

Tauchert, Ashley. *Mary Wollstonecraft and the Accent of the Feminine*. New York: Palgrave, 2002. Print.

Taylor, Barbara. *Mary Wollstonecraft and the Feminist Imagination*. Cambridge: Cambridge UP, 2003. Print.

Wolfson, Susan J. *Borderlines: the Shiftings of Gender in British Romanticism*. Stanford, CA: Stanford UP, 2006. Print.

Wollstonecraft, Mary. *The Works of Mary Wollstonecraft*. Ed. Janet Todd and Marilyn Butler. 7 vols. London: William Pickering, 1989. Print.

———. *Letters Written During a Short Residence in Sweden, Norway and Denmark*. Ed. and introd. Tone Brekke and Jon Mee. Oxford: Oxford UP, 2009. Print.

———. *An Historical and Moral View of the Origin and Progress of the French Revolution and the Effect It Has Produced in Europe*. Introd. Janet Todd. New York: Delmar, 1975. Print.

———. *The Wrongs of Woman and Mary*. Ed. Michelle Faubert. Peterborough, ON: Broadview P, 2011. Print.

———. *A Vindication of the Rights of Men and A Vindication of the Rights of Woman*. Ed. and introd. Sylvana Tomaselli. Cambridge: Cambridge UP, 1995. Print.

Woodman, Ross. "The Idiot Boy as Healer." *Romanticism and Children's Literature in Nineteenth-Century England*. Ed. James Holt McGavran, Jr. Athens: U of Georgia P, 1991. 72–95. Print.

Wordsworth, William. "Lines Written a Few Miles Above Tintern Abbey." *Lyrical Ballads, and Other Poems, 1797–1800*. Ed. James Butler and Karen Green. Ithaca: Cornell UP, 1992. Print.

———. "Preface to Lyrical Ballads (1802)." *The Norton Anthology of English Literature*. Ed. Stephen Greenblatt, et al. Vol. 2. New York, London: Norton, 2006. 262–72. Print.

———. *The Thirteen-Book Prelude*. Ed. Mark L. Reed. Ithaca: Cornell UP, 1991. Print.

———. "We Are Seven." *William Wordsworth*. Ed. Stephen Gill. Oxford: Oxford UP, 1984. Print.

Young, Art. *Shelley and Nonviolence*. The Hague: Mouton, 1975. Print.

ANDREW J. SMYTH

That This Here Box Be in the Natur of a Trap

Maria Edgeworth's Pedagogical Gardens,
Ireland, and the Education of the Poor

> "Aye," said Rosamond; "and would it not be very unjust indeed,
> that we should work for them all day."
> "And, perhaps, at last," continued Orlando, "if we did not eat
> animals, they might eat us." (Maria Edgeworth, "The Rabbit" 158)

The breakfast conversation of young Rosamond and her two brothers, Orlando and Godfrey, in this typically Edgeworthian educational setting—where the whole house is a site of learning through experience and inquiry (Narain 58)—sounds like either an animal rights debate gone awry, a grisly B-grade sci-fi movie, or, given that the prompt for this discourse is a rabbit that has been chomping on Rosamond's laburnum saplings, a Monty Python sketch. Within the tale, "The Rabbit," in Maria Edgeworth's *Early Lessons* (1801), the conversation is indeed about animal rights and the ethics of eating meat; particularly, whether the children should kill the rabbit that has invaded Rosamond's garden or give up meat and allow rabbits and all kinds of animals to feed on the human-cultivated gardens. Edgeworth simultaneously expands and complicates the debate with embedded metadiscourses on practical education (following the success of her and her father's pedagogical tract of the same name) and the education of the poor, the subject of an unfinished essay she drafted around 1800. The rabbit—both a signifier of contrived naturalistic innocence and an agricultural pest that invades and disrupts pleasurable production, in this case, Rosamond's personal pedagogical garden—evokes the questions of how best to care for and educate the poor and what dangers to the status quo come with educating the working class. In *Practical Education* as well as in a number of her children's stories, Maria Edgeworth promotes gardening for children, just as her father had set aside separate plots in Edgeworthstown for his children and tenants to cultivate (Colvin and Nelson 58–59; Butler, "Irish" 162). The distribution of land for familial educational purposes, though, raises troubling questions about the situation of the Edgeworths in Ireland after the Act of Union.

The discourse on the rabbits in the children's personal gardens reveals the uneasiness of landowners like the Edgeworths in Co. Longford, Ireland, and others like them throughout the newly United Kingdom, about the implications of educating the poor and dispossessed and allowing them to share in the carefully cultivated gardens of their privilege. Meredith Cary highlights this anxiety in Edgeworth's later Anglo-Irish texts—*The Absentee, Ennui,* and *Ormond*—which attempt to lay out a case for both conciliation and continued rule by families such as the Edgeworths (36–37). By numerous accounts, though, the Edgeworths were some of the most benevolent and empowering landlords in Ireland at the turn of the 19th century. As Mitzi Myers notes, during the 1798 rebellion, the Edgeworths and their property were spared twice, thanks to their good relations with their Irish tenants ("Child's Play" 29). Following the end of the rebellion and the subsequent Act of Union, Richard Lovell Edgeworth was deeply involved in education reform in Ireland, both at the local level, setting up a school for the poor in Edgeworthstown in 1816, and at the national level with his service on the Select Committee on the Education of the Poor and the Commission of Inquiry on Irish Education in 1806 (Taylor 44–48). Still, the character of Rosamond, who is based upon Maria herself (Butler, *Maria* 160, 248) and who undergoes a "female bildungsroman" in a range of stories Edgeworth published between 1796 and 1821 (Myers, "Socializing" 52), reveals in "The Rabbit" an anxiety about the distinction between human and animal that mirrors the divide between the formerly ascendant class of Anglo-Irish to which the Edgeworths belong and the Irish who are now legally copartners in the Union.

Competition between humans and animals stirs strong feelings in children and adults. Harriet Ritvo describes how children's natural history books in the late eighteenth and early nineteenth centuries frequently included man-eating animals, far more so than was justified by the habits of the animals themselves. Since study of zoology was also meant to reinforce human social structures, "then man-eating offered . . . a graphic and extreme illustration of the consequences that might follow any weakening of the social hierarchy" (6). Rosamond's response to the possibility of proliferating rabbits overcoming the means of agricultural production and, in essence, eating up the population, too, illustrates the sophistication of an experientially educated child who considers the evidence offered, acknowledges the ethical complications of the issue, and comes down with a self-interested, pragmatic compromise that removes her from the slaughter that must accompany the exploitation of animals for food: She decides, "I think we should go on eating meat . . . but I am glad I am not a butcher" ("Rabbit" 144). Rosamond's decision, as with so many other insights that inform these tales (Colvin and Nelson 58; Narain 61), derives directly from *Practical Education*:

> It is fortunate for us that there are butchers by profession in the world, and rat-catchers, and cats, other-wise our habits of benevolence and sympathy would be utterly destroyed. Children, though they must perceive the necessity of destroying certain animals, need not be themselves executioners; they should not conquer the natural repugnance to the sight of the struggles of pain, and the convulsions of death; their aversion to being the cause of pain should be preserved both by principle and habit. (166)

Yet, as Erica Fudge explains, the spectacle of cruelty to animals inseparably bonds anthropocentrism and anthropomorphism; that is, inhumane treatment of animals deconstructs the distinction between human and animal: "A human-ness based upon cruelty recognises the link with the animal and is not truly human at all. To enjoy cruelty there must be a recognition of suffering, but such a recognition implies sameness. The distinction of *anthropos* and anthropoid breaks down" (17). For a realistic vision of what human cultivation has wrought upon animal species, Rosamond needs to confront the suffering of the rabbit who, from an anthropocentric mode of thinking, has encroached upon the territory she has taken and marked as her personal garden. Edgeworth's genius in this child's tale brings about for Rosamond recognition not only of her effects on the animals in the gardens but also of the economies of exchange that are rapidly creating a new class of human urban poor in an industrialized era. In 1799, Maria accompanied her father and his new wife, Frances Beaumont Edgeworth, to England, where they stopped to visit the factories at Birmingham on their way to London (Butler, *Maria* 141). Her divided response to this glimpse of industrialization in England can best be seen in *Harry and Lucy Concluded* (1825), where, on a similar visit, Harry admires a factory, while Lucy is horrified by it (Butler, *Maria* 143–44). Such sentiments are immediately visible in "The Rabbit."

Published in 1801, "The Rabbit" turns Rosamond's garden and the eponymous animal therein into a parable of contemporary industrial infringement on the dignity of the working class. A benevolent trap designed by Orlando for the rabbit leads Rosamond and her family directly to a hardworking manufacturer worn down by her job—a mantua-maker who "was obliged to sit in a close room, in a narrow street in London, all day, and often worked whole nights as well as days," much to the detriment of her health, forcing her to flee the city with her daughter to try to revive in the country ("Rabbit" 159–61). Ultimately, Rosamond's mother creates convenient and consoling distance between her family and the apparently single mother and her daughter by guaranteeing her rent at an airy new lodging in Hampstead, complete with gardens. The gardens are meant to offer an idyllic yet productive alternative to the industrial revolution, a nostalgic quest that runs through much of Edgeworth's fiction, but the rental agreement reminds readers that the broken down mantua-maker must continue to be productive on someone else's land, much as a rabbit must steal from the gardens of those who displaced it in order to subsist.

The miserable industrial working conditions alluded to in "The Rabbit" provide the backdrop for the unfinished and unpublished essay, "On the Education of the Poor," which Edgeworth drafted around the same time, 1800. Edgeworth begins her essay by mockingly representing the fears of those who would argue against any form of education for the lower classes: "'Education for the Poor!' They will exclaim. 'The more you educate them the worse they *become*—Make them scholars & they will never mind their business—They will be above work, above their station & they will be idle, and good for nothing'" (5).[1] In other words, the rabbits will run amuck in the gardens. Edgeworth counters this argument by noting up front that her essay will explore the necessary *differences* between lower- and higher-class educations (1), and she argues for the formation of "dispositions, habits & characters which are wanted in that kingdom" (99). As Mitzi Myers illustrates in her analysis of *Practical Education*, Maria and Richard Lovell Edgeworth applauded the connections Jeremy Bentham made between secular education and a national governance that benefited the greatest number of people ("Anecdotes" 239–40). The education that Edgeworth promotes in her draft essay relies on the parallel developments of institutional improvements (city-provided clean housing for new factory workers coming in from the countryside, for example) and informed parental involvement to instill morals in their young children. The question that must be asked, then, is whether the Lockean education that the Edgeworths support and illustrate in Maria's short stories like "The Rabbit" is fundamentally compromised by nationalist, colonialist, and class issues when they take up the matter of educating the poor.

John Locke's influence on the Edgeworths' educational philosophy and practice has been widely acknowledged. As Elizabeth Eger illustrates in her introductory note to *Early Lessons*, Locke points to the kind of heuristic education leading to independent judgment for children that Maria and Richard Lovell Edgeworth advanced (xiv). Indeed, Eger highlights, Maria Edgeworth used an epigraph from Locke for the four volumes of *Harry and Lucy Concluded* in 1825: "The business of Education, in respect of knowledge, is not, as I think, to perfect a learner in all or any one of the sciences; but to give his mind that disposition, and those habits, that may enable him to attain any part of knowledge he shall stand in need of in the future course of his life" (Qtd. in Eger xv–xvi). Such a vision of learning is exactly what Edgeworth draws for her character Rosamond in *Early Lessons*. The precocious girl in "The Rabbit" and other tales in the collection learns how to make informed, independent judgments through experience and dialogue with her mother, father, and brothers—all positioned as what we would later call Vygotskean More Knowledgeable Others (Allan and Tarulli 131–32). The circumstances for Rosamond's ideal learning situation, though, are for a landed family with resources and leisure to devote to education, much as the Edgeworths had at their plantation in Co. Longford.

Edgeworth is also in dialogue with Jean-Jacques Rousseau in her didactic discourse. The disappointing outcome of her older brother Richard's *Émile*-style upbringing led Edgeworth to react against Rousseau in *Practical Education*, even while she shared similar ideas about child-centered education (Myers, "Anecdote" 228–29). According to Catherine Toal, in *Émile* the theme of geographical space is intricately linked with educational philosophy and methods, and the young boy gains a preference for a rural setting by beginning his education in a carefully controlled rural environment (215). Edgeworth challenges Rousseau in the use of that space. Toal notes that Rousseau's tutor wants to maintain the control established in the local setting set against the dangers of the world beyond, whereas *Practical Education* embraces the unknown outside of the local: "Forming a tacit alignment between knowledge and imperial expansion and renovation," *Practical Education* employs mapping metaphors which "express the ease and equanimity with which the Edgeworthian paradigm contemplates the absorption of influences from 'abroad' into the confined space of 'home' . . ." (Toal 216–17). This imperialist approach to knowledge is in line with the Edgeworths' colonial outlook in Ireland and further abroad, and *Practical Education* firmly rejects the contrived lessons that can be culled from Rousseau's garden:

> There is one particular in which Rousseau especially . . . [has] given very dangerous counsel . . . to teach truth by falsehood. The privilege of using contrivance, and ingenious deceptions, has been uniformly reserved for preceptors; and the pupils, by moral delusions, and the theatric effect of circumstances treacherously arranged, are to be duped, surprised, and cheated, into virtue. The dialogue between the gardener and Emilius about the Maltese melon seed is an instance of this method of instruction. Honest Robert, the gardener, in concert with the tutor, tells poor Emilius a series of lies, prepares a garden, 'choice Maltese melon-seed,' and 'worthless beans,' all to cheat the boy into just notions of the rights of property, and the nature of exchange and barter.
> (114)

Edgeworth's fiction emphasizes the lack of contrivance in her characters' experiential educations. While the mother arranges opportunities for learning, the child must reason for herself the lessons to be taken from the ground.

Rosamond is *rooted* in her education, having been provided a literal plot of land to create a pedagogical garden that will lead to long-term material benefits through her opportunities to develop strategic decision-making abilities. That rooting, of course, echoes the plantation policies of the Anglo-Irish that have dramatically altered the nature of Ireland since the Elizabethan Era, a practice that permeates Edgeworth's fiction. In another story in *Early Lessons*, "The Hyacinths," Rosamond's mother pushes her to use critical, long-term planning to replant the roots of the hyacinths at the expense of the soon-to-wither flowers. Rosamond picks up on her mother's lesson with a decisive question that her environment provides for her: "do you mean, that if I choose the roots, you will give me leave to keep them in your ground?—You know if I have no ground to plant them in, they would be of no use to me; and I then had better chuse the flowers" (146). The child ascertains quickly that there is no point in laboring and sacrificing for long-term gains if one does not have the property from which to reap the rewards, and her mother confirms the lesson: "Very true, Rosamond . . . I am glad that you are so considerate—I *do* mean to give you some ground to plant the roots in, if you chuse the roots" (146). The mother-child transaction here parallels the familiar Anglo-Irish landlord-tenant relationship that Edgeworth attempts to recast in terms of educational expertise. J. H. Plumb notes that for Locke and pedagogical practitioners who followed him, education became a way to prepare children for commercial opportunities sprouting up everywhere, and parents were willing to invest heavily in education as well as children's books for this reason (xviii). In this children's tale, the young learner must be guided in how to use property in a profitable manner by the more knowledgeable partner in the dialogue who alone appears to have the power to parcel out land. Returning to Vygotsky, one would have to say that the child Rosamond has learned the value of land ownership quite handily in this particular zone of proximal development. This lesson is critically important at a time when the Edgeworths and Anglo-Irish families like them were in danger of losing the land and class privilege that they had accrued since

Elizabethan times. According to Teresa Michals, "For Edgeworth, 'class' can refer either to status or to character, either to a fixed social position based on the ownership of property or to a collection of personal traits shared by a group of people. Usually, however, it means both. As the market erodes the first sense of the word, Edgeworth supports it with the second" (3). "The Hyacinths" and "The Rabbit" cultivate character, even as the texts raise problematic issues of land ownership and displacement.

In "The Rabbit," Rosamond learns how to manage her plot of land, her garden zone, along with the inhabitants of that land. The invasive rodent is first hated—"Mischievous rabbit! good for nothing animal!" Rosamond exclaims (155)—then feared—"He'll come to me next, I'm afraid, as soon as he has done with you," cries her brother Orlando (155). Still, as Mitzi Myers shows in "Portrait of the Artist as a Young Robin," Rosamond as a shadow of Edgeworth has a deep-seated love for animals (249), and the thought of killing the rabbit to prevent it from eating her garden is repulsive. This impulse to kindliness is a direct nod to Locke, who, as Colleen Glenney Boggs points out, mandated an anti-cruelty-to-animals ethic in his 1693 *Thoughts on Education*: "Children should from the beginning be bred up in Abhorrence of killing or tormenting any living Creature. . . . And indeed, I think People should be accustomed, from their Cradles, to be tender to all sensible Creatures" (Qtd. in Boggs 535). Boggs sees Locke's dictate as one that makes a major transformation in childhood pedagogy, where animals can be used to teach inner values to children, particularly against harming others (535). Writers such as Sarah Trimmer (1741–1810) had instilled bourgeois values such as cleanliness or economy through animals, including a sense of kindness to animals (Kramnick 219–22). Boggs advances, arguing contrary to Erica Fudge, that by the late eighteenth century, "animals began to take on a central function *as animals* in the instruction of children" (535), adopting what she calls a "didactic oncology":

[Animals] stand in for children—their behavior models for the child how to behave—and they remain animals, whose vulnerability and exposure to potential cruelty teaches children to be kind. Children relate to these animals through a double sense of identification and disidentification: because the animal is like them, they are asked to extend kindness, but the kindness they extend makes them human stewards of the animal and marks their separation from it. (536)

In Edgeworth's tale of "The Rabbit," following this scheme, Rosamond's simultaneous identification with the innocent rabbit, which, she acknowledges, does not know that it is doing harm to her garden, and her disidentification with it—the rabbit is still the destructive other—allow her to position herself as the social superior who must decide what's best for the rabbit. What, then, to do about this intruder who seems to make his own the land that Rosamond was granted by her mother? The colonialist parallels are obvious, as are the possible solutions offered at the breakfast table: killing it, imprisoning it, eating it, or risk being eaten by the ever growing population of animals who would compete with humans for food.

Rosamond, with the help of her father and brothers, decides on returning the rabbit to a nearby warren—dislocating the colonized other to prevent it from encroaching on the lands marked for productive gardening by the colonizers, and containing it in a reproductive site that will produce more meat to be consumed by the voracious appetites of the privileged. In the process of returning the animal, though, they discover that the rabbit was a tamed rabbit brought to the farm to be a companion to the daughter of the poor, broken mantua-maker from London. As a product of domestication, the rabbit narrows the distance between human and animal and also serves as a transitional token of entrance back to the country from industrial London. Farmer Early, who recognizes the rabbit he brought for his impoverished visiting relative from London, marvels at the cleverly designed container Orlando has constructed to capture and transport the animal: "this here box be in the natur of a trap . . . a curous, new fashioned one " (160). The tamed rabbit, entrapped in a crafty product of Enlightenment thinking and practice, ultimately is returned to its origination point because Anne, the girl to whom the rabbit was given, decides, "since he does mischief, we had better carry him to the warren again" (160). The question of what to do with the rabbit stands in for what to do with the working poor and the dispossessed, who are mistrusted for their potential for mischief.

Maria Edgeworth in championing the education of the poor is not, of course, explicitly trying to trap and transport them, but the example of the "tamed" rabbit raiding the plantation gardens undercuts the notion of education as a means to develop critical, independent thinking. In the draft essay "On the Education of the Poor," Edgeworth is much more direct about the kind of education the children of the working poor need. She emphasizes instilling moral precepts through the family unit, as she does in the educational household setting of *Early Lessons*, but the Lockean dialogue is replaced with a top-down, patriarchal system that demands obedience to authority: "The punishment which awaits theft, perjury, murder should be exactly stated and these should be made known to the children of the poor as soon as they can understand the nature of the crimes, and punishments—But long before that time they may be prepared for obedience to the laws by the habit of obedience to the orders of parents" (30). What matters, continues Edgeworth, is the manner in which these lessons of crime and punishment, authority and obedience, are delivered, and she promotes a spirit of love that should permeate the family setting as an ideal environment. What she does *not* promote—and I realize the perils of emphasizing what was left out of an unfinished essay—is the kind of critical dialogue in which Rosamond so profitably engages. Instead, one reads of morals being "impressed" on children: for example, "The horror of the crime of perjury should be forcibly impressed on the young mind" (40). Acknowledging the power of oral culture among the agrarian working class, Edgeworth recommends axiomatic learning: "Those who spend most of their time in active employments & who have neither leisure nor materials for refined speculation govern themselves much by the ready made axioms which they have learned in their childhood or which they hear repeated frequently by their neighbors" (42). Through such methods, she prompts parents to inculcate an aversion to crime in their children, who otherwise are highly likely to succumb to the temptations of theft. Education of the poor becomes a better way to tame the rabbits, who would otherwise follow their own impulses and devour the landscape. This education is one of restriction rather than inquiry: "All eateables expecially those of which children are most fond such as fruit etc should be cautiously & absolutely kept from their reach,—They should not be left alone in the room with things which they have been forbidden to take, until they are old enough to have acquired some sense of honor & steady habits of forbearance" (35–36). Despite this prohibitive tone, Edgeworth continues to recognize in this tract the *potential* for the transformative power of literacy and early education among the working poor—including the elimination of opportunities and motives for violent rebellion—and in the process she challenges prevailing economic assumptions of the late eighteenth century.

Responding to the recent horrors of the French Revolution (not to mention the rebellion in Ireland), Edgeworth offers in contrast the possibility for advancement by the rules in England, as long as literacy provides a foundation for personal improvement: "in England a man who can read & write *may* make his way to the first offices of the state, but there is no possibility that this eminence should be attained by an illiterate boor" (52). Deirdre Raftery discusses the role of English texts in literacy reform movements in Ireland, in some of which Richard Lovell Edgeworth played an important role. According to Raftery, while various religious societies and the National System of Education sought to promote literacy among the Catholic poor using readers with texts by English authors ranging from Hannah More, Sarah Trimmer, and Maria Edgeworth to Dr. Johnson and John Milton, many of whom reinforced class and gender stereotypes, the reformers' sustained focus on literacy made it possible for Irish Catholics to break out of social immobility and to gain access to universities and civil service jobs (160). Literacy was highly esteemed: "The official returns made by parishes in 1824 indicate that while many parents were too poor to buy food and clothing, parents were the main purchasers of children's books" (152), even if they were English books. Catholic families recognized English attempts to establish cultural hegemony through education, and they resisted that movement even while urging their children to learn to read and write in English in order to advance themselves (147).

According to Fraser Easton, Maria Edgeworth followed Adam Smith in believing that international trade would correct colonialist oppression and prevent English hegemony, even though England clearly had a material advantage in trade negotiations (101–02). Easton argues that Edgeworth followed Smith "religiously," which led her to set up an imperial paradigm, one that legitimated a presumptive hierarchy of nations headed by Britain" (103). Famously, Adam Smith's *Wealth of Nations* was one of the first books Richard Lovell Edgeworth presented to his daughter Maria when she returned to Co. Longford in 1782 (Butler, "Irish" 160), and she has characters in her Irish novels, such as McLeod in *Ennui*, quote Smith approvingly for the reform of Ireland (Michals 5–6; Butler, *Maria* 368). In her children's fiction, Adam Smith figures significantly, but perhaps under critical scrutiny. Myers describes how the communal work scene organized by the children in "The Cherry Orchard" is "a tongue-in-cheek reworking of the famous pin-making introduction to his *Wealth of Nations*," one that sets "communal solidarity" against the Romantic, male-centered individualism of the story's antagonist, Owen ("Child's Play" 34). Nevertheless, Smith's brief discussion on education in *A Wealth of Nations* had a strong impact on Maria and her father: "Though no friend to state intervention in education generally, Smith made an exception on the behalf of poor children, because he saw in them the victims of one of the central features of the commercial system, the division of labour" (Butler, "Irish" 163). Despite the clear influence of Smith on Richard Lovell and Maria Edgeworth as they engaged in educational reform in Edgeworthstown and beyond, Maria openly questions the Smithian capitalist enterprise in her own musings on the instruction of the poor. Her belief in appropriately geared education for future workers clashes with the all too evident degrading conditions of an industrialist workplace and capitalist framework, and as with the rabbit and the broken down mantua-maker in "The Rabbit," Edgeworth retreats to an agrarian solution, one in which families like her own retain control of the land and economy.

Edgeworth's critique of Adam Smith is quite open in "On the Education of the Poor." While she praises Ben Franklin and other examples of individual self-determination, thus following Smith's central philosophy of individualism, she also states, "Much has been written concerning the wealth, and but little respecting the happiness of nations" (66). She then condemns the demand for luxury with which she associates the growing prosperity of industrial England and contrasts the happiness of country peasants with the depraved lifestyles of poor factory workers that have come in from the country to try to make more money. Anticipating Dickens, Edgeworth writes of drunken dissolution, squalid living conditions, and the dullness of mind inspired by constant application of one task in a factory every day—all leading to crime and vice during the hours outside of work. Thus, while the initial portion of her draft essay promotes top-down education to instill solid character in the working poor, the picture Edgeworth develops of urban manufacturing conditions expands the problem to one of environment after any attempts at childhood education have taken place. With this vision in mind, she asks, "is it not worth while to sacrifice a portion of national wealth to secure a far greater proportion of national health & happiness [?]" (76).

The answer to that question involves a return to agrarian productivity. Edgeworth cites at length *The Essential Principles of the Wealth of Nations; Illustrated, in Opposition to Some False Doctrines of Adam Smith, and Others* by John Gray, who proposes shifting the manufacturing centers to country settings in order to reform the workers: "whereas if those journeymen were to be settled in the country, with a garden adjoining to their house, more of them would be induced to marry, & would find delight in their hours of relaxation in cultivating their garden, or instructing their children" (80). Essentially, in this vision of familial and agricultural fertility, the rabbit is being returned to the warren, but here Edgeworth, following Gray, grafts together the industrial and the agricultural and adds the kind of home-schooling possibilities that readers of *Practical Education*, with much more wealth and leisure at their disposal, would recognize. Indeed, in his own application of Smith's principles on education, Richard Lovell Edgeworth initiated estate changes that included "the granting of a plot to smallholders on which to grow vegetables or keep an animal" (Butler, "Irish" 162). Furthermore, the family did start a school in Edgeworthstown in 1816, the year before Richard Lovell Edgeworth died; and its mixture of students from different backgrounds, classes, and religions continued with some success (170 boys, according to Maria, by 1820) under the direction of Maria's brother, Lovell, until 1833, when poor finances caused her to shut down the school (Taylor 47–48). The estate, though, during this time and beyond, remained in the hands of the Edgeworths.

Maria Edgeworth should be credited for breaking new ground in pedagogical theory and practice, especially in her advocacy for universal education, involved parenthood, and child-centered literacy. Her unpublished essay on educating the poor is a fitting extension of what she and her father accomplished for families of growing means in *Practical Education*, and her recognition of the horrors of manufacturing workplaces shows the kind of skepticism of massive, dehumanizing forces that her children's stories are designed to instill in their audience. While both her stories and educational advancements are compromised by her desire to maintain

Anglo-Irish control of the agrarian landscape, a vision which may explain why "On the Education of the Poor" was neither finished nor published, Maria Edgeworth shares a wealth of good pedagogy in the gardens of her literary landscape.

NOTE

1. I would like to thank Sir David Edgeworth Butler for permission to quote from Maria Edgeworth's draft manuscript, as well as the Bodleian Library, Oxford.

WORKS CITED

Boggs, Colleen Glenney. "Emily Dickinson's Animal Pedagogies." PMLA 124.2 (2009): 533–41. Print.

Butler, Marilyn. "Irish Culture and Scottish Enlightenment: Maria Edgeworth's Histories of the Future." Economy, Polity, and Society: British Intellectual History 1750–1950. Ed. Stefan Collini, Richard Whatmore, and Brian Young. New York: Cambridge UP, 2000. 158–80. Print.

———. Maria Edgeworth: A Literary Biography. Oxford: Clarendon, 1972. Print.

Cary, Meredith. "Privileged Assimilation: Maria Edgeworth's Hope for the Ascendancy." Eire-Ireland 26 (1991): 29–37. Print.

Cheyne, J. Allan, and Donato Tarulli. "Dialogue, Difference and Voice in the Zone of Proximal Development." An Introduction to Vygotsky. Ed. Harry Daniels. New York: Routledge, 2005. 122–44. Print.

Colvin, Christina, and Charles Nelson. "'Building Castles of Flowers': Maria Edgeworth as Gardener." Garden History 16.1 (1988): 58–70. JSTOR. Web. 20 Dec. 2009.

Easton, Fraser. "Cosmopolitan Economy: Exchangeable Value and National Development in Adam Smith and Maria Edgeworth." Studies in Romanticism 42.1 (2003): 99–125. JSTOR. Web. 13 Dec. 2010.

Edgeworth, Maria. "The Hyacinths." Early Lessons, Part III. London: Joseph Johnson, 1801.

———. The Pickering Masters Novels and Selected Works of Maria Edgeworth. Vol. 12. Ed. Elizabeth Eger, Clíona ÓGallchoir, and Marilyn Butler. London: Pickering and Chatto, 2003. 145–47. Print.

———. "On the Education of the Poor." c. 1800. Bodleian Lib., Oxford. Microform. MS Eng. misc. e.1461 (X. Film 13/1A).

———. *Practical Education*. 1798. *The Pickering Masters Novels and Selected Works of Maria Edgeworth*. Vol. 11. Ed. Susan Manly. London: Pickering and Chatto, 2003. Print.

———. "The Rabbit." *Early Lessons, Part III*. London: Joseph Johnson, 1801. *The Pickering Masters Novels and Selected Works of Maria Edgeworth*. Vol. 12. Ed. Elizabeth Eger, Clíona ÓGallchoir, and Marilyn Butler. London: Pickering and Chatto, 2003. 151–64. Print.

Fudge, Erica. *Perceiving Animals: Humans and Beasts in Early Modern English Culture*. New York: St. Martin's, 1999. Print.

Kramnick, Isaac. "Children's Literature and Bourgeois Ideology: Observations on Culture and Industrial Capitalism in the Later Eighteenth Century." In *Culture and Politics from Puritanism to the Enlightenment*. Ed. Perez Zarorin. Berkeley: U of California P, 1980. 203–40. Print.

Michals, Teresa. "Commerce and Character in Maria Edgeworth." *Nineteenth-Century Literature* 49.1 (1994): 1–20. JSTOR. Web. 13 Dec. 2010.

Myers, Mitzi. "'Anecdotes from the Nursery' in Maria Edgeworth's *Practical Education* (1798): Learning from Children 'Abroad and At Home.'" *Princeton University Library Chronicle* 40 (1999): 220–50. JSTOR. Web. 10 Dec. 2009.

———. "Child's Play as Woman's Peace Work: Maria Edgeworth's 'The Cherry Orchard,' Historical Rebellion Narratives, and Contemporary Cultural Studies." *Girls, Boys, Books, Toys: Gender, Culture, Children's Literature*. Ed. Beverly Lyon Clark and Margaret R. Higonnet. Baltimore: Johns Hopkins UP, 1999. 25–39. Print.

———. "Portrait of the Artist as a Young Robin: Maria Edgeworth's Telltale Tailpiece." *Lion and the Unicorn: A Critical Journal of Children's Literature* 20.2 (1996): 230–63. Print.

———. "Socializing Rosamond: Educational Ideology and Fictional Form." *Children's Literature Association Quarterly* 14.2 (1989): 52–58. Print.

Narain, Mona. "Not the Angel in the House: Intersections of the Public and Private in Maria Edgeworth's *Moral Tales* and *Practical Education*." *New Essays on Maria Edgeworth*. Ed. Julie Nash. Burlington, VT: Ashgate, 2006. 57–71. Print.

Plumb, J. H. "The First Flourishing of Children's Books." *Early Children's Books and Their Illustration*. By Gerald Gottlieb. New York: Pierpont Morgan Library, 1975. xvii–xxx. Print.

Raftery, Deirdre. "Colonizing the Mind: The Use of English Writers in the Education of the Irish Poor, c. 1750–1850." *Educating the Child in Enlightenment Britain:*

Beliefs, Cultures, Practices. Ed. Mary Hilton and Jill Shefrin. Farnham, Surrey: Ashgate, 2009. 147–61. Print.

Ritvo, Harriet. "Learning from Animals: Natural History for Children." *Threepenny Review* 21 (1985): 4–6. JSTOR. Web. 13 Dec. 2010.

Taylor, Brian W. "Richard Lovell Edgeworth." *Irish Journal of Education* 20.1 (1986): 27–50. Print.

Toal, Catherine. "Control Experiment: Edgeworth's Critique of Rousseau's Educational Theory." *An Uncomfortable Authority: Maria Edgeworth and Her Contexts.* Ed. Heidi Kaufman and Chris Fauske. Newark: U of Delaware P, 2004. 212–31. Print.

ELIZABETH A. DOLAN

→ Financial Investments vs. Moral Principles

Charlotte Smith's Children's Books and Slavery

Charlotte Smith's remarkably productive twenty-three-year writing career coincided with the most intense decades of British Parliamentary debate about the slave trade.[1] Smith's *Elegiac Sonnets* (1784) appeared the year after a Quaker group presented the first abolitionist petition to British Parliament (1783); her volume *Beachy Head and Other Poems* and her sixth children's book, *A Natural History of Birds*, were published posthumously in 1807, the same year Parliament abolished the slave trade. In her children's literature, Smith addressed a wide range of contentious social issues such as poverty, women's oppression, slavery, and war.[2] In her depiction of poverty and women's lack of rights, she clearly drew on her own financial, legal, and emotional suffering. Separated from her profligate husband in 1787, she struggled to support her large family—including two sons who went to war—by writing, all while battling severe rheumatoid arthritis and depression. By 1794, when she began writing children's literature, Smith was sliding into real poverty. Thus, in her children's books, she urges girls to learn self-supporting skills, decries the illogic of nationalism that leads to war, and explains the relationship between illness and poverty.

Unlike Smith's support for women's rights and for pacifism, her anti-slavery stance in the children's literature ran counter to her best interests. A major aspect of Smith's struggle during the last decades of her life was to settle her father-in-law's, Richard Smith's, estate on her children. This estate included holdings in Barbados, including two sugar plantations from which she regularly received earnings. With the hopes for her children's financial future dependent upon West Indian slave money, Smith might have been silent in her published works on the topic of slavery. And yet, instead, she spoke up repeatedly against slavery in her juvenile literature, a rare practice among children's authors in the 1790s. Thus, this essay will investigate the strategies Smith employed to mediate between the antislavery principles she determined to inculcate in child readers and the financial interests of her children and grandchildren.

Scholars of her novels disagree about Smith's position on the slave trade and slavery in the colonies. For example, Eamon Wright and Moira Ferguson offer passages in Desmond (1792), the Old Manor House (1793), and The Wanderings of Warwick (1794) as evidence of Smith's antislavery views (Wright 73–74; Ferguson 192–93). In contrast, M. O. Grenby characterizes Smith as an ameliorationist, at least in The Wanderings of Warwick (xiv–xvi). More subtly, in their scholarship about The Wanderings of Warwick and Letters of a Solitary Wanderer (1800), Charlotte Sussman investigates Smith's representation of the relationship between colonial violence and "free labor" (183), while George Boulukos examines Smith's depiction of the effect of local plantation politics on emancipation, and Smith's apparent fear of racial hybridity ("Horror"). The conversation about Smith's position on slavery is ongoing.

Unlike the novels' polyvocal representation of slavery, Smith's children's literature depicts teachers who offer explicit advice to children about how to reason through this and other difficult social issues. Although no one has written about her depiction of slavery in children's literature, Smith includes a lengthy discussion between a teacher and children about both slavery and race in the first dialogue of her second children's book, Rambles Farther (1796). In addition, in Conversations Introducing Poetry (1804) and A Natural History of Birds (1807), Smith mentions slavery briefly, endorsing slave uprisings and protesting the treatment of slaves as animals. Although the teacher-centered structure of her children's books allows for a more straightforward response to slavery than does the structure of her novels, Smith's financial interest in the products of slave labor still complicates our ability to assess her position. Smith wrote Rambles Farther, the primary focus of this essay, while negotiating the sale of a plantation and slaves in Barbados. I will argue that Smith teaches children a method of reasoning in *Rambles Farther* that serves as a strategy for managing the conflict between her antislavery principles and her family's financial interest, and, more subtly, allows Smith to acknowledge her own moments of ambivalence about this issue.

As with her innovations in the novel and poetry, Smith's foray into children's literature reveals her sensitivity to generic conventions and to the market. Her correspondence with publisher Thomas Cadell, Sr. suggests that she encountered these texts while homeschooling her children.[3] In a letter to Cadell about *Rural Walks* (1795), she proposes "A sort of School book, calculated not for mere children, but for young persons from twelve to sixteen" (*Collected Letters of Charlotte Smith* 127; hereafter referred to as *CLCS*). Two weeks later Smith situates her work more precisely, stating that it will be "A Work less desultory than Mrs. Barbauld's 'Evenings at Home' (which have had & still have an amazing sale) & calculated for young persons three or four years older" (*CLCS* 131). With Anna Letitia Barbauld and John Aiken's *Evenings at Home* (1792–1796) as her model, Smith imagined a multivolume work, containing "dialogues" that, like Barbauld's and Aiken's individual tales, could be read aloud for a family's evening entertainment. However, Smith's children's book would differ from this model by sustaining a plot and cast of characters in the tradition of Sarah Trimmer's *Fabulous Histories* (1786) and Mary Wollstonecraft's *Original Stories* (1788). The multigenerational cast, including a mother-teacher to shape the conversation, gave every auditor a character with whom to identify. Smith, then, wrote for children ages twelve to sixteen, but expected younger children and adults to encounter the texts as well.

Perhaps thinking about this mixed audience, Smith focused on current social issues in her children's books. In contrast, most late-eighteenth-century children's authors sought to encourage in child readers individual qualities such as hard work, temperance, and charity, and thus often reinforced rather than criticized existing social institutions.[4] Although abolition would become a major focus in children's literature by the 1820s, particularly in the United States, Smith's *Rambles Farther* entered the children's literature market in the 1790s with very little precedent for raising the issue of slavery in this genre.[5] Three children's authors—the exceptions—joined Smith in mentioning slavery before it became common practice in the genre.[6] The sixth volume of Barbauld and Aiken's *Evenings at Home* includes a forthright dialogue between a "Master and Slave" that boldly counters major aspects of the proslavery and ameliorationist arguments in the spirit of dissenting religion. Barbauld and Aiken teach children that the slave trade and slavery in the colonies are unambiguously immoral. Exploring the master-slave bond through plot rather than through dialogue, Maria Edgeworth's "The Grateful Negro," from her 1804 *Popular Tales*, vividly depicts a slave rebellion in Jamaica. Edgeworth contrasts the bond between a kind planter and a "grateful negro" with the antagonistic relationship between a cruel planter and a rebellious slave.[7] While Barbauld and Aiken allow children to "overhear" a discussion between a master and slave, and Edgeworth creates a drama about plantation life, Smith speaks directly to children about how to reason through the proslavery and abolitionist rhetoric, encouraging them to challenge habitual thought with observation and comparison.

This pedagogy of moral reasoning allows Smith to navigate the complexities in her own understanding of slavery, an understanding that was inextricably linked to her marriage. Smith would have learned very little about the slave trade or life in the slave colonies as she grew up on her family's estate in Stoke Park. Yet, when she married into the Smith family at age sixteen, Charlotte Smith began socializing and living among West Indian planters in Cheapside, London. Her husband, Benjamin, grew up in Barbados, the son of West Indian merchant and plantation owner, Richard Smith. She likely met individual slaves in person, as her father-in-law brought five slaves with him when he moved back to London from Barbados (Fletcher 30–31).[8] In addition, she heard many stories about plantation life from Benjamin's stepmother, who prided herself and other "ladies of Barbados" on their firm management of slaves (Fletcher 28). In her two earliest recovered letters, Smith expresses alienation from this West Indian society in Cheapside (CLCS 2). Most poignantly, as an educated young woman with an abusive husband living among West Indian traders, Smith depicts herself as a slave: "the more my mind expanded, the more I became sensible of personal slavery" (CLCS 2). The conception of herself as a slave and of her husband, the son of a West Indian planter, as her owner profoundly shapes her response to African slavery.

Indeed, Smith likely drew on these experiences to write the first dialogue of *Rambles Farther*. A direct encounter between child characters and a former slave leads the children to ask their mother-teacher, Mrs. Woodfield, questions about slavery and race. As this narrative opens, Mrs. Woodfield's brother, Colonel Cecil, writes to say that he has adopted his deceased friend's young daughter, Ella, who was born in Jamaica. He explains that Ella has come to England with Mimbah, "a black female servant, who brought her up, and from whom it will be very painful to wean her" (*Works of Charlotte Smith* 12:118; hereafter referred to as *WCS*). Mimbah, a slave in Jamaica, could not be expatriated back into slavery following the 1772 Mansfield Judgement and thus was essentially free in England. Mrs. Woodfield agrees to welcome Mimbah and Ella into her home in order to educate the white Creole girl along with her own children and niece.

With this former slave among them, Mrs. Woodfield describes unflinchingly the suffering of slaves to the children. Remarkably, she raises the topic in the midst of a discussion about sharks, noting that "These hideous monsters follow the ships which we send to Guinea to convey slaves to our colonies" (*WCS* 12:121). With the collective pronoun "we" in the phrase "we send to Guinea" Mrs. Woodfield does not separate herself from British slavers; instead she displaces their cruelty onto the monstrous sharks. She describes to the children the outcome of the horrible conditions on board slave ships: "of these unhappy men, women, and children, a great number died on their passage, and are thrown into the sea" (*WCS* 12:121). Mrs. Woodfield's blunt account of enslaved Africans being thrown to the sharks suggests that Smith had read about the deaths of Africans on slave ships due to illness, malnutrition, and suicide in Clarkson's 1788 *Essay on the Slavery and Commerce of the Human Species* (*Abolition* 51–53). Clarkson explains that "[the bodies] being thrown into the sea, the tragedy was supposed to have been immediately finished by the not more inhuman sharks" (*Abolition* 59). Mrs. Woodfield's mention of sharks directs adult auditors to Clarkson's pointed comparison between the "not more inhuman sharks" and the slavers in his graphic and disturbing expose. Smith's 1796 portrayal of the brutality inherent in the middle passage signals her familiarity with abolitionist treatises and her support for the abolition of the slave trade more than ten years before it was eradicated by law.

Having been trained to ask questions, Mrs. Woodfield's niece, Caroline, follows up on her aunt's description of the death of Africans during the middle passage: "And what right have we to do this? It is shocking even to think of it" (WCS 12:121). Mrs. Woodfield replies that "To your young and generous nature it appears so, as it must indeed to every unadulterated mind" (WCS 12:121). Characterizing Caroline's question as springing from an "unadulterated mind," Mrs. Woodfield reveals herself as a Rousseauvian, that is, an educator who believes that children come into the world morally pure. Their ability to retain and develop this innate goodness depends upon the quality of their education, broadly conceived (including their home life, reading material, interactions with others, and formal schooling). For Smith, as we will see, teaching children to resist habitual thought was crucial to helping children maintain their "generous nature[s]" and "unadulterated mind[s]."

Indeed, Mrs. Woodfield models the technique of challenging habitual thought by responding to Caroline's question with a commentary on proslavery arguments. "First," Mrs. Woodfield explains to the child characters and readers of all ages, people argue for slavery based on the grounds "of custom; which is an argument that might equally be brought forward to support any abuse or wickedness" (WCS 12:121). Mrs. Woodfield dismisses the common argument that Europeans have the right to hold slaves because they have been engaged in the slave trade for almost 200 years. Planter Bryan Edwards, for example, argues that slavery is "a necessary evil that has always existed" (Abolition 326, 339). Mrs. Woodfield continues to teach children to question received knowledge, explaining that some people justify slavery based "on necessity; as if God had created one race of men, with necessities which could not be relieved but by the blood and tears of another" (WCS 12:121). Here Mrs. Woodfield disagrees with arguments such as George Turnbull's An Apology for Negro Slavery (1788), which situates slavery as "part of the providential order" (Abolition xxiv). Although Mrs. Woodfield takes a clear antislavery position in this discussion, I want to emphasize her effort to teach children to question received information, largely because Mrs. Woodfield's comments are not always this easily categorizable.

In order to question arguments based on "custom," the children learn to rely on observation or other forms of empirical evidence. Summarizing a third proslavery assertion, Mrs. Woodfield informs the girls, "it is said, that the negroes are happier, as slaves to Europeans, than they are in their own country" (WCS 12:121). Mrs. Woodfield's words resonate with a number of abolitionist summaries of proslavery arguments, including Samuel Taylor Coleridge's *On the Slave Trade* (1796). In his treatise, Coleridge challenges five proslavery claims, the second of which is "That the Slaves are more humanely treated and live more happily in the Plantations than in their native Country" (*Abolition* 214). While Coleridge dismantles this assertion by suggesting that Africans reproduce more plentifully in Africa than they do in the colonies, Mrs. Woodfield counters the proslavery claim based on a simple lack of evidence: "This remains to be proved; and we can certainly never prove it" (WCS 12:121). This statement is less clearly antislavery than her dismissal of proslavery arguments based on custom and providential order, and thus suggests some ambivalence in Smith's thinking about the abolition of slavery in the colonies. Indeed, opposing the slave trade while supporting the amelioration of slavery in the colonies would be a position consistent with Smith's acceptance of earnings from Richard Smith's estate. To manage this moment of ambivalence, Mrs. Woodfield invokes her method of reasoning, relying on eyewitness testimony to counter the assumption that slaves are happier in the colonies than in Africa: "I have conversed with persons who have been present at negro sales, and they have assured me, that so far from feeling themselves happier, these miserable victims of commercial avarice exhibit the most affecting symptoms of despondence and anguish" (WCS 12:121). Ultimately, Mrs. Woodfield relies on the testimony of "persons who have been present at negro sales" to manage her uncertainty. Smith teaches children that when they do not know something firsthand, they should gather empirical evidence such as eyewitness accounts.

Right after Mrs. Woodfield's three-point summary of proslavery rhetoric, Henrietta asks, "But, mamma, why are [slaves] black?," inviting Mrs. Woodfield to link the enslavement of Africans to race, or at least to clarify the viewpoint that one race is meant to serve another (WCS 12:121). Notably, Mrs. Woodfield leaves all mention of hierarchy out of her explanation of race: "I can give you no other reason, than that it has pleased God to make them so; as it was his pleasure to make us white.—Another race of men in North America are of a copper colour; and the Asiatics, within certain degrees of the line, are of another shade of yellow" (WCS 12:121). Mrs. Woodfield extends the conversation about race beyond the binaries of black and white, a strategy consistent with abolitionist rhetoric. Once Mrs. Woodfield has broadened the discussion of race, the children begin to consider other racial groups. Caroline asks: "Pedro; my cousin Rivers's servant, whom he brought with him from the East Indies, is an Asiatic, is he not?" (WCS 12:121). Mrs. Woodfield explains, "Yes, you remember he is not black like Mimbah, nor fair like English people, but of a tawny complexion, with strait course black hair; he came from Bengal: but in the northern parts of the Continent of Asia, which is a part of China, the Chinese and Tartars become fair, yet still with a particular cast of countenance" (WCS 12:121). Here Mrs. Woodfield echoes Clarkson's and Olaudah Equiano's attempts to "decenter the binary hierarchy of white and black by positing 'tawny' as an intermediary complexion" (Kitson 116). As with the question of slaves' happiness, Mrs. Woodfield emphasizes observation before evaluation.

In an apparent shift, Mrs. Woodfield extends her lesson about the dangers of habitual thought into a conversation that seems to advance proslavery ideas. As with the question of slaves' happiness, this conversation focuses on slaves' own feelings about their lives in the colonies. Mrs. Woodfield considers why Mimbah might still "love her own country best" though she is free on British soil (WCS 12:119):

> You see now, my dear girls, how strong is that habit which attaches even slaves to their native country, and that our ideas of the horrors of that state we call slavery, cannot all be well founded, since this negro woman, who knows that she is free here, who is mistress of her time, and has every thing found for her, without any other work than the little attendance such a child requires, prefers her own country where she was a slave, and liable to be beaten or turned into the field on the caprice of her mistress. (WCS 12:119)

Here Mrs. Woodfield enacts the methodology she has been teaching— challenge conventional wisdom ("our ideas of the horrors of that state we call slavery") based on an observation (Mimbah misses Jamaica). This passage might be interpreted as a proslavery argument that resonates with the liberal impulse to support independence in Europe, but not in the colonies or in Africa, because non-Europeans would not appreciate liberty or use it wisely (Saïd 80).

Although she dismisses arguments in favor of the slave trade, Smith again entertains uncertainty about slaves' lives in the colonies. She uses her moral reasoning methodology to allow readers to question the "horrors" of slavery. Yet, her lesson on habitual thought—focused here on demonstrating to the children "how strong is that habit which attaches even slaves to their native country"—presumes that slaves' lives are full of horror. In other words, Mrs. Woodfield suggests that "[O]ur ideas of the horrors of that state we call slavery, cannot all be well founded," yet she accepts that in Jamaica, "where [Mimbah] was a slave," she was "liable to be beaten or turned into the field on the caprice of her mistress." Ultimately, then, Mrs. Woodfield uses Mimbah's homesickness to exemplify the dangers of habitual thought, the repeated lesson in this dialogue. Thus Smith, through Mrs. Woodfield, encourages children to consider that desiring the familiar can compromise their freedom—the habitual thought that is nostalgia can create its own kind of enslavement.

In addition to relying on observation and empirical evidence to fight habitual thought, Mrs. Woodfield recommends comparison. She suggests that English colonists' early habituation to slavery and lack of exposure to other social and economic structures with which they might compare slavery make the institution possible:

> A person brought up [in the West Indies], and accustomed to [slavery], has not the least idea, that these unhappy men are of the same species; they no more feel hurt at seeing them compelled to labour or suffer punishment, than persons in this, not accustomed to think, do, when they see a team of horses, or a yoke of oxen, and the driver exercising his whip. (WCS 12:119)

Seeing the same oppression and suffering day after day normalizes it, dulling rather than sharpening one's moral sensibility. Mrs. Woodfield's comparison between the suffering of slaves and of animals in this passage recurs as she explains slave life to the children. Mrs. Woodfield compares the lives of house slaves in the colonies to the lives of servants in England, and the existence of field slaves to that of animals:

There are different sets of slaves—some are employed, as we employ our servants, for domestic purposes, and are called house negroes; another set are occupied, I am sorry to say, as we employ our horses and oxen; while others are directed like our carters and plowmen, to drive them. When an house servant misbehaves, it is a frequent punishment to send them into the field, a circumstance so mortifying to their pride, that it has often been known to drive them to despair and death. (WCS 12:119)

Mrs. Woodfield describes the hierarchy of slaves in comparative terms that British children can understand. House slaves do the work of domestic servants, field slaves do the work of horses and oxen, and drivers do the work of carters or plowmen. The comparison of field slaves to animals is particularly damning of slavery, a point that Mrs. Woodfield emphasizes by implying that some house slaves would rather commit suicide than be sent to work the fields like an animal.

In fact, comparing slaves to animals was a common practice on both sides of the abolition debate.[9] Smith refines the abolitionist focus on the common suffering of animals and slaves by focusing in *A Natural History of Birds* on the inhumanity of the economic structure of slavery: "A horse is sometimes overworked by his barbarous owner, that he may make all the present profit he can of him; and the same thing has, I fear, been done in those countries where the unhappy negroes are purchased, and compelled to labour to raise sugar, and coffee, and cotton, for the use of Europeans" (WCS 13:281). In this passage, Smith's teacher figure uses the analogy between horses and slaves to condemn the dehumanization of Africans when they are valued only for their use within the institution of slavery. Ultimately, Smith decries the commerce that is the root of slavery, describing slaves as "miserable victims of commercial avarice" (WCS 12:121). This point makes the conflict between Smith's antislavery position in her literature and her financial entanglement in plantation profits all the more striking.

During the period that Smith wrote *Rambles Farther* and *A Natural History of Birds* her efforts to settle her father-in-law's estate on behalf of her children focused on the sale of his slave plantations. In 1790, Smith threatened to publish a pamphlet accusing the "conduct of the trustees" of this estate of withholding from her children money she thought rightly theirs. She identifies a number of sources of money that the trustees have not pursued, including the plantation called Gays in Barbados (Stanton and Guest 15). Smith felt she had a right to be consulted about the management of this plantation because Benjamin used her wedding dowry to buy it, a point to which I will return (Stanton and Guest 9). In July 1797, shortly after the publication of *Rambles Farther*, she wrote to trustee John Robinson demanding control of Gays. She orders him "to deliver the Plantation & Negros, and stores into such hands as I shall direct" (CLCS 282). Presumably she did gain control of Gays, because in 1799, she negotiates via letter with the planter William Prescod about its sale:

> The valuation [of Gays plantation] last year was £22,048.15.0. Your present Proposal is near 1,000£ less. It is true the value of the Negroes is by death lessen'd; but only three of considerable value have died: a Man worth (as pr valuation of 1798) 70£ called Kit James, a young Woman called Catharina, stated to be worth £100, and a Woman called Sarah or Sareey worth £80. The three other Girls or Women were of inferior value, and one Slave named Bennah, tho stated in the Managers Account to be a Man, was a very old Woman worth nothing; her death therefore . . . is rather a relief than a disadvantage to the Estate. (CLCS 353)

Stanton has convincingly documented Smith's business acumen in the realm of publishing, but to witness Smith negotiate for the sale of a plantation and its slaves is shocking (Stanton, "Charlotte"). Most startling, Smith assesses three girls to be "of inferior value" and "Bennah" . . . "a very old woman" to be "worth nothing." A master of discursive register, Smith wisely speaks the planter Prescod's own language in her negotiations with him. Nonetheless, this passage makes it clear that Smith understood that a monetary value was assigned to people, and she hoped that her children would benefit from an advantageous valuation of the slaves.

In short, the excerpt from Smith's letter to Prescod potentially situates Smith's stated sympathy for the "miserable victims of commercial avarice" as a moment of great hypocrisy. Writing *Rambles Farther*, Smith encourages children to rethink the customs and assumptions that sustain slavery, and then within two years she seeks to benefit from the sale of a plantation, including the slaves. Rather than label her a hypocrite, however, I will suggest that it is more productive to consider how pressured Smith must have felt knowing that her children's and her own livelihood depended on her husband's and her father-in-law's slave plantations—an institution she opposed. In the end, she chooses her children's well-being over other options she might have considered, such as freeing the slaves on the Barbados plantation. The interpretive key for understanding this choice, I argue, is her self-conception as a slave. Smith believed strongly that she had been sold—"as a slave" not "like a slave"—into marriage to Benjamin.

In fact, outside of discussions of the sale of the Barbados plantations, Smith uses the word "slave" in her letters in reference only to herself. Describing her marriage to Benjamin Smith, she characterizes herself as "a slave and a martyr to a man contemptible in understanding" (CLCS 654), as "sold into bondage," and as "a wretched slave" (CLCS 455). When eventually separated from her husband, Smith asserts that nonetheless, "I am still in reality a slave" because she was compelled to write constantly in spite of severe illness in order to support her large family (CLCS 350). Speaking generally about her life she decries "this weary pilgrimage, this worse than African bondage" (CLCS 522). These references begin as early as 1768, shortly after her marriage, but become more frequent, significantly, in her correspondence about trust business between 1802 and 1804. The occasions for thinking about herself as a slave, then, are her marriage to Benjamin Smith, the resulting struggle to survive financially, and finally her Herculean effort to salvage some money from Richard Smith's estate for her children.

Ferguson argues that as early as 1670, feminist authors commonly drew a connection between women's oppression and colonial slavery, yet, in their comparisons, authors "failed to [condemn] colonial slavery itself" (23–25). Smith does not quite fit this pattern. She does not, like Wollstonecraft, compare marriage to slavery because a husband subsumes a wife's legal rights, nor does she compare marriage to prostitution because women trade themselves to marry a man with money. Instead, she likens her own relentless work, physical suffering, and lack of hope—all of which she attributes to her "sale" into marriage to Benjamin—to the working and living conditions of a slave in the colonies. Smith's willingness to condemn the slave trade in her children's literature yet to question slaves' own attitudes toward living in the colonies reveals the degree to which she experienced her work life as enslavement. As I mentioned above, in 1781, Benjamin Smith bought Gays plantation from George Walker using Charlotte Smith's £3000 marriage settlement (Stanton and Guest 9). The money that was included in the "sale" of Smith into marriage, then, was used to buy the plantation she eventually sold for the benefit of her children. In selling this plantation and its slaves, Smith hoped to gain some small restitution—at least for her children—for "this weary pilgrimage, this worse than African bondage" (CLCS 522). She felt that she and the slaves had a common oppressor in planter families. Psychologically, in order to choose her children's well-being over the liberty of the slaves on Gays plantation, she might have needed to entertain the idea that not all slaves were subject to horror.

A serious consideration of Smith's response to slavery, then, must take into account her personal identification with the bonds of slavery as well as her effort to teach children ethical reasoning tools. Because she addresses issues that are unfolding right before her—including the debate about ending the slave trade—Smith teaches children first to observe and then to compare before they accept customary judgments about the world. Smith herself seems more comfortable with the abolition of the slave trade than with the emancipation of slaves in the colonies, but uses her reasoning method to manage her own ambivalence. Ultimately, Smith intended her lesson to children to be useful for developing an ethical response to slavery in all its forms. As Mrs. Woodfield's comment to Caroline about her "unadulterated mind" demonstrates, Smith—like Jean-Jacques Rousseau and William Wordsworth—understood children to be born pure, yet she also understood that this moral vision would dim as the realities of life impinged on the growing child. Therefore, she determined to teach children a method of reasoning based on observation and comparison to help them resist the kind of acculturation that would compromise their moral selfhood. In a more hopeful vein, Smith envisioned a time when these future adults would not be so terribly constrained by their financial and cultural inheritances, when their livelihood could be unentangled from the oppression of others. She would have agreed with Opie's 1823 charge to children: "You will make the world what we of the present generation wish it to be, but are not able to make it ourselves" (4). Smith sought to ensure that children would be ready for this important work.

NOTES

1. I would like to thank Monica Najar, Rosemary Mundhenk, and Judith Stanton for their invaluable feedback on this essay at various stages.

2. Smith's children's books include *Rural Walks* (1795), *Rambles Farther* (1796), *Minor Morals* (1798), *Conversations Introducing Poetry* (1804), *History of England* (1806), and *A Natural History of Birds* (1807).

3. Smith's daughter Harriet Amelia (b. 1782), whom Smith educated at home, was twelve when her mother began writing *Rural Walks*, fourteen when *Rambles Farther* appeared, and sixteen when *Minor Morals* was published.

4. See Kramnick 203–40.

5. On American abolitionist literature for children, see, among others, Roth, Keller, and DeRosa.

6. Poets such as William Blake in "The Little Black Boy" from *Songs of Innocence* (1789) and Amelia Opie in "The Negro Boy's Tale: A Poem" (1802) feature sympathetic child slaves to inspire readers' opposition to slavery, but do not identify children as their primary audience. Although she published the poem with no mention of children in 1802, Opie republishes "The Negro Boy's Tale: A Poem," in 1825 with an "Introduction: Addressed to Children," a move that reflects the growing number of abolitionist children's texts in the 1820s.

7. Edgeworth's story has been labeled both "emancipationist" and "ameliorationist" (Ferguson 232; Boulukos, "Maria" 22–23).

8. The year before Smith moved to Cheapside, the *Gentleman's Magazine* reports that there are 20,000 "Negroe servants" living in London (Gerzina 41).

9. See Ginsberg 89–98 and Perkins 18.

WORKS CITED

The Abolition Debate. Vol. 2. *Slavery, Abolition and Emancipation: Writings in the British Romantic Period.* Ed. Peter J. Kitson. London: Pickering and Chatto, 1999.

Aiken, John, and Anna Laetitia Barbauld. "Master and Slave." *Evenings at Home; or, the Juvenile Budget Opened.* Vol. 6. London: J. Johnson, 1796. 81–88.

Bentham, Jeremy. *An Introduction to the Principles and Morals of Legislation.* Ed. J. H. Burns and H. L. A. Hart. London: U of London, Athlone Press, 1970.

Boulukus, George. "Maria Edgeworth's 'Grateful Negro' and the Sentimental Argument for Slavery." *Eighteenth-Century Life* 23 (1999): 12–29.

———. "The Horror of Hybridity: Enlightenment, Anti-slavery and Racial Disgust in Charlotte Smith's *Story of Henrietta* (1800)." *Slavery and the Cultures of Abolition: Essays Marking the Bicentennial of the British Abolition Act of 1807.* Ed. Brycchan Carey and Peter J. Kitson. Cambridge, UK: Brewer, 2007. 87–109.

DeRosa, Deborah C. *Into the Mouths of Babes: An Anthology of Children's Abolitionist Literature.* Westport, CT: Praeger Publishing Group, 2005.

Ferguson, Moira. *Subject to Others: British Women Writers and Colonial Slavery, 1670–1834.* New York: Routledge, 1992.

Gerzina, Gretchen Holbrook. *Black London: Life Before Emancipation.* New Brunswick, NJ: Rutgers UP, 1995.

Ginsberg, Lesley. "Of Babies, Beasts, and Bondage: Slavery and the Question of Citizenship in Antebellum American Children's Literature." *The American Child: A Cultural Studies Reader.* New Brunswick, NJ: Rutgers UP, 2003. 85–105.

Grenby, M. O. Introduction to *The Wanderings of Warwick.* Vol. 7. *The Works of Charlotte Smith.* Gen. ed. Stuart Curran. London: Pickering and Chatto, 2007. vii–xviii.

Keller, Holly. "Juvenile Antislavery Narrative and Notions of Childhood," *Children's Literature* 24 (1996): 86–100.

Kitson, Peter J. *Romantic Literature, Race, and Colonial Encounter.* New York: Palgrave, 2007.

Kramnick, Isaac. "Children's Literature and Bourgeois Ideology: Observations on Culture and Industrial Capitalism in the Late Eighteenth Century." *Culture and Politics from Puritanism to the Enlightenment.* Ed. Perez Zagorin. Berkeley, CA, 1980. 203–40.

Opie, Amelia Alderson. "The Negro Boy's Tale" (1801/1824). In Deborah C. De Rosa *Into the Mouths of Babes: An Anthology of Children's Abolitionist Literature.* Westport, CT: Praeger Publishing Group, 2005. 1–12.

Perkins, David. *Romanticism and Animal Rights.* Cambridge: Cambridge UP, 2003.

Roth, Sarah N. "The Mind of a Child: Images of African Americans in Early Juvenile Fiction." *Journal of the Early Republic* 25.1 (Spring 2005): 79–109.

Saïd, Edward. *Culture and Imperialism.* New York: Vintage, 1994.

Smith, Charlotte. *Collected Letters of Charlotte Smith.* Ed. Judith Philips Stanton. Bloomington: Indiana UP, 2003.

———. *The Poems of Charlotte Smith*. Ed. Stuart Curran. New York: Oxford UP, 1993.

———. *The Works of Charlotte Smith*. Gen. ed. Stuart Curran. 14 vols. London: Pickering and Chatto, 2007.

Stanton, Judith. "Charlotte Smith's Literary Business." *The Age of Johnson* 1 (1987): 375–401.

Stanton, Judith, and Harriet Guest. "'A Smart Strike on the Nerves': Two Letters from Charlotte Smith to Thomas Cadell, with a Title Page." *Women's Writing* 16.1 (2009): 6–19.

Sussman, Charlotte. *Consuming Anxieties: Consumer Protest, Gender, and British Slavery 1713–1833*. Stanford: Stanford UP, 2000.

Tague, Ingrid H. "Companions, Servants, or Slaves? Considering Animals in Eighteenth-Century Britain." *Studies in Eighteenth-Century Culture* 39 (2010): 111–30.

Wright, Eamon. *British Women Writers and Race, 1788–1818: Narrations of Modernity*. Basingstoke: Palgrave Macmillan, 2005.

ELIZABETH GARGANO

The Innocent Child in the House of History

Storytelling and the Sensibility of Loss in Molesworth's The Tapestry Room

Mary Louisa Molesworth's two best-known children's novels, *The Cuckoo Clock* and *The Tapestry Room*, appeared in print within two years of each other and bear striking similarities: both depict innocent children who come to inhabit vast and ancient houses that seem burdened by the weight of their own history, and both depict children who suffer from a paralyzing *ennui* that at times amounts almost to despair. Imprisoned in houses that are comfortable only for adults, and rather elderly adults at that, they find little room for self-expression and few opportunities to play. Yet, as they continue to explore these vast and in some ways forbidding domiciles, the children find secret spaces within the houses that open on vistas of fairyland; through dreamlike journeys, often at night, they escape to a visionary realm linked with a romanticized childhood innocence. Significantly, however, these songs of innocence inexorably fade into narratives of compromised adult experience; the promised escapes into fairyland lead back to the cul-de-sac of history, as magical, fairylike figures narrate scraps of tragic family history to the listening children.

Like so much children's literature, Molesworth's novels might be irreverently described as practicing a bait and switch on their naïve child protagonists (and child readers). Enchantment is the sugar coating for the bitter pill of a moral admonition. Yet, the situation is not quite so simple as this formulation implies, for if *The Cuckoo Clock* punctuates its magical adventures with didactic advice, *The Tapestry Room* does not. Further, neither novel ends with a simple moral or clear lesson; rather, Molesworth's narratives seek to cultivate a generalized sensibility of loss that can deepen children's emotional connections with others. At the same time, these two conflicted novels glamorize and, to a degree, fetishize childhood innocence, even as they seek to erode it by acquainting children with the struggles of daily existence and the tragic nature of history.

While *The Cuckoo Clock* is generally regarded as a more polished and coherent work, I choose to focus on the relatively ignored later novel. A more fragmented and problematic work, *The Tapestry Room* is also less didactic. Working not through direct moral injunctions but rather through generalized appeals to a culture of sympathy, the novel grapples more directly with its own conflicted agendas, revealing contradictory longings for innocence and experience. In *The Tapestry Room*, the dark and shadowy house of history is a difficult place to inhabit. Often lonely and even frightening, it dwarfs the child's body, and tempts children to escape into its secret passageways in search of fairyland. Yet, all such journeys are only temporary digressions, and the house itself constitutes the children's final destination, since its secret doorways to magical worlds close inevitably as the children grow up.

Like its predecessor, *The Cuckoo Clock*, *The Tapestry Room* draws on a long tradition of children's literature that situates innocent children in houses that typify a dreary or oppressive adult society. From Alice's discovery of a mysterious looking-glass house that lurks behind the drawing room mirror in Lewis Carroll's *Through the Looking-Glass* (1871), children's literature has offered rich depictions of small children exploring mysterious houses that have a talent for shape-shifting: as the daring child explores further, these shadowy structures reveal hidden recesses and secret stairways—or in Alice's case, a drawing room in reverse that opens onto an exciting but disorienting complementary world. While the child is small, fragile, and innocent, the house often looms large, freighted with the weight of social conventions and adult dispensations. In *Looking-Glass*, Alice repeatedly associates herself with her black kitten, whom she playfully describes as a "wicked little thing" (Carroll 107). The kitten is "wicked" because she disrupts the orderly, utilitarian activities that Alice regards as adult; she resists being washed and unrolls balls of yarn. Similarly, in a house that seems locked into perpetual stillness, Alice, too, is playfully disruptive. In Tenniel's classic illustration, the drawing room oozes propriety and solemnity; Alice is tiny enough to fit on the lace-draped mantelpiece, between the glass domes covering a clock and a vase of flowers. Under her playful ministrations, the solid barrier of the mirror melts into "a bright silvery mist" (Carroll 111). Illuminated against the shadows, the child's body forms a vivid contrast with the dark stillness of the rest of the house.

Especially in the so-called golden age of children's fantasy literature, Alice's literary siblings—the children who enact their vivid games against the looming edifices that adults have built—are legion. In George Mac-Donald's *The Princess and the Goblin* (1872), the young princess, Irene, discovers a hidden stairway leading to the turret room of a magical lady, who may be her great-great-grandmother. As is well known, C. S. Lewis's Narnia stories draw on this tradition: in *The Magician's Nephew* (1955), two children navigate the secret spaces of the attic to sneak into a magician's secret room. In *The Lion, the Witch, and the Wardrobe* (1950), the route to Narnia is through an old wardrobe in a rambling country house. Similarly, Mary Norton's novel *The Borrowers* (1952) reveals another smaller, hidden world in a house that seems tediously respectable. Later examples might include the sinister house of shadows that lurks within an ordinary family home in Neil Gaimon's *Coraline* (2002), or Harry Potter's Hogwarts, with its shifting staircases, secret passages, and a room that appears and disappears as needed. Significantly, numerous works in the realistic tradition, such as Frances Hodgson Burnett's *The Little Princess* (1905) and *The Secret Garden* (1911) develop a similar motif: the child exploring previously hidden spaces and making discoveries in an old house weighted with mysteries and secrets.[1]

Narratives that follow this common plotline frequently minimize the role and presence of adults to an extreme degree. Reduced to conventional, static figures, the adults may appear nearly as lifeless as the furnishings; in some cases, in fact, the chairs, tables, and curios may even have a magical, vital existence that the adults themselves lack. The general effect, then, is to foreground the child as the vital center of a static house, or even perhaps as the single inhabitant who is fully alive. In some iterations, the child's journey offers redemptive possibilities. Alice's journey to Looking-glass Land enables her to escape the boredom and conventionality of the adult world, while Mary Lennox's discovery of a secret garden revivifies a sterile house burdened with loss and despair. In contrast, Coraline's dangerous explorations send her running back to the conventional world.

Molesworth's novels exemplify an original and striking variation on this tradition; they highlight contradictions inherent in the plotline that set exuberant childhood physicality at odds with the static presence of the houses dominated by adults. As Judith Flanders notes in *Inside the Victorian Home*, throughout the nineteenth century, children's living quarters became increasingly distant from those of the adults in prosperous middle-class homes. Situated atop the house near the servants' quarters, the Victorian nursery served as a status symbol.[2] The house in *The Tapestry Room*, the venerable mansion of an aristocratic French family, embodies this emotional geography of familial distance. The child protagonist, seven-year-old Jeanne, occupies a room on the highest story: "In that great rambling house it was really quite a journey from [Jeanne's] room to her mother's salon" (*The Tapestry Room* 10; hereafter referred to as TR). During the course of the novel, Jeanne's father ascends to the upper stories only once, to investigate Jeanne's claim that Dudu, the ancient raven who lives in the backyard, has perched on the tapestry room's windowsill; the elderly father's journey up so many stairs is presented as an inconvenient sacrifice to childhood whimsy (TR 14).

The strikingly similar houses in *The Cuckoo Clock* and *The Tapestry Room* are presented as both old and chilly, symbolizing adult control and lack of emotional warmth. "Once upon a time in an old town, in an old street," *The Cuckoo Clock* begins, "there stood a very old house."[3] *The Tapestry Room* renders Jeanne's old French mansion even bleaker by situating it in an icy wintry landscape where "not the least little ray of sunshine" can penetrate "the leaden-grey sky" (TR 2). As we soon learn, Jeanne's internal state parallels the wintry external world: "upstairs, inside the old house," the little girl, already chilled, is making herself "colder still"; she is "pressing [her nose] against the icy window-pane and staring out on to the deserted, snow-covered garden, and thinking how cold it was, and wishing it was summer time again" (TR 3). Repeatedly, winter, the end of the year, is associated with the old house, its faded furnishings, and its aging inhabitants, both animal and human. The cold makes Jeanne's white-haired father "very rheumatic" because he is "not so young" anymore (TR 14). Even Dudu, the raven, is "depressed in spirit by the cold," reduced to hobbling painfully across the snowy garden.

Some form of the word "old" occurs at least twenty times in the novel's first chapter, frequently linked with images of cold and isolation. Since her parents are busy with adult concerns, Jeanne's most constant companion is her nurse, Marcelline, who, Jeanne speculates, may be "quite a hundred" years old (TR 6). Given their age and emotional distance, adults tend to merge with the furnishings of the house: Marcelline is described as having "reached a settled oldness, like an arm-chair which may once have been covered with bright-coloured silk, but which, with time and wear, has got to have an all-over-old look" that never changes (TR 4).[4]

Jeanne is particularly fascinated by the mysterious room down the hall "hung with tapestry, very old, and in some parts faded" (TR 10). Attracted to the room by the reflected moonlight from "the snow-covered garden" shining through its window (TR 10), Jeanne fancies that the peacocks in the tapestry are alive and moving (TR 12). Thus, the old house, which leaves Jeanne feeling cold and isolated, leads her to seek warmth and emotional connection in the realm of fantasy. In a rare image of warmth, we are told that Jeanne loves to stir up the nursery fire to release a "bevy of lovely sparks . . . like a thousand imprisoned fairies escaping at some magic touch" (TR 5).

The magical narratives that Jeanne craves are also a way of breaking the house's oppressive silence, associated with the absence of other children before the arrival of her cousin Hugh. When she first appears, Jeanne has "been all alone in [her] room for some time, with not a sound about her" (TR 3). Addressing her kindly but rather taciturn nurse, Jeanne highhandedly demands fairytales to break the silence: "Naughty Marcelline . . . [y]ou are to speak. I want you to speak very much, for it is so dull, and I have nothing to do. I want you to tell me stories, Marcelline" (TR 6). Tellingly, Marcelline refuses the request in part because her storytelling days are in the past: Jeanne, she claims, "got [all the stories] out of my old head long ago" (6). Similarly, when Jeanne attempts to tell her parents about Dudu's, the raven's, supposed magical powers, they dismiss her fancies with benevolent but boring commonsense explanations, and Jeanne sub-sides momentarily into the silence that permeates the house because she is "too well brought up . . . to contradict her father" (TR 15).

Both Jeanne and her newly arrived English cousin, Hugh, seem physi-cally exhausted by their immersion in the frigid realm of adult space. Jeanne complains that she is "so tired" because "[t]hese winter days . . . are dull" (TR 9) and even longs to become ill because of the attention she might receive from her nurse and family (TR 3). In contrast, Hugh is liter-ally ill, in part as a result of his emotional deprivation: "since his parents' death," we are told, his life "had not been a very happy one, and he had learnt to bear his troubles without complaining" (TR 20). In a sense, both children need to be healed by storytelling and fantasy, a cure that can take place only when the wintry house of adulthood reveals the secret passages that lead to a realm of summer and childhood magic. The tapestry room where Hugh sleeps becomes the initial gateway to this magical realm, trig-gering the children's three adventures, each associated with a different embedded narrative.

Spatially, then, the old house serves as an embodiment of adult values and social arrangements. Symmetrically, Molesworth also literalizes and physicalizes childhood imagination. Jeanne's magical adventures begin only after the arrival of Hugh, her companion in fantasy, when the two children put their joint powers of imagination to work. Gaps in the walls appear where the children imagine them, and become in turn the space of embedded narratives, as Jeanne and Hugh embark on a series of dreamlike journeys, each of which begins in the magical tapestry room. According to their nurse, Marcelline, the room is filled with "stories without end" pictured on its rich hangings, stories that come to life "on a moonlight night" (19). Significantly, every exciting adventure ends with a mysterious and unsettling story, a narrative that elicits the children's rapt attention and sympathy. Eschewing a strong linear plotline, the book's structure revolves around three very diverse narratives to which the children must listen and respond. Thus, as this section of my essay contends, narrative serves to unravel the apparent solidity of plaster and stone, carving gaps in the structure of the house, and opening secret spaces that are vaster than the house itself. The landscape depicted on the tapestry hangings contains a multitude of realms through which the children travel, including a rainbow forest and the mountains and rivers of Frog-land. Similarly, the children explore houses within houses like a series of Chinese boxes: the venerable French mansion encloses the visually stunning tapestry palace, which in turn encloses the vast spaces of the "Castle of Whiteness" that the children visit in their second adventure (TR 132).

In my view, critics have underestimated the originality of Molesworth's unique fusion of embedded narrative and shifting spatial relations. While *The Cuckoo Clock* is generally praised as Molesworth's most accomplished novel for children,[5] *The Tapestry Room* has been relatively ignored by critics. As Roger Lancelyn Green notes in his classic study *Tellers of Tales*, he finds *The Tapestry Room* "less satisfactory" than the more celebrated *Cuckoo Clock* (Green 113). Similarly, Angela Bull praises the later novel for its "brilliantly evoked atmosphere," but regrets its "flawed structure." In her view, "*The Tapestry Room* is chaotic, with many different ingredients thrown together."[6] In fact, this effect of chaos and confusion is created by the novel's extensive use of embedded stories, a device that Molesworth employed frequently, but foregrounded to a greater degree in *The Tapestry Room* than in the earlier *Cuckoo Clock*. For Marghanita Laski, writing in the 1950s, the frequent "breaking of the narrative by the interpolated story" constitutes a "very noticeable" and distracting "fault" in "many of [Molesworth's] . . . books" (Laski 64).[7] While the earlier novel incorporates both adventures and interpolated stories into its plotline, the later novel lavishes far more time on the tales told by magical characters to the child protagonists. One such story, "The Brown Bull of Norrowa," a traditional Scottish fairytale, takes up most of three chapters.

Nevertheless, the interpolated stories serve important structural and thematic purposes in *The Tapestry Room*; they reinforce the narrative's movement from fairytale to history, along with the children's conversion from a state of isolated innocence to sympathetic experience. Different as they are, the stories share a common theme; each story positions its listeners within a world of flux and change, in which mortality looms like a dark shadow on the edge of a romanticized fairytale landscape.[8] Jeanne and Hugh listen to the first embedded narrative in a magical country where animals can speak; beautiful and haunting, reaching to the heights of ecstatic and visionary experience, this narrative is a song performed by a dying swan, the tale of a rich life nearing its close. In contrast, the second tale represents a familiar genre. A classic fairytale, "The Brown Bull of Norrowa" is told by a magical fairy godmother figure in a tower. The third narrative, near the novel's close, is perhaps the most prosaic and yet the strangest within the context set up by the novel: narrated by Dudu, the magical raven who "may be a fairy" (TR 18), it is a tale of ordinary human loss and sorrow, a slice of family history linked to the violence of the French Revolution.

Thus, Molesworth's oddly episodic and in some ways disjointed tale becomes a series of meditations on and responses to narrative in its many guises. For Molesworth, storytelling is a perilous art, one that brings experience and loss into the sheltered realm of childhood innocence. In the conflicted world of the novel, if stories and storytelling expand the child's range of sympathy and understanding, they risk at the same time extinguishing the innocence that Molesworth clearly celebrates as a precious characteristic of childhood. In fact, then, the novel celebrates two contradictory impulses: the preservation of childhood innocence and the narrative art that will help, ultimately, to extinguish it. Narrative, which initially appears as a gateway into magic childhood fantasies, is revealed as a bridge to the traumas of adult life. Though thematically related, all the adventures and their culminating stories are diverse in terms of approach and genre; Molesworth differentiates them by means of the adventures' settings and major characters, as well as by the content and genre of each story that the children hear. At the same time, the children's own sympathetic connection with the realm of experience and loss heightens with each adventure, and each story.

The children's first journey immerses them in a rich physicality and sensuous detail associated with the realm of lush nature. If the house itself has been linked with the rational, highly segmented, and civilized world of adults, the children's escape offers a much needed natural corrective that helps to cure the once frail Hugh's lingering weakness, as well as Jeanne's enervating *ennui*. In contrast to the gray, wintry atmosphere of the house, depicted in a color palette of gray, white, and black, the children now enter a world saturated with color. One moonlit night, in what may or may not be a dream, Hugh steps inside the castle in the magical tapestry, an experience akin to stepping inside a rainbow: he traverses a great hall lit by lamps that shade from "the richest crimson to the softest pale blue" (TR

61) and enters a forest where the foliage sparkles in prismatic hues from "canary yellow" to silver, from "the richest corn-flower" to gold and "brilliant crimson" (TR 70). Molesworth underlines the difference between this fairytale world and the wintry landscape of home: "[these] were not winter trees, such as he had left behind him . . . bare and leafless," for "no winter's storms or nipping frosts had ever come near" their foliage (TR 64).

Spatially, Hugh must enter this natural world by means of a series of descents, suggesting his need to embrace the world of nature and physicality. Although Hugh initially mounts the wall to the tapestry castle with the aid of magical shoes "made after the pattern of the fly's wall-climbers" (TR 57), once he has passed out of the castle's great hall, he descends a stairway to reach the forest. Later he encounters Jeanne riding in a fairytale coach, but all too soon the children must "get down" from their carriage and walk (TR 72), a prospect that makes them anxious in this strange new world. Soon afterward, they descend a steep spiral staircase hidden under a slab of stone: "we're to go down," Hugh asserts bravely, and the once timid boy now takes on the task of reassuring his cousin, Jeanne. Having abandoned their carriage in the world above, the children find a boat that carries them downriver into a fertile and watery world, culminating in a shimmering lake surrounded by hills.

In keeping with their immersion in the world of nature, the children encounter only animals on this visit and must, in fact, learn to experience the world through the eyes of their new animal companions. Bored with life in their solemn and lonely house, Hugh and Jeanne previously imagined Dudu, the raven, as an ancient fairy and assigned personalities to the chickens and tortoise who live in a backyard coop, along with Hugh's pet guinea pig. Now the children are proved correct: Dudu is revealed as the "guardian" of the tapestry world (TR 57), and the pet animals transform themselves in Cinderella fashion into a coachman, footman, and horses. As Hugh notes, their adventure is "like a real fairytale," or, as the narrator suggests, a story "like those which one reads of in The Arabian Nights" (TR 77). Their adventure combines comic elements with a lesson about the nature of the animals they encounter. When their boat founders in the marshy water of Frog-land, an army of "bright green" frogs invades the boat, and Jeanne utters "a scream of horror" (TR 84). In fact, the frogs are there to help them; by working together, the tiny creatures free the stymied boat and escort the children to a feast as their honored guests. As the culmination of this animal entertainment, the children listen to the haunting song of a swan and enter into the swan's experience.

In the first of the three embedded narratives, the swan song signifies a dramatic shift in tone, from the comic and playful, to a note of transcendent joy mingled with sorrow. For the swan's song of death also sums up a whole life: it "tell[s] of suffering and sorrow, of beautiful things and sad things, of strange, fantastic dreams, of sunshine and flowers and summer days, of icy winds from the snow-covered hills, and days of dreariness and solitude" (TR 97). Although the swan's tale of a full life nearing its end is wordless, the narrator informs us that "the notes . . . in themselves" are "words," creating a purer form of communication, a species of transcendent speech "which no words of mine could describe" (TR 97). Enhancing the paradox, the description of the swan's death creates a measure of synesthesia as the senses of sight and sound merge: the song ends with soaring flight, as the swan is transformed into the image of a "dying star," and the "joyous song . . . melt[s]" along with the swan itself into "opal radiance" (TR 98). Jeanne finds the narrative both "wonderful" and "sad" (TR 99), and wonders if the singer is "an angel, and not a swan" at all (TR 98). The song expands the children's capacity for imaginative sympathy through an understanding of life's fleeting nature; at the same time, they are able to distance themselves from the experience of death, since it takes place only within the magical world of animals, where a dying swan might also be an angel or a star.

The children's next adventure will bring them closer to a human experience of loss and the threat of mortality, although it, too, incorporates distancing mechanisms that safeguard their innocence. Once again, the tropes of dream and fairytale shroud the adventure in a cloud of mystery. This time Hugh and Jeanne enter the tapestry together when Jeanne appears at Hugh's bedside, wearing sparkling wings that recall the angelic swan in their previous adventure: in her "snow-white wings," Jeanne "look[s] like a fairy queen, or like a silvery bird turned into a little girl" (TR 119). Just as Hugh's fly-like wall-climbers reinforced his task of entering into the natural world of the animals, so now the angelic wings signal the children's entrance into an elevated spiritual domain. Unlike the earlier journey, a descent into a realm of vibrant physicality, this journey invites the children to ascend to new spiritual heights of self-discipline and moral consciousness. As noted, during the previous adventure, Hugh informed Jeanne, "we're to go down" (TR 74). Now Jeanne fits Hugh with his own wings before instructing him, "We're to fly" (TR 124). As Hugh took the lead before, so Jeanne must lead him now, evoking the familiar Victorian association of women and girls with spiritual mentorship. "Jeanne . . . you're a perfect puzzle," Hugh muses. "I do wonder whether you're half a fairy, or an angel, or a dream. . . . But, oh, dear, I cannot understand" (TR 129). Enjoining him to forget mere logical understanding, Jeanne encourages him to take their journey on trust. The children fly up through the vast spaces of the tapestry castle only to find another spiral staircase—this time, they ascend, rather than descend—leading to a magical turret room. In contrast to the brilliant colors of the "Forest of Rainbows" (TR 71), they now find themselves in "The Castle of Whiteness," an ethereal realm pale as the clouds (TR 132).

The white-robed, white-haired lady who spins stories in the castle tower is a literary descendant of Irene's magical great-great-grandmother in MacDonald's *The Princess and the Goblin*.[9] As in MacDonald's tale, this fairy godmother figure is both ancient and eternally young. Her seclusion with her magical spinning wheel in the tower also evokes echoes of such fairytales as "Sleeping Beauty" and "Rumpelstiltskin," not to mention the heroine of Tennyson's Lady of Shalott, who weaves narratives of the world that she is forbidden from entering. In fact, as the lady explains, her spinning wheel smoothes out the "tangle" of story threads that she receives, in order to make each tale "pretty" for her child listeners. In contrast to the jolly frogs in the children's previous adventure, the storyspinner resides high above the human domain, sending her stories down to refine human existence, and then pulling up the tangled strands to arrange, disentangle, and clean them again. Thus, she exercises a purifying function.

Although the storyspinner's narration of "The Brown Bull of Norrowa" eschews any heavy-handed moral, it serves as a parable of moral discipline and self-sacrifice. Nina Auerbach and U. C. Knoepflmacher see Molesworth's version of the tale as a feminist story, since its princess protagonist resists the temptations of traditional feminine passivity in order to determine her own fate and that of her kingdom.[10] As Molesworth emphasizes, the princess is "clever . . . quick-witted, and very brave" (TR 143). In a story reminiscent of the Greek Minotaur legend, she learns that she must sacrifice herself to the fierce brown bull ravaging her father's kingdom. Only if she accompanies him will the destruction end. For our purposes, what is noteworthy about Molesworth's tale is the extensive time devoted to the king and queen's ingenious attempts to protect their daughter's innocence, keeping her enclosed, and metaphorically imprisoned, in a paradisal garden, ignorant of the destruction and chaos of the world around her. Callously, the parents send substitute maidens to the brown bull in her stead, hoping that he will claim their lives rather than hers. When the princess learns the truth, she insists on leaving the garden of childhood innocence in order to sacrifice herself for the greater good. Her noble act is rewarded by a fairytale outcome. Like the terrifying monster of "Beauty and the Beast," the brown bull proves to be an enchanted prince who craves the princess's love; yet many more trials await the princess when the lovers are separated, and she must undertake a terrifying journey to find him through a bleak and menacing landscape.

Although the fairytale trappings and happy conclusion soften its message, the story makes clear that childhood innocence is not only a luxury but also a dangerous indulgence when allowed to persist too long. The arduous journey to the kingdom of adulthood must be undertaken and can succeed only when accompanied by self-discipline and a willingness to sacrifice for others. Because the protagonists are now struggling human beings rather than magical and symbolic animals, the second tale moves Hugh and Jeanne one step closer to an understanding of human loss in a world of tumult and change.

The children's third adventure is the most prosaic and yet the most surprising. While their previous journeys were wrapped in a haze of moonlight and dream, this one takes place in the waking world on a winter evening. Instead of entering into the tapestry, the children now step behind it. The spatial implication is clear: the luminous castle and gorgeous gardens of the tapestry exist as metaphorical space, given dimension by the narrative processes of childhood imagination. Now, the domain of imaginative space is once again flattened out, reduced to a curtain that hides new, more significant, unknown spaces within the house. When Hugh "pull[s] back the tapestry," the children are astonished to find yet another flight of stairs. Unlike the spiral staircases of their previous adventures, this one "run[s] straight upwards, without twisting or turning" (TR 201). Pointing out the contrast with the children's previous journeys, Molesworth explains that "the steps were easier to mount than the corkscrew staircase up to the white lady's turret." Although Jeanne speculates that "this is another way into Fairyland," the stairs lead merely to the roof of the house (TR 202). Rather than the luminous colors of the first adventure or the ethereal whiteness of the second, the color palette is now one of neutral tones, of gray shadows and winter darkness.

The character who dominates this adventure is the old raven, Dudu, but rather than serving as a magical guide to fairyland, he now disparages the romance of fairytales: "What did you expect?" he asks testily. "Fairies, I suppose, or enchanted princesses, or something of that kind. What creatures children are for wonders, to be sure" (TR 203). During the children's first journey, the swan's narrative serves as the culminating moment of a protracted adventure. The second adventure in the white castle is far briefer, merely the frame for the lengthy "Brown Bull," which occupies the bulk of three chapters. In contrast, the third adventure is the story. Hinting that he has no more magical places to show them, Dudu entertains the children with a tale, since as they themselves agree, a story is "as nice as an adventure" anyway (TR 205).

Neither a transcendent song nor a fairytale, Dudu's story is a bleak history of Jeanne and Hugh's aristocratic forebears during the French Revolution. Although the Revolution is never explicitly named, it appears as a metaphorical "storm"—the "terrible days" that broke up the homes of "hundreds and thousands" (TR 225). Haunted by loss and death, the raven's tale revisits elements of both the swan song and "The Brown Bull." Echoing the princess's innocence at the start of "The Brown Bull," this third embedded narrative begins with an idealized sketch of the children's great-grandmother, Jeanne, strolling as a young woman in the garden with her sister Eliane. Somewhat uncharacteristically, the old raven sketches in a lyrical, pastoral scene, describing a lovely day when the young ladies "came out like the flowers and the birds to enjoy" the sunshine (TR 213). Yet, the reality of a ravaged world soon intrudes as the revolution sends the family fleeing to Switzerland. Now grown up and married, Jeanne grieves that her husband, a fugitive from the government, has been trapped in France. History echoes fairytale, as the raven's narrative embodies elements of

"The Brown Bull of Norrowa." Just as the princess abandoned a safe haven to sacrifice herself for the common good, and later climbed a mountain of glass to find her lost lover, so Jeanne returns to France, facing peril to seek her husband, and finding him at last, very ill in the old house where the young Jeanne and Hugh now listen to their story. Although the couple eventually escapes to England, Jeanne's husband—the children's great-grandfather—dies young, weakened by his sufferings; and more deaths are to come. The story ends with Jeanne and Eliane reunited in the house as old women, conversing with a childhood friend who is on her way to Italy to die. The friends' final parting, after lives filled with mingled joy and sorrow, evokes the swan song that so moved and saddened the children during their first adventure.[11]

This time, the children's own connection to the embedded narratives is impossible to deny. The suffering protagonists are their own flesh and blood, and one of them even bears Jeanne's name. Spatially, the children now find themselves in a new situation: perched on the roof along with the old raven, they glimpse a wider vista, but it is an unsettling panorama of the world outside the house, not the fairytale landscape they yearned for. Although Hugh and Jeanne now claim to prefer history to fairytales, proclaiming dutifully that Dudu's sad tale is "nicer even than fairy adventures" (TR 236), a solemn air hangs over the novel's close, especially when Dudu disappears, apparently never to return. As the children acknowledge sadly in the final pages, "We shall have no more stories . . . [n]or fairy adventures" (TR 236). In fact, the very stories that they sought as a magical escape from adulthood have sapped their innocence.

Ambiguously, in the novel's last sentence, the narrator speaks directly to her characters (and her child readers), promising the children more stories if the raven should someday return. At the same time, the novel's imagery hints that the bird has flown away to die. Thus, even in its last moments, the novel speaks with two voices, inviting children to construct an imaginative fantasy of the bird's return while simultaneously undermining it. The narrator's intervention here not only reveals her as the true storyspinner, the adult who has constructed the magical narratives that her fictive children have wished for and dreamed of; it also foregrounds the many-layered texture of her narration, which allows child readers to react to children reacting to stories. Problematic and disjointed as it may appear to some critics, Molesworth's canny novel illuminates the contradictory dynamics of numerous works of Victorian children's fiction, whereby narrative itself, as it stirs a child's powers of sympathy, facilitates an inevitable initiation into sorrow.

NOTES

1. It is not my intention to blur the substantial differences among these diverse works. Secret architectural spaces play an important role in all these novels, but they function sometimes in diametrically opposed ways. In the Alice novels, the subversive secret spaces of childhood fantasy and dream cannot be integrated into the house as a whole, but rather serve as a parodic commentary on adult realities. In *The Secret Garden*, in contrast, Mary Lennox's discovery of Colin's secluded bedroom and her explorations of the mysterious secret garden lead to a metaphorical "regreening" of adult sensibilities, as previously secret spaces are opened to all. In the gothic and surreal *Coraline*, the secret shadow house that exists as potential within Coraline's literal house must be sealed off from experience if the child protagonist is to survive.

2. See "The Nursery" (chapter two) in Flanders, *Inside the Victorian Home* (62–99).

3. Mary Louisa Molesworth, *The Cuckoo Clock*, in *The Cuckoo Clock and The Tapestry Room*. Facsimile edition. Garland Classics of Children's Literature (New York: Garland, 1976) 1.

4. Despite Marcelline's comfortable, old-fashioned aura, Molesworth makes a point of affirming that she is not only cheerful and attractive, but even, in Jeanne's eyes, "beautiful" (TR 4). As the novel progresses, she becomes associated with the maternal and ageless storyspinner of the children's second adventure.

5. According to Sanjay Sircar, this "first and best-known classic fantasy novel for children" by Molesworth is a *bildungsroman* reminiscent of works by Dickens and other major Victorian writers ("The Classic Fantasy Novel as Didactic Victorian Bildungsroman," 163). In keeping with other critics, he notes that "*The Cuckoo Clock* [has always] stood out for the care with which it assembled the credible psychological antecedents of its leap into fantasy proper" ("Locating a Classic," 173).

6. See Angela Bull's brief but insightful introduction to the Garland edition of the novel (v–vii).

7. Although more recent critics tend to eschew such clear aesthetic judgments, *The Tapestry Room*'s lengthy embedded stories may provide a reason why so many still refrain from writing about the novel.

8. Molesworth's Victorian understanding of the fairytale leaves little room for the dangerous, uncanny creatures who populate medieval tales of Faerie, or for the violent and bloody justice in the tales of Perrault and the Grimms. Nevertheless, like traditional fairytales, Molesworth's literary tales are also haunted by death and loss.

9. As Anita Moss points out in her essay "Mothers, Monsters, and Morals in Victorian Fairy Tales," Molesworth had alluded to MacDonald's storyspinning great-great-grandmother in earlier works. In *The Enchanted Garden* (1892), the child protagonists, Rafe and Alix, encounter Mrs. Caretaker, an avowed "relation of George MacDonald's white lady in the attic who spins stories" (51–52). Similarly, as Moss notes in "Mrs. Molesworth: Victorian Visionary," the figure of the "Godmother" in *Christmas-Tree Land* (1884) is also reminiscent of "MacDonald's goddess-like maternal figures" (107).

10. Nina Auerbach and U. C. Knoepflmacher, *Forbidden Journeys*, 17. This collection of Victorian fairytales by women authors includes "The Brown Bull," along with their engaging analysis. See "Refashioning Fairy Tales," 11–20.

11. The dying friend who visits the sisters at the end of the tale has herself played a major part in their lives. An Englishwoman who visited the neighborhood as a child, she returns during the Revolution and helps to smuggle Jeanne and her husband out of the country.

WORKS CITED

Auerbach, Nina, and U. C. Knoepflmacher, eds. *Forbidden Journeys: Fairy Tales and Fantasies by Victorian Women Writers*. Chicago: U of Chicago P, 1992.

Carroll, Lewis. *Through the Looking-Glass, and What Alice Found There*. In *Alice in Wonderland: Authoritative Texts*. New York: Norton, 1992.

Flanders, Judith. *Inside the Victorian Home: A Portrait of Domestic Life in Victorian England*. New York: Norton, 2003.

Green, Roger Lancelyn. *Tellers of Tales: Children's Books and Their Authors from 1800 to 1968*. London: Kaye and Ward, 1969.

Inglis, Fred. *The Promise of Happiness: Value and Meaning in Children's Fiction*. New York: Cambridge UP, 1981.

Laski, Marghanita. *Mrs. Ewing, Mrs. Molesworth, and Mrs. Hodgson Burnett.* New York: Oxford UP, 1951.

Molesworth, Mary Louisa. *The Tapestry Room.* (1879). In *The Cuckoo Clock and The Tapestry Room.* Facsimile edition. Garland Classics of Children's Literature. New York: Garland, 1976.

Moss, Anita. "Mothers, Monsters, and Morals in Victorian Fairy Tales." *The Lion and the Unicorn: A Critical Journal of Children's Literature* 12:2 (December 1988): 47–60.

———. "Mrs. Molesworth: Victorian Visionary." *The Lion and the Unicorn: A Critical Journal of Children's Literature* 12:2 (June 1988): 105–10.

Ostry, Elaine. "Magical Growth and Moral Lessons; or, How the Conduct Book Informed Victorian and Edwardian Children's Fantasy." *The Lion and the Unicorn: A Critical Journal of Children's Literature* 27 (2003): 27–56.

Rosenthal, Lynne. "Writing Her Own Story: The Integration of the Self in the Fourth Dimension of Mrs. Molesworth's The Cuckoo Clock." *Children's Literature Association Quarterly* 10:4 (Winter 1986): 187–92.

Sircar, Sanjay. "The Classic Fantasy Novel as Didactic Victorian Bildungsroman: *The Cuckoo Clock.*" *The Lion and the Unicorn: A Critical Journal of Children's Literature* 21:2 (April 1997): 163–92.

———. "Locating a Classic: The Cuckoo Clock in Its Literary Context." *Children's Literature Association Quarterly.* 21:4 (Winter 1996–1997): 170–76.

DOROTHY H. MCGAVRAN

→ Oversleeping Oneself

Elizabeth Gaskell's Wake-Up Call
in Wives and Daughters

Wives and Daughters begins with a little girl waking up to the "old rigma-role of childhood," a time when "unseen power[s]" rule the circumscribed world she lives in. It is a bewildering world full of danger for the daughters who wake up in it. Many do not wake up and are doomed to passivity, hypochondria, listlessness, ignorance, and tedium. In the terms of accusation used by the grown-ups when twelve-year-old Molly Gibson, the novel's hero, visits the Towers, these young girls "oversleep" themselves. The unseen powers manipulate truth in a way that transforms the girls into young women incapable of goodness except with "a great jerk, an effort," an experience that leads Cynthia Kirkpatrick, Molly's stepsister, to call herself "a moral kangaroo" (221). *Wives and Daughters* is, in its most interesting and deep sense, an analysis of the exchange of information in a credit economy. But it is an economy which gives women of the upper and middle classes no kind of credit—either monetary or moral. In this economy the very definition of honesty is split to mean one thing for men and another for women. This economy puts marginalized women—such as widows and governesses—into the position of maneuvering a place for themselves. Wives and daughters of Hollingford must manipulate the truth and dissimulate in order to find economic security. Through Molly's and Cynthia's childhood challenges, Gaskell develops the subtext that all of her novels share: the use and abuse of language to achieve power. On behalf of her sister, Cynthia, Molly must run the verbal gauntlet of lies, secrets, gossip, and blackmail to become a self-directed moral agent, valued for her own powers of intellect and virtue.

Wives and Daughters might be called a conduct book for daughters, and was in actuality a literal legacy to her unmarried daughters (Uglow 586). Gaskell wrote this novel for her daughters in more ways than one. She was secretly paying for a house, The Lawn, for her husband and daughters with the proceeds from the novel when she died before writing its last chapter. In her concern for her unmarried daughters having a secure home of their own, she received the impulse to explore other marginalized women's need for economic security and the way they had been forced to maneuver to get it. So cynical was Gaskell about the honesty of her society that she put in the mouth of one of her straightest-talking characters, Lady Harriet, the injunction, "Tell the truth, now and evermore. Truth is generally amusing, if it's nothing else" (163). But she also put in the mouth of the most devious liar, Mrs. Gibson, the following revelation: "If there's one thing that revolts me, it is duplicity" (563). Duplicity did revolt Elizabeth Gaskell, but her comical look at Mrs. Gibson is understanding of her plight at the same time it is scathing in its condemnation.

Wives and Daughters has been variously described as Molly Gibson's rite of passage in fairytale form (Stoneman 172); her "resistance to fairytale rhetoric and to the adult characters who use this rhetoric" (Wasinger 282); her "initiation to the 'grown-up world'" (Uglow 578); her hard lesson in "learning how to be a woman" (Spacks 89); "an autobiography of a suicide" (Bonaparte 56); and the developing story of language, representing for daughters a "shift from the language of one kind of mother to that of the other" (Homans 263, 269). Like Margaret Homans and Jenny Uglow, I believe that Molly's story initiates her to a new awareness of the uses of language in her culture. But unlike Homans and Bonaparte, I believe Molly's learning a new way of communicating does not come at the expense of, or co-opting of, herself. I agree also with Spacks that Molly is offered various female models for her education into womanhood (89), but rather than following Homans in believing that Molly enters "the symbolic order . . . presided over by the new Mrs. Gibson . . . along the chain of the father's desire" (257), I maintain that Molly forges a new use of language that sets her in the modern age, apart from her father and the older class-based power in Hollingford. Moreover, the novel has double heroines, with the paired half-sisters Molly and Cynthia, whom Gaskell alludes to as Una and Duessa, respectively. It is male characters who categorize the girls, and it says more about their desire to control women than it does about Molly and Cynthia. Mr. Gibson first refers to Molly as Una when disciplining Mr. Coxe after the father intercepts a love letter from the young apprentice addressed to his daughter. Mr. Gibson says, "Remember how soon a young girl's name may be breathed upon, and sullied. Molly has no mother, and for that very reason she ought to move among you all as unharmed as Una herself" (55). But Mr. Gibson would have his daughter move through life with no control by any man but himself. Even when he admits he "can't help" Roger's attachment to Molly and describes his losing his daughter as "a necessary evil," he thinks sadly, "lover versus father! . . . Lover wins" (644). Cynthia is named Duessa by Roger in the same conversation with Mr. Gibson late in the novel. He says, speaking of Molly, "What must she think of me? How she must despise me, choosing the false Duessa" (642). Cynthia has not been created in simple opposition to the innocent Molly as the Spenserian allusion suggests. The situation is more complex and involves the setting and circumstances of the novel; its class and gender issues are equally complex.

Gaskell set *Wives and Daughters* in the late 1820s, on the cusp of the new credit economy. As topical references in the novel indicate, that time of transition came just before the Reform Bill of 1832, the penny post, and the railroad. In the new economy and in science, honesty is even more important than it was in earlier days of the aristocratic control of information. Gaskell shows awareness of the economic importance of honesty, of the reliability of sources of information, and of the risks of betrayal. *Wives and Daughters* contains more secrets than any of her earlier novels. In the time of transition, about which she writes, control of knowledge, literacy, and information was shared more and more among middle-class professionals rather than exclusively dictated by the aristocracy. Still, Gaskell shows Hollingford continuing to enjoy the patronage of Cumnor Towers. Thus Lady Harriet becomes Molly's champion and, in what she jokingly calls her playing Don Quixote to Miss Phoebe's Sancho Panza (529), she acts "in defence of a distressed damsel" and, by her mere presence, restores Molly's reputation. But the Cumnors belong to the past of feudal romance. Gaskell's deeper concern is to warn of a new control by what Alexander Welsh in his fascinating book, *George Eliot and Blackmail*, calls the "pathology of information" (title of Section II, 31). Welsh contrasts the period Gaskell writes about—the 1820s—with earlier times that he calls Old Leisure. Before the explosion of sources of information and the very need to keep records, a different consciousness of social life prevailed; more depended on firsthand acquaintance and less on information. According to Welsh, reputations were maintained in mostly face-to-face meetings by a gentleman's word and occasionally by a duel (108). Welsh cites Georg Simmel, a German sociologist of the late nineteenth century, who claims that honesty is even more important under "modern" conditions. The economy and science must rely on trustworthy reports and repeatable experiments. Lying is much more devastating in this time of the credit economy (Welsh 73). What is required in the new economy is discretion. Being accountable for information possessed in whatever manner and understanding the impact of its release upon a given audience contribute to the "modern" virtue of discretion.

Welsh argues for the importance of honesty in this time of transition, but he makes no difference between standards of honesty for men and women. Gaskell's novel focuses on this difference by contrasting the honesty of "wives and daughters" as opposed to that of "fathers and sons." Adrienne Rich outlined these differences in her 1975 address, "Women and Honor: Some Notes on Lying." Rich contrasts "the old, male idea of honor. A man's 'word' sufficed—to other men—without guarantee" with "women's honor, something altogether else: virginity, chastity, fidelity to a husband. Honesty in women has not been considered important" (186). Rich claims women "have been depicted as generically whimsical, deceitful, subtle, vacillating. And . . . [they] have been rewarded for lying" (186). Rich's insights put in the form of theory what Gaskell had illustrated in *Wives and Daughters* over a century before. Both analyses of honesty have been holistic. Rich claims, "Men have been expected to tell the truth about facts, not about feelings. They have not been expected to talk about feelings at all" (186). If women are forced to tell lies to maneuver a place for themselves, it is at the expense also of the men and children who closely touch their lives. Gaskell's analysis goes further than Rich's to reveal the changing concept of honor for men in the nineteenth century's growing credit economy. Women, however, remained even more dependent on men for economic security during this time. Gender distinctions in standards of honesty, therefore, were even more pronounced as men developed the new virtue of discretion, and women continued to rely on calculations and maneuvers.

Mary Wollstonecraft had identified the same problem more than half a century before Gaskell wrote this novel. In *Vindication of the Rights of Woman* (1792), she argued that their education brought women to believe cunning was the only form in which their intellect would serve them. "Women are told from their infancy, and taught by the example of their mothers, that a little knowledge of human weakness, justly termed cunning, softness of temper, outward obedience, and a scrupulous attention to a puerile kind of propriety, will obtain for them the protection of man; and should they be beautiful, everything else is needless, for, at least twenty years of their lives" (100). Wollstonecraft might have been describing Hyacinth Clare Kirkpatrick Gibson or her daughter Cynthia Kirkpatrick. By the time we meet Mrs. Kirkpatrick, her cunning is sharpened into a habit of lying that she is the last to recognize. Her survival has depended upon it, and she succeeds in her objective—financial security in a second marriage.

Despite a shaky beginning, Molly's education spared her from developing cunning at the expense of intellect. As a child, motherless from an early age, Molly had always been an avid reader. This was despite her father's instructions to her governess, Miss Eyre:

> Don't teach Molly too much; she must sew, and read, and write, and do her sums: but I want to keep her a child, and if I find more learning desirable for her, I'll see about giving it to her myself. After all, I'm not sure that reading or writing is necessary. Many a good woman gets married with only a cross instead of her name; it's rather a diluting of mother-wit, to my fancy; but, however, we must yield to the prejudices of society, Miss Eyre, and so you may teach the child to read. (34)

Susan Colón argues that the reader should "read his speech as an example of the doctor's characteristic irony" and that his "orders are intended for Molly's optimal rather than minimal education" (14). Allowing Molly full entrance to his library afforded a much better education than "a country finishing school in the eighteen-teens would" (Colón 14–15). Society, however, is more likely to uphold Mr. Gibson's first instinct to leave Molly illiterate and in complete and undiluted possession of her "mother-wit." This feminine quality of mind, we suspect, much resembles cunning and is shown to perfection by Molly's stepmother, another governess and teacher of young girls. Knowing no more than she ought to, the female pupil is prepared for her future role. Miss Eyre, for her part, serves her master to the letter and spirit of his instructions to teach Molly only to read and write: "she tried honestly to keep her back in every other branch of education" (34). But Molly, "fighting and struggling hard," gains a better education by insisting on French and drawing lessons and by reading or trying to read every book in her father's library (34). Reading books, however, does not provide quite enough education for Molly to read her complex society. Before Molly Gibson takes control of her future by speaking out with directness and discretion, she runs into several verbal trials.

As the novel opens, twelve-year-old Molly is put into a situation which tests her poor powers of education in reading her society. For the first time she is made aware of "unseen powers" who use languages that she is not accustomed to read. Though eagerly anticipating the School Visiting Day at Cumnor Towers, Molly is not prepared for any power other than the familiar maid, Betty, who rules her childhood order until Mr. Gibson remarries. Lost on the Tower grounds and sick and tired, Molly is subjected, one after another, to characters who might have sprung from books. Lord Cumnor, whom she already has classified as a "cross between an archangel and a king" (9), becomes the big Father Bear with his deep voice, from a tale she had never read (22). Abandoned by her fairy godmothers, the Misses Browning, Molly meets with several women's dazzling use of language that she cannot translate. All she knows is that she is put at fault for acts she is not responsible for. She is laughed at for "over-eat[ing] herself" (18), when Clare ate all her lunch. She is wrong for "over-sleep[ing] herself" (20–21), when Clare was supposed to wake her up. She is judged stupid when she fails to respond to one guest who, finding Molly "wild and strange" (22) and thus probably foreign, addresses her in French. Clearly, Molly is not accustomed to the unseen powers of language spoken at the Towers, which put her in the wrong. Gaskell's use four times in four pages of the reflexive "oversleeping herself" (20–24) calls the reader's attention to the harm being done to the self if Molly succumbs to this verbal damp-ening. Indeed Molly internalizes the "implied blame," which felt like "needle-points all over her" (23).

The rest of the novel shows the depth of the problem, which Molly only glimpses on that first day, across her whole society. Those in control of the discourse can say what they like; others less strong must maneuver to hold their own even to acquire the very necessities of life like food and rest. Bewildered by her day at the Towers, Molly is shown in almost surreal or nightmarish detail the power relations that rule her society, and the way language facilitates them. At the time, she can only assert her identity, "I'm only Molly Gibson, ma'am" (22). Her evaluation of the experience, spo-ken to her father on the way home, reveals how threatening her experience was: "I felt like a lighted candle when they're putting the extinguisher on it" (27). Molly's experience at the Towers brings home to her that reading her society correctly can be a question of life and death. Uglow emphasizes that in the world of *Wives and Daughters* there is a "need [for] a strong sense of self to survive. The deeply held view that the chief role of women is to serve, please and succor is potentially lethal if taken to extremes" (588). And Hilary Schor points out that "to be female is primarily to be an invalid, to be passive, to suffer victimization" (190). Both Molly and Cynthia at-tempt to get out of the suicidal script written by their society.

At Hamley Hall Molly meets the squire's wife, a perfect example of a woman whose candle has been extinguished, to use Molly's metaphor. Married to a man who loves her, but whose own education was not equal to hers, Mrs. Hamley diplomatically gives up all association with people of culture in order to keep her home harmonious. Gaskell explains, "de-prived of all her strong interests, she sank into ill-health; nothing definite; only she never was well" (43). The pathology of Mrs. Hamley's condition was similar to that of many Victorian wives. At Hamley Hall Molly sees the operation of secrets and subterfuges designed to keep the truth from those most concerned. But she also sees that the containment of information is not healthy. Hamley Hall is the "moated grange" (83), and danger lies in Molly's becoming a Mariana and adopting a position there as a replace-ment for their dead daughter, Fanny.

The crisis comes for Molly when she learns her father is to be married to Mrs. Kirkpatrick. Molly receives advice from Roger Hamley, the young second son of Hamley Hall, who is soon to make a name for himself as a scientist. From Roger Molly learns the proper role for a woman is to take after the example of his mother and Harriet, a fictional character who finds herself in much the same situation as Molly when her father remarries. Roger's advice is "to try to think more of others than of oneself" (117). Molly, however, is not willing to give up her own will to others even though she sees the conventional wisdom of Roger's advice. She refuses to admit she will be the happier for living as Roger advises her: "It will be very dull when I shall have killed myself, as it were, and live only in trying to do, and to be, as other people like. I don't see any end to it. I might as well never have lived. And as for the happiness you speak of, I shall never be happy again" (135). At Hamley Hall, Molly experiences two influences: the example of Mrs. Hamley coupled with the advice of Roger to think of others. When Gaskell describes Mrs. Hamley's death later in the novel, we can see echoes of Molly's lament, "I might as well never have lived." "At length . . . the end came. Mrs. Hamley had sunk out of life as gradually as she had sunk out of consciousness and her place in this world. The quiet waves closed over her, and her place knew her no more" (219). *Wives and Daughters* inquires on every page what that place in the world is for women. Molly intends to fight for her place and to be conscious of understanding it. She will not sink out of consciousness.

Molly returns to her father's house, now redecorated with new furnishings, including a new wife for her father. There she is faced with her stepmother, Hyacinth Gibson. From her Molly learns the insidious means to power practiced by many Victorian women. At the Towers, Mrs. Kirkpatrick had realized that "money is like the air they breathe," and she considers it is not natural that she "go on all [her] life toiling and moiling for money" when it is the husband who should have "all that kind of dirty work to do" (98). From the start of her renewed acquaintance with Mr. Gibson, she thinks of a second marriage as a business deal: "how pleasant it would be to have a husband once more;—some one who would work while she sate at her elegant ease in a prettily furnished drawing-room; and she was rapidly *investing* this imaginary *breadwinner* with the form and features of the country surgeon" (104 my emphasis). As Patricia Spacks points out, Mrs. Gibson's "predicaments, emotional and financial, are real; her solution for them is the only one available to her" (91). Having taken care of her own situation in marrying the doctor, Mrs. Gibson turns her attention to the two unmarried girls in her care.

Molly gradually becomes aware of the pathological deceit that rules Mrs. Gibson's life. Because Molly possesses the secret of Osborne Hamley's marriage, she must bear in silence Mrs. Gibson's designs on Osborne as a husband for Cynthia. Molly also must bear the taunts that slight Roger although they "made Molly's blood boil. . . . She read her stepmother's heart" and perceived her strategy (314). Molly also reacts in disbelief when she perceives Mrs. Gibson is capable of thinking of others' deaths only in relation to her own desires or convenience. When the new Mrs. Gibson comes home and Molly has prepared a tasteful tea-dinner for the honeymoon couple, Mr. Gibson is called out to attend the dying Craven Smith, an old patient. Mrs. Gibson complains, "I think your dear papa might have put off his visit to Mr. Craven Smith for just this one evening." Molly responds, "Mr. Craven Smith couldn't put off his dying." Mrs. Gibson believes Molly's concern is "droll" and that the only reason to rush to the side of the dying man is if Mr. Gibson "expects any legacy, or anything of that kind" (173). Mrs. Gibson is capable even of wishing for others' early deaths to advance her strategies. Osborne cannot die too soon to suit Mrs. Gibson after she learns of his heart condition and has promoted the second son, Roger, as Cynthia's husband:

> A young man strikes us all as looking very ill—and I'm sure I'm sorry for it; but illness very often leads to death. Surely you agree with me there, and what's the harm of saying so? . . . I should think myself wanting in strength of mind if I could not look forward to the consequences of death. I really think we're commanded to do so, somewhere in the Bible or the Prayer-book. (427)

Later, when Osborne's secret marriage is revealed after his death, Mrs. Gibson anticipates his child's death when he falls ill. "When one thinks how little his prolonged existence is to be desired, one feels that his death would be a boon" (638). Molly cannot accept her stepmother's explanation that thoughts of inheritance cannot help but cross people's minds because of "the baseness of human nature." Molly believes people can help discipline such thoughts as she replies to Mrs. Gibson: "All sorts of thoughts cross one's mind—it depends upon whether one gives them harbor and encouragement" (639). Mrs. Gibson's mind is always harboring and encouraging the thoughts that feed her self.

In reaction to her stepmother's language, Molly is forced to find a deeper way of communicating. Unlike Mrs. Gibson, she does not use "words like ready-made clothes . . . never fitted [to] individual thoughts" (306–07). Nor does she, like her stepmother, cover her lack of knowledge with misquotations and clichés. Though secrets and silences lead Molly into involuntary deception, she never abandons her ability to translate herself into the position of her listener. Thus she translates Cynthia's feelings to Preston despite his unwillingness to hear them; she similarly translates Aimée's French letters to Osborne for the French-hating Squire Hamley upon his son's death. She stands up to her father and refuses to submit Cynthia's secret to his control. Far from being co-opted by the language of deceit, Molly tries to work within her power to "avoid the practice" in order "to save pain" to others.

Gaskell sets up an interesting contrast between the word of the father and the word of the (step)mother as guides to a daughter's education. Mr. Gibson is, in universal Hollingford opinion, an honorable man. But his reasons for marriage are as self-seeking as those of his second wife. And Mr. Gibson harbors secrets about his past and about the love of his life that are only hinted and never completely revealed to the reader, let alone to his daughter or to either of his wives. His neighbors know nothing of where he came from, though Mrs. Goodenough pronounced him "the son of a Scotch duke, my dear, never mind on which side of the blanket" (38). He first marries the daughter of his predecessor, Mr. Hall, but we are led to believe that marriage was also one of convenience. The Misses Browning consider Mr. Gibson "faithful to the memory of his first love," as Miss Phoebe puts it, but Mr. Gibson winces on hearing this and thinks: "Jeannie was his first love; but her name had never been breathed in Hollingford. His wife—good, pretty, sensible, and beloved as she had been—was not his second; no, nor his third love" (143). It is safe to assume that Mr. Gibson never realizes what a problem his silence and reserve about his feelings might bring him until he grows to know the ways of his second wife. Even when he realizes her style of manipulation, he believes he can keep her in a separate sphere. "He never allowed himself to put any regret into shape, even in his own mind" (178).

However, when Mrs. Gibson moves into his professional affairs, eavesdrops on his professional conversation about Osborne Hamley, and even enters his surgery to pry into his professional vocabulary, he feels violated. Mr. Gibson's anger against her comes on two accounts; both are centered on his view of himself as a professional man and as a man of honor. Mr. Gibson's medical conferences are confidential information: "If it would be a deep disgrace for me to betray a professional secret, what would it be for me to trade on that knowledge?" (383) he asks his wife. If Mr. Gibson could see it, he might realize Gaskell's point, which comes quite accidently and poutingly out of Mrs. Gibson's mouth when her husband asks for the current state of the relationship between Cynthia and Roger: "I don't think I ought to tell you anything about it. It is a secret, just as much as your mysteries are" (384). In Victorian society, Mr. Gibson's mysteries of profession and manly honor do outrank Mrs. Gibson's and Cynthia's desires for secrecy in her engagement. As a professional man, Mr. Gibson has always known his place in the community of Hollingford. He manages by secrecy about his past and his private life to be accepted by the town at the same time he proves by deference and tact to get along well with the Towers. Mr. Gibson manages his uneasy position as a link between town on the one hand, and Tower and Hall, on the other, by following the ideal of honor at each. Thus his word to Squire Hamley is his bond. His silence in the town gives gossips a chance to romanticize his past; but meanwhile, he earns credit by marrying his predecessor's daughter. Thus Mr. Gibson does not see any reason why a man's word should not override a woman's wish (388). He does not credit women with the right to exercise discretion.

Gaskell did see reasons for woman's honor to be as important as man's honor, and she also was strongly disapproving of dishonesty in women and men. She recognized the harm to men of what Patsy Stoneman calls the "masculine lie . . . [which] prevents humane emotion" (180). Though Molly may not realize her father's part, Mrs. Gibson is not entirely to blame for the lie of the Gibson marriage. Molly is troubled by her awareness of her stepmother's constant deceit: "At first she made herself uncomfortable with questioning herself as to how far it was right to leave unnoticed the small domestic failings—the webs, the distortions of truth which had prevailed in their household ever since her father's second marriage" (362). Practicing the discretion she has learned through the possession of secrets and love for her father, she does not think it her place to tell "her stepmother some forcible home truths" (362).

Gossip is the operation of conversation that goes beyond its immediate purpose of conveying information to have long-lasting credit in the judgment of people's worth. Homans argues that gossip is like money, "a chain of signifiers that can easily operate without referring to anything" (268). And Molly is caught in her go-between role in the middle of scandal that moves from Mrs. Dawes, to Miss Phoebe, to Miss Browning, and finally to her father. It is Mrs. Dawes who has the lead in passing on the scandal. Even though Miss Browning warns her not to repeat it—"My dear, don't repeat evil on any authority unless you can do some good by speaking about it" (511)—Mrs. Dawes has her position in society to earn, and nothing makes her more of an insider than to best Mrs. Goodenough in repeating the juiciest gossip. As Schor points out, "Gossip . . . is generated out of the need to prove one's right to speak out" (200). Molly refuses to get enmeshed in the power plays of Hollingford gossip. She has learned enough from the role models of Mrs. Hamley, Mrs. Gibson, and Lady Harriet to realize that there are greater dangers. Molly's defense to her father expresses her belief that she has done nothing to violate morality: "What I did, I did of my own self. . . . And I'm sure it was not wrong in morals, whatever it might be in judgment. . . . If people choose to talk about me, I must submit; and so must you, dear papa" (518). Nor will Molly tell her father any reason for the scandal, because of her solemn word to Cynthia. Mr. Gibson is confounded by his not being able to seek satisfaction from Mr. Preston in the usual way of men of honor (Molly: "he behaved well to me" 519) or to confront Cynthia (Molly: "you will drive her out of the house if you do" 520). They must both bear it. Molly advises her father, "It's like tooth-drawing, it will be over some time. It would be much worse if I had really been doing wrong" (520).

By the end of the novel, Molly learns to read her audience so well that she edits her conversation to stay within the demands of her position in it. One scene demonstrates her newfound sensitivity to the complexities involved in a simple exchange of information. She has just returned from the Towers, where she has spent the time of Cynthia's London wedding recovering from an illness. Molly is in the position of telling the Misses

Browning all about her exciting visit, but she has her stepmother's over-sensitivity to her favor at the Towers to contend with; consequently, Molly feels compelled to alter her story: "So Molly began an account of their say-ings and doings, which she could have made far more interesting to Miss Browning and Miss Phoebe if she had not been conscious of her stepmoth-er's critical listening. She had to tell it all with a mental squint; the surest way to spoil a narration" (623). Molly has discovered what feminists have termed "telling it slant," after Emily Dickinson's poem. Gaskell presents "telling it with a mental squint" as a survival skill in Hollingford society. However, as Molly is well aware, it spoils the narration.

The barriers to open and honest communication for marginalized women can best be illustrated by the case of Cynthia Kirkpatrick. Both Molly and Cynthia attempt to get out of the suicidal script written by their society for young women in the marriage market. Gaskell is careful to develop justification for Cynthia's falling into subterfuge and becoming victim to blackmail. Cynthia is herself aware of her mother's manipula-tions, even to the point of recognizing the harm done to her own character. Yet she does not put the blame on her mother. If Gaskell implies blame, it is directed at the unfortunate snares that prevent marginalized people from full development of their moral backbones. These snares most often occur in the breakdown of communication. Just as economic conditions, along with a weak character, force Hyacinth Clare into subterfuge, so the same forces control Cynthia's moral growth. Gaskell's literary method ex-plores every aspect of the context of the lie. For example, when Cynthia first comes under the control of Preston, the reason is that her mother has left no forwarding address. Homans claims that her mother is "a shift-ing signifier" who makes Cynthia "unable to 'refer to' her" (265). Cyn-thia, who was not yet sixteen, contracts a marriage with Preston, which she really intends at the time to honor, in exchange for a loan of twenty pounds. Though Cynthia denies she sold herself for twenty pounds (463), the very concept of selling oneself is brought out in the open. The Gibson marriage was such a deal, though neither participant in it admits such a blatant truth. Twenty pounds was a significant amount of money even to a woman who had a method of earning money, and, of course, Cynthia did not. According to M. Jeanne Peterson, average salaries for governesses ranged from twenty to forty-five pounds a year (8). For Cynthia, however, it's not the money that causes the problem—she scrimps and saves like Nora Helmer in Ibsen's *A Doll's House* to repay the money. It is the letters which are put to pathological uses.

The letters Cynthia wrote to Preston in gratitude and appreciation were not discreetly written. But how would a fifteen-year-old girl understand what dangers her words could create? She tells Molly, "Those unlucky letters . . . only seven of them! They are like a mine under my feet, which may blow up any day; and down will come father and mother and all" (473–74). In Cynthia's personal world, blackmail will affect not only herself but also her family. By alluding to the surprisingly violent lullaby, "Rock-a-bye Baby," Gaskell reveals the deep-reaching danger of the pathological uses of information. Cynthia's marginalized situation makes her susceptible to that chief pathology of information, blackmail. While her person genuinely attracts Preston, her position makes her vulnerable.

Cynthia's situation says much about the trap society has set for women of her class. Welsh points out that "a blackmailer has this curious role, for a villain, of aligning himself with society and also befriending his victim. . . . The blackmailer seems to be enforcing the kinds of behavior demanded by society" (84). Gaskell argues in *Wives and Daughters* that lying has the same function as blackmail in enforcing the standards that society thinks it values: cunning and passivity in women. But she also traces the causes of verbal pathology and suggests a way to healthier communication.

Healthier communication does not categorically rule out what Gaskell calls "telling it all with a mental squint." Nor does it rule out consciousness of power in controlling the uses of information. In her confrontation with Preston, Molly is forced to use a power play to achieve her goal of obtaining Cynthia's letters. While Preston details the audience who may be shocked and dismayed to read them—Osborne Hamley, Mr. Gibson, and Mrs. Gibson—Molly thinks of the audience that would similarly dismay Preston: "So I will tell it all, from beginning to end, to Lady Harriet, and ask her to speak to her father. I feel sure that she will do it; and I don't think you will dare to refuse Lord Cumnor" (482). As Preston wonders "how she, the girl standing before him, had been clever enough to find" the exact way to blackmail him, the two are interrupted. Preston admires her: "There she stood, frightened, yet brave, not letting go her hold on what she meant to do" (482). Molly's resources are the lessons learned from Lady Harriet and even from her stepmother. And when her goal is just, she stands firm enough to beat Preston at his own game.

It is appropriate, perhaps, that Gaskell did not live to finalize the marriage between the two young people she educated to go forward together into a new age of information. On the grounds of protecting Molly's health, Mr. Gibson keeps Roger from speaking with Molly before he leaves on the extension of his Darwinian African journey of discovery. Wasinger finds a similar satisfaction in the nonending: "Molly unmarried remains Molly not-yet-fully-socialized, still on the threshold of adult sexuality, still unmarked by her husband's name, still autonomous" (282). Gaskell did, however, accomplish Molly's transformation into that autonomous woman of discretion and integrity.

WORKS CITED

Bonaparte, Felicia. *The Gypsy-Bachelor of Manchester: The Life of Mrs. Gaskell's Demon.* Charlottesville: UP of Virginia, 1992.

Colón, Susan E. "Elizabeth Gaskell's *Wives and Daughters*: Professional and Feminine Ideology." *VIJ: Victorian Institute Journal* 35 (2007): 7–30.

Gaskell, Elizabeth. *Wives and Daughters.* New York: Penguin, 2001.

Homans, Margaret. *Bearing the Word: Language and Female Experience in Nineteenth-Century Women's Writing.* Chicago: U of Chicago P, 1986.

Peterson, M. Jeanne. "The Victorian Governess: Status Incongruence in Family and Society." *Suffer and be Still: Women in the Victorian Age.* Ed. Martha Vicinus. Bloomington: Indiana UP, 1973.

Rich, Adrienne. *On Lies, Secrets and Silence: Selected Prose 1966–78.* London: Virago, 1980.

Schor, Hilary M. *Scheherezade in the Marketplace: Elizabeth Gaskell and the Victorian Novel.* New York: Oxford UP, 1992.

Spacks, Patricia Meyer. *The Female Imagination.* London: George Allen and Unwin, 1976.

Stoneman, Patsy. *Elizabeth Gaskell.* Bloomington: Indiana UP, 1987.

Uglow, Jenny. *Elizabeth Gaskell: A Habit of Stories*. London: Faber and Faber, 1993.

Wasinger, Carrie. "That 'Old Rigmarole of Childhood': Fairytales and Socialization in Elizabeth Gaskell's *Wives and Daughters*." *Studies in the Novel* 40 (Fall 2008): 268–84.

Welsh, Alexander. *George Eliot and Blackmail*. Cambridge: Harvard UP, 1985.

Wollstonecraft, Mary. *A Vindication of the Rights of Woman*. Ed. Miriam Brody. London: Penguin, 1992.

MARY ELLIS GIBSON

The Perils of Reading

Children's Missionary Magazines and the Making of Victorian Imperialist Subjectivity

In December 1849 the *Ragged School Union Magazine* reprinted a poem from the *Ladies Needlework Penny Magazine* written by one Mrs. E. S. Craven Green. Mrs. Green's poem, "The Claims of the Needy," will have a familiar ring in the context of middle-class "condition of England" poems of the decade. Mrs. Green exhorted Christian mothers to acts of charity in language that conflated home, country, queen, and empire. She began with the biblical epigraph, "suffer the little children to come unto me" and exclaimed:

Yes, suffer them—the dust upon thy purple,
    Oh Island Queen of the far-surging sea,
Imperial Albion!—by the wayside scattered
    Though vile and noisome weeds they seem to be;
There is in each a germ of mighty power,
A soul to answer at the judgment hour.
[. . .]
Oh, Christian mothers! England's honour'd matrons,
    Whose hands free aid to the far heathen pour,
How long shall little children be forbidden
    To tread with naked feet, the sacred floor

Of those high temples where the Spirit moves,
Of Him who ever pleads and ever loves?

(30)

For Mrs. Green, Britain, the "Island Queen" of the "far-surging sea," has a "world-saving mission" both at home and abroad, a mission conceived as integral to motherhood. Metaphorically, the mother country and the queen herself guarantee the goodness of Britain's children. Middle-class philanthropy ritually cleanses the imperial mantle by saving children everywhere.

The same issue of the *Ragged School Union Magazine* defended Lord Ashley's emigration scheme for "ragged boys" who were sent to something like indentured servitude in Australia. The magazine printed testimonials from boys sent to Australia attesting to their happiness, but the writer acknowledged the "strong suspicion" in the minds of poor children and their parents that "something more than philanthropy" had to do with the emigration scheme. Some parents and children, the writer admitted, considered the emigration scheme "a secret system of transportation, without the benefit of council or jury. . . . Among the parents the report was current, that it was a new system of British slavery, and that Lord Ashley was to have [10 pounds] for every young 'Arab of the city' he could capture" ["The Emigrants. No. III," *Ragged School Union Magazine* 1 (December 1849): 2]. As I shall argue, the *Ragged School Union Magazine* was only one of many in nineteenth-century Britain that worked—as these examples suggest—to constitute a gendered, classed, and defensively British subjectivity in its readers.

Children's missionary magazines, formed in evangelical Christian understandings of the world, worked within the parameters Mrs. Green well understood. For Mrs. Green and the editors of the *Ragged School Union Magazine* the bourgeois family was *the* family. The destitute family in Britain and the heathen child abroad measured the limits of domesticity. Mrs. Green's language was, if anything, even more common in magazines for children than in magazines for adults. In such magazines, doing good and converting the heathen were central impluses that defined the family itself. The editorial practices, dominant tropes, and organizational principles of children's magazines (whether overtly religious or secular) over the course of the nineteenth century were rooted in the practices of missionary magazines.

Here I trace the publishing history of missionary magazines for children. I argue 1) that they were crucial to the formation of enduring journalistic practices in children's publishing and 2) that they crucially formed children as imperial subjects. Assuming my reader is likely to have little familiarity with missionary periodicals, I quote from them at length, analyzing at once the development of their print formulas and their implications for imperial subjectivity.

Missionary magazines for children proliferated in the first half of the nineteenth century. Mrs. Green had a wide array of magazines from which to choose if she desired uplifting reading for her own middle-class children, or indeed for the destitute children in the ragged schools themselves. By 1849 she could have chosen from among the *Children's Friend*, the *Church Missionary Juvenile Instructor*, the *Juvenile Missionary Magazine*, the *Juvenile Missionary Herald*, the *Wesleyan Juvenile Offering*, to name a few among the most prominent. And she would have just missed Mrs. Sherwood's *Youth's Magazine*, which had commenced in 1822 but ceased publication in 1848.[1]

In these children's missionary magazines, such "heathen" practices as infanticide, child marriage, and sati (the immolation of Hindu widows on the funeral pyres of their husbands) provided the exotic limit to bourgeois domesticity and guaranteed by contrast a norm for British domestic life. Broadly speaking, the bourgeois domestic family was coeval with the orientalized exotic child. Children of the middle classes and the elite, and of the literate or better off working classes to a significant extent, were central to a normative discourse of domesticity that was constituted against the limit of the foreign. Nowhere is this more apparent than in periodicals for children, both religious and ostensibly secular. Evangelical discourses of charity and missions redefined the most intimate domestic task, child rearing, within a global context.

Editors were happy to put their case for a normative Christian domesticity in the baldest way, whatever its implicit contradictions. The editor of the *Primitive Methodist Children's Magazine*, for example, wrote in 1847: "Imagine, my dear children, what a glorious thing it would be, if the gospel were spread throughout the world! If all men's hearts were under the influence of saving grace we should no more hear of children being given to idolatrous priests, to be offered as sacrifices; no more would our feelings be harrowed up at the thought of widows being burnt to death on the funeral piles [pyres] of their husbands; no more should we hear of the horrors of war" (5: 82). Like "street Arabs" of the ragged schools, ignorant heathen provided the limits by which the domestic was defined. The roots of late Victorian imperial anxieties, moreover, are amply evident in depictions of early Victorian domesticity in children's missionary publications. These magazines evince the changes in aesthetics, rhetoric, and geography attendant upon imperial expansion.

One way to account for the influence of missionary magazines on Victorian children's subjectivity is to appeal to technological change and the expansion of education. Rapid changes in production, communication, and transportation—from the telegraph to the steamship to the penny post—at once compressed space and time and allowed the rapid recirculation of themes and tropes. In the 1840s and 50s, British taxes on knowledge—that is on newspapers, paper itself, and advertising—were gradually reduced; at the same time Britain saw growing prosperity after 1850. The second phase of the industrial revolution also had a significant impact on publishing: the invention of linotype, the rotary press, and paper made from pulp enabled a vast increase in the amount of material published. Coupled with increased literacy, these developments led to the creation of a mass market for periodicals, including periodicals for children. These periodicals ranged from respectable magazines like *The Boy's Own* to less respectable penny dreadfuls.

But this historical narrative, based on technological change in the commercial publishing industry, underestimates the formation of a mass audience earlier in the century, a formation mediated by evangelical print culture. A focus on mass markets in the later half of the nineteenth century for magazines like penny dreadfuls obscures the way evangelical print culture had already formed Victorian children's subjectivity. Nancy Armstrong, writing about the world of adults and conduct books, has argued in *Desire and Domestic Fiction* that the domestic novel acted as both agent and product of cultural change, creating forms of bourgeois subjectivity. Such a process is if anything more striking in children's periodicals between 1800 and 1850, if only because of their overt religious didactic claims. The formation of subjectivity, which Armstrong attributes to domestic fiction (and to conduct books), was the explicit purpose of periodicals that set as their goal the religious and social education of children.

Missionizing literature for children was intended to *create* the forms of subjectivity that domestic fiction and conduct books for adults were understood to *regulate*. Formation of subjectivity, particularly the forms of interiority encouraged in evangelical Christianity, is understood to be imparted at the same time as literacy. The children's missionary magazines, building on the lessons of the primer, inculcated ideas about the soul in the world and about moral action. These ideas maintained their importance even in ostensibly secular novels and magazines later in the century—from R. M. Ballantyne's *Coral Island* to Harmsworth's halfpenny mass market magazines.[2] The Christian evangelical formulation for children's imperial subjectivity thus was extraordinarily long lived.

Magazines for children published between 1790 and 1850 anticipated later developments in publishing by creating mass market forms even in advance of technological change. Many early children's magazines were the creations of evangelical religion and were published in large numbers before technological and economic developments made secular ventures profitable. Religious organizations, ranging from the London Missionary Society (LMS) to the Church Mission Society (CMS) to denominations like the Wesleyans, subvented the publication of magazines and tracts for children in great numbers. Charitable individuals and individual congregations, particularly Sunday schools, purchased these publications by the job lot and often distributed them free of charge.

No life is long enough for a scholar to read the deluge of print that engulfed the Victorian young; every denomination and various missionary and charitable organizations had their own publications, and many were published in numbers suitable for large circulation. The *Juvenile Missionary Magazine*, published by the London Missionary Society, for example, claimed at the end of its first volume in 1844 that it had already a demand for 200,000 copies.[3] What's more, the editors declared, their magazine was priced so cheaply that readers could purchase numerous similar magazines *in addition*. Though an unspoken class bias here anticipates a largely middle-class readership, free distribution in Sunday schools and publications sponsored by groups such as the Wesleyans and the Primitive

Methodists ensured that working-class children also could be included in the evangelical audience. By 1850 the *Juvenile Missionary Magazine* claimed it was publishing hundreds of thousands of copies a year, and that at a profit. The editor observed:

> This is a wonderful age. Never were so many wonderful things seen, or so many wonderful things done, as there are now. And amongst these things cheap books, especially books for the young, are not the least wonderful. Their number, their beauty, their usefulness, and their price, must surprise every body who thinks about them. Just consider for a little your own Juvenile Missionary Magazine, the Seventh Volume of which is now finished. In every Number there are twenty-two pages, closely and beautifully printed. These pages are not filled up with scraps and patches from other books, old stories which have been often told, or foolish ones which were not worth the telling; but nearly every line has been written, with great care, expressly for our little readers. And they would be surprised if they saw the quantity of writing which every month is sent to the printers, before they have enough to make one Magazine. But, besides the printing, there is in every Number, one, and sometimes two Engravings, which cost from £2 to £3 each, and now and then there is added a piece of music, for which the printer is paid an extra price. All this is nicely stitched in a coloured cover, and together makes one of the prettiest and most instructive books ever prepared for the young. Is it not wonderful, then, that such a book, with so much paper and print, can, with the pictures and music into the bargain, be sold for a halfpenny? But perhaps you may suppose that the Directors of the London Missionary Society lose money by it. Now, even if they did, they would still publish the Magazine; because it makes the young think about the poor heathen, and brings many of them to pray, and give, and collect for the spread of the gospel. But this is not the case; and the most surprising thing of all about this little book is, that, though it contains so much. and sells for so little, it yields a good profit to the funds of the Society. (7: iii–iv).

Formation of children's character went hand in hand with raising money for missionary causes.

Children's missionary magazines were largely the productions of the many missionary societies established between 1792 and 1880. At least fifty such organizations were created over the course of the century, beginning with broadly designed organizations founded at the end of the eighteenth century. The dominant early organizations included the Baptist Missionary Society (1792), the London Missionary Society (Non-Conformist, 1795), the Scottish Missionary Society (1796), the Church Missionary Society (1799), and societies focused exclusively on publications—the Religious Tract Society (1799) and the British and Foreign Bible Society (1805). By the mid-nineteenth century such broad-spectrum missionary endeavors were supplemented by more specialized funds, such as the Coral Missionary Fund, the Indian Female Normal School Society, the Christian Vernacular Education Society for India, and so forth. A great many Protestant groups in Britain, like their similar counterparts in the United States, devoted significant effort to publications, both at home and abroad, and great excitement in evangelical circles accompanied these founding efforts.[4]

The most successful religious publications were joined in the course of the century by a number of secular ones. By 1900, as working-class children, especially boys, attained both literacy and the wherewithal to buy their own magazines, the religious press and these more secular magazines faced stiff competition from mass market publishers, particularly the Rupert Murdoch for the young, Harmsworth.[5] These publications drew upon and reshaped earlier publishing formulas. Meanwhile, evangelical publications also transformed themselves, in packaging and sometimes in content as well. At mid-century children's religious magazines had such titles as the *Church Missionary Juvenile Instructor*, the *Wesleyan Juvenile Offering*, and the *Juvenile Missionary Magazine*. By the 1870s they had transformed themselves into *Children's World*, *At Home and Abroad*, and *News from Afar*.[6] These changes, in part, appealed to changing fashion—"juvenile" was no longer the popular term. But more importantly, they acknowledged that a different sense of "children's world"—and hence of adult world—had been created in the course of the century. The world was constituted in a taken-for-granted binary creating "home" as the other half of "foreign."

Enabled by evolving technologies of production and distribution and focusing their application, an early Victorian evangelical sensibility persisted and transformed itself in supposedly secular publications. This evangelical sensibility was the foundation of a significant cultural mythology that persisted in the publishing formulas for girls' and boys' magazines. Here I trace the contours of this highly successful publishing formula, relying on a sample of more than thirty British magazines for children, most of them published by specifically religious institutions.

Examining magazines for children across the century, it is easy to identify a movement from the overt and, to us, heavy-handed didacticism of the 1820s to a different, less pious tone in the 1890s. Nonetheless, rather than simply becoming more secular, late Victorian children's periodicals repeated tropes, narrative structures, and publishing formulas that began in improving literature for children, especially as it drew on missionary lore. Far from being a marginal concern of evangelical nonconformists and their counterparts in the Church of England, early to mid-Victorian missionizing created the crucial discourse through which empire was to be popularly understood. Early religious publications for children and their more secular successors created what I would call a global subjectivity; they prepared the way for British children to see themselves as subjects defined through global relationships.

Religious and secular children's magazines functioned in the building of empire by mediating the relationship between home and empire, thus providing empire with moral justification. They provided the language through which the new domesticity could be constituted as already implicated in and fueling the foreign knowledge, trade, and conquest of a growing empire. As directed toward children, missionary publications were a new form for a new market, which both effected and represented the creation of children as a separate group and as, again, gendered within this category. The creation of British and North American childhood, as we ourselves knew it up to about 1980, was established in the languages of religion, domesticity, and Christian civilization. The new magazines for children created a space in which children could imagine themselves as imperial subjects, as religious souls, and as gendered beings.

So what were the publishing formulas for these magazines? And how were gendered patterns established within them? As early as 1824 in the evangelical *Select Magazine for the Instruction and Amusement of Young*, the formula was clear: a memoir or character sketch of a famous person (including Walter Raleigh—later a staple of boys' imperial adventures); historical tidbits (especially relating to the Bible); English botany and other scientific subjects; articles on historical subjects such as chivalry (again a later staple of boys' magazines); fictionalized domestic stories; improved stories of children's deaths; selections from books of travel, adventure, or missionary labors; and poetry. Ostensibly secular magazines such as *Parley's* (in both American and British versions) and church publications alike relied on this routine publishing formula. Most numbers included geographical descriptions, travel, voyages, and adventures, historical tidbits, biography, natural history both exotic and domestic, description of familiar objects, original tales including both domestic and adventure stories, accounts of trades and pursuits, and rhymes.[7] As this formula became a cultural commonplace, children, like their parents, could imagine themselves as domestic, religious, and imperial subjects. These magazines, like less overtly didactic texts, can be thought of as making a cultural and emotional geography out of the material geography of commerce, politics, and the implicit demands of religious endeavor.

Four examples, one North American (in origin), one British and conservatively working-class evangelical, one middle-of-the-road semisecular, and one for very young children, can demonstrate the continuity and ubiquity of the evanglical publishing formula. In 1833, the American publisher of *Parley's Magazine for Children and Youth* had nailed his market share (so successfully he was pirated and plagiarized in Britain). Omitting the Calvinist death scenes of earlier evangelical writing, Parley included quaint stories of heathen customs and indulged in natural history both exotic and domestic. The publisher promised original tales along already gendered lines—"home scenes" and "stories of adventure." The *Wesleyan Juvenile Offering* brought forth similar fare in the next decade. Figure 1 illustrates the continuity of this effort across the ocean as it ranged from the implicitly religious effort of *Parley's* to the explicitly religious. The contents of volume 4 (1847) of the *Wesleyan Juvenile Offering* are typical. The appeal is miscellaneous, though here focused more on missions than in many nonsectarian journals. This formula continued through the century for church-based periodicals. Competing secular publications, however, relied on a similar mixture of morality, adventure, and natural history. Routledge's *Every Boy's Annual* enticed its middle-class readers by printing on its cover the contents (1862):

1. The Wild Man of the West by R. M. Ballantyne
2. Our Domestic Pets: The Squirrel by Rev. J. G. Wood
3. Our First Great Sea-Fight by A. B. Edwards [set in 1617]
4. Amongst the Show Folks by Sterling Coyne [which includes a carnival owner and his daughter the "Princess of the Caribee Isles"]
5. A Word about the Gorilla

Every Girl's Annual a decade later (1872) included a cover featuring birds and inside provided a song, an orphan story, "A Plea for our Sailors" (which solicited girls to provide libraries for ships' crews); "Aunt Winifred's Hours" (a domestic hortatory tale); "The Broken Soldier," another "orphan" or half-orphan story in which the heroine's mother dies and her father ships out to India; and a miscellany of poems and recipes.

Everyone indeed had a magazine, not just older boys and girls. *The Child's Own*, published by the Sunday School Union, had a similar but simpler formula in 1875. Volume 4 in the new series included in this order: Mrs. Battersby's moralistic poem, "A True Story: Minnie's Prayer," a poem titled "The Frozen Brook," "Ants in Ceylon," "God's Promise to Abram: A Sunday Lesson," two more poems and moral anecdotes, "The Serpent in the Toy Box (from the Journal of a Missionary)," "A Noble Example Set by a Heathen Boy" [Chinese], and "The Bear," which was "taken from Captain Butler's interesting book "Wild North Land.""

The ideological freight of these magazines is a posited coherence between domesticity and empire, a coherence that, even within the magazines themselves, is shown to be fraught with contradiction. Though in actual fact empire disrupted the family—sending sons and sometimes daughters abroad in the military, trade, or missions—editors presented empire as contributing to familial harmony. The domestic was, in fact, more like a colander than a castle; but in a kind of ideological compensation, children's magazines idealized the family.

In managing the contradictions of empire, mothers are frequently effaced and patriarchs displaced. The catalyst for boys' adventures is, as often as not, an "imperial uncle"—say, for example, the sea captain who

WESLEYAN JUVENILE OFFERING:

A MISCELLANY

OF

MISSIONARY INFORMATION

FOR YOUNG PERSONS.

VOL. IV.

FOR THE YEAR MDCCCXLVII.

CONTENTS OF THE FOURTH VOLUME.

A 2

1. The contents of volume 4 (1847) of the *Wesleyan Juvenile Offering*.

returns to take his nephew on a voyage toward adventure and restoration of family fortunes. Occasionally the imperial uncle is a villain (as in Stevenson's *Kidnapped*). But in either case, the boy's heroism replenishes family fortunes and restores the coherence of domesticity and empire. The mother's role is to send her son off with her prayers, making do with any daughters left at home. Peter Parley in his American versions and British knockoffs took the avuncular role, while Aunt Judy (though the nickname was taken from the pet name of Mrs. Gatty's child) held a somewhat similar role; in countless stories the aunt or uncle provides a path to an outside world of learning, amusement, or adventure.

While the miscellaneous form of children's magazines yoked the domestic and the exotic, formulas for older children became increasingly divided over the century along gendered lines. In the *Boys of Empire* (1, no. 1 [1888]) we find a school story, a sea story, domestic scenes, English history recast, and a suitable number of exotic or ferocious animals. *Boys of Empire* went further than most magazines to eschew explicit religious language, in part because it was appealing to working-class boys who purchased it with their own money. Yet, its inaugural issue (1888) provided a bonus color illustration of "King Richard of England Fighting the Saracens in Palestine." The magazine identified the British boy with Richard's Christian chivalry and with England's greatness. In their preface to the magazine, the editors declared that the modern English boy is "brave yet refined, muscular, yet withal gentle"; he and his country are hailed as "harbingers" of civilization. At about the same time, *Every Girl's Magazine* was renamed by its new publisher the more heroic *Atalanta*. The editors followed the lead of missionary magazines in soliciting girls' contributions to charity and to self-improvement. The girls were also treated to English history, travel, stories of brave women, an African adventure by Rider Haggard, exotic animals, and the like. While working-class boys were called on by *Boys of Empire* to be "brave yet refined," middle-class girls were exhorted by *Atalanta* to "Truth, Duty, and loving service sweet." Thus girls received a double message—be courageous, be subservient. Boys were to compass a less fraught dichotomy, uniting courage with good manners. For boys and girls chivalry and service figured empire as mission and provided an imaginary coherence that obscured the routine and menial tasks, the actual labor, required by imperial expansion. Service may have been philanthropic, then as now, but it also defined the boundaries between "street Arabs" or exoticized heathen and the children of the Victorian middle classes and respectable working classes.

Both gendered moralizing and narrative excitement, obscured imperial violence and imperial profit, and effaced domestic disruption. But these elements—money and violence—returned coded. They were transformed into the violent exotic or domesticated through the technology of missionary fund-raising. Money or profit and violence were key to the ideological contradictions within the publishing formulas of children's magazines. Materialism had always been a sin from an evangelical point of view, as was made clear in repeated messages to girls criticizing fancy dress; often religious magazines contrasted English girls' modest simplicity with the elaborate costumes or coiffure of the "heathen" or, conversely, assured girls who primped that they themselves were no better than heathen. More problematic was the issue of material wealth itself. Despite the emphasis on heavenly rewards, missionary magazines, with their language of debt and salvation and their insistent fund-raising efforts, encouraged young readers to sell missions to their friends and relations, however poor.

Children's missionary magazines developed elaborate and successful technologies for fund-raising. By one estimate the children of the Methodist Missionary Society alone raised "well over a million pounds" for missions between 1814 and 1900—representing by the turn of the century a fifth of the society's annual receipts (Prochaska 107). The missionary societies pioneered the fund-raising card technology taken over in the twentieth century by the March of Dimes. A continued refrain in missionary magazines was the need to raise money for missionary causes. Typical was the poem "To a Collector of Small Contributions" published in the *Wesleyan Juvenile Offering*:

> Though trifling in your eye
> The little mite appear,
> Yet to my charming words
> A moment lend your ear.
>
> Look on the mighty deep,
> And contemplate the sea;

2. Hairstyles on females from Rotuma (now part of Fiji), as depicted in the *Wesleyan Juvenile Offering* as a caution for young girls.

If 'twere not for the DROPS,
  Where would its *vastness* be?
[. . .]
Despise not then THE PENCE,
  They help to make *the pound;*
And each may help to SPREAD ABROAD
  The GOSPEL'S JOYFUL SOUND!
(4 [1847]: 44)

Thrift had its reward—in the child's salvation, her subsumption in a larger cause, and the conversion of the heathen.[8]

Thus missionary magazines taught the children of England about accumulation and saving, if not about risk. The profits of empire were subsumed in questions of charity. In money matters, the magazines yoked the domestic and the exotic by means of children's imaginations, as they treated British children to verbal and visual displays of the missionary work the children supported in faraway places. Financial risk—the dimension of capitalism most violent in its effects—was like the patriarch himself relegated to the margins of stories, often as a missing adult who has lost his fortune before the story begins. For girls, a restoration of fortune depended on discovered inheritance; for boys, on their own efforts.

Even more than money, a focus for imperial anxiety was violence itself. Children's magazines marginalized the reality of risk in figures of financial failure, but risk returned in force through the fascination with shipwreck. In shipwreck, violence (and financial risk) is evoked without reference to larger social institutions. This sublimation of imperial risk and violence is also the driving force in many tales of adventure involving animals.

By focusing on shipwreck, ferocious animals, and cannibals, children's magazines elided the reality that empires operate through administrative detail and organized violence. Such tales as the story of Volney Becker, devoured by a shark after rescuing his father, project violence onto the radically different other. The shark depicted in figure 3 accompanied Volney's story in more than one publication, without necessarily illustrating the letterpress. This tale of a boy heroically rescuing both a young girl and his father from the depredations of a shark was recycled incessantly throughout the century. In the *Primitive Methodist Children's Magazine* it took an especially

THE SHARK.

3. The shark from the story of Volney Beckner that appeared in *Primitive Methodist Children's Magazine*, 1847.

horrific form. The story commences when the "daughter of a rich American merchant" falls overboard. Volney's father leaps into the water to save her and has almost succeeded when a shark appears. All hands call for help, but only young Volney answers the call effectively: "In this terrible extremity, filial piety excited little Volney to arm himself with a broad and pointed sabre; and, throwing himself into the sea, he dived with the velocity of a fish, slipped under the animal, and thrust his sword up to the hilt in his body." Ropes are thrown overboard, and as the trio is lifted from the water, "at least one victim" is "to be sacrificed for the rest."

> Enraged to see his prey about to escape him, the shark plunged to make a vigorous spring; then issuing from the sea with impetuosity, and darting forth like lightning, with the sharp teeth of his capacious mouth he

tore asunder the body of the intrepid and unfortunate boy, while suspended in the air. A part of poor little Volney's palpitating body was drawn into the ship, while the father and the fainting child in his arms were saved.

The adult storyteller concludes: "Surely, my dear children, this noble deed of Volney Beckner will induce you to come forward to save thousands of immortal souls from that eternal death to which they are daily exposed" (*Primitive Methodist Children's Magazine*, 4 [1847]: 85–86). The story of Volney Becker, or Beckner, was retold many times in the nineteenth century and illustrated with ferocious drawings. In the *Primitive Methodist Children's Magazine* the editors moralized Volney Becker even beyond the celebration of filial piety and masculine heroism.[9] In most examples of imperial violence sublimated, the triumphant British boy or man kills or controls the exotic animal, and home—both family and country—becomes peaceful once more.

Again, exotic violence is gendered, as stories and letterpress most often connect the male protagonist with an animal opponent. No doubt these stories also appealed to little girls, but one wonders how they responded to what one critic has called the magazines' "morbid fascination" with Asia and Africa.[10] Perhaps more directly addressed to the domestic sphere, throughout the century magazines reiterated the tropes of child sacrifice, ritual sacrifice of adults, sati or widow burning, child marriage, and infanticide. In all of these horrific recitals, disruptions of domesticity—or perversions of it, from the Victorian point of view—are projected on exotic others. Girls' general missionariness was evoked to counter such evils.

In the course of reading magazines, then, Victorian children learned that to be a girl or a boy, a family member, a "success" in a capitalist economy, and a British person was to be a subject in empire. Lions, tigers, bears, and murdered infants and children constituted the shadows in this sunny picture, naturalized its violence, diminished its risk, and prepared a generation for the global conflicts of our own century. An explicit missionary agenda was not necessary to accommodate missionizing sentiment.

An anonymous poet distilled all these elements in a few short lines, writing for the *Pictorial Magazine for Little Children* in 1858. In the writer's verses, the child becomes an imperial subject subsumed by the poem's speaking voice:

> Tis to the grace of God I owe
> > That I was born on British ground,
> Where streams of love and mercy flow,
> > And words of sweet salvation sound.
>
> I would not change my native land
> > For rich Peru with all her gold,
> A nobler prize lies in my hand
> > Than East or Western Indies hold.
> (5 [1835]: 36)

Patriotism and religion, though separable when William Blake wrote in the same meter more than half a century earlier, coalesce here in a seamless hymn. The delights of home are, in more ways than one, guaranteed for young readers by a vision of the exotic foreign.

Victorian missionizing discourse, especially as directed toward children—and whether in its explicitly religious or ostensibly secularized variants—assumed a stable sense of the imperial gendered subject. It would be a mistake, however, to imagine that this language fully incorporated previous or even contemporary imaginings. Blake's *Songs of Innocence and Experience*, the most apposite analog of Isaac Watts and his heirs writing in the *Pictorial Magazine*, create an opposing voice, as they further an antimonarchical and radical language. As Saree Makdisi has proposed, Blake moves within the evangelical formation and beyond it, within the antimonarchical frame and beyond it. As Makdisi puts it, rather than "the imperial 'warrior' discourse essential to the dominant strand of 1790s radicalism as well as to at least a major strand of romanticism . . . Blake proposes an opening out away from the discourse of sovereign power" (5).

The dominant discourse of evangelicalism, which eventually undergirded various versions of Victorian imperialism, was also contested in less dramatic ways. Though Blake is surely the clearest antidote either to Watts or to the poet of the *Pictorial Magazine*, poets and editors such as George MacDonald persuaded their youthful readers to inhabit a different ground.

In *Good Words for the Young*, with some considerable tension, and in his own stories, MacDonald moved the imperialist context to a less contested geography and imagined, in stories like "The Princess and the Goblin" or "The Princess and Curdie" or *At the Back of the North Wind*, a theodicy that, like Blake's, does not depend upon the theological import of empire, but rather upon a broader, more forgiving and less nationalistic formation. And yet, MacDonald's positioning of the child and the child's "other" can more easily be understood as a liberal middle ground (however critical of Calvinist theology) than as Blakean radicalism. Despite MacDonald's efforts to counter Calvinism for the young, the adventure plot for empire's boys and the supporting stories for empire's girls continued for many years beyond the relatively brief run of *Good Words*. The Victorian authors we have adopted for our own canon of Victorian children's literature—among them MacDonald, Lewis Carroll, E. Nesbit, and Thackeray—stand in an oblique relationship to a dominant mode of writing for children founded in Victorian missionizing. It is within this orbit that we might once more, contrarily or reluctantly, define Victorian children's literature.

NOTES

1. See Demers on Mrs. Sherwood and the shift from overt didacticism to a more realistic mode.

2. Ballantyne's *Coral Island* (1857) in fact drew upon evangelical depictions of the South Seas, and particularly on the Wesleyan missions to Fiji and other islands, as well as other sources. The *Children's Missionary Magazine* of the Church Missionary Society was renamed the *Coral Missionary Magazine* in 1860 and continued under that name until 1894. For this data and other highly useful details see Missionary Periodicals Database, http://divdl.library.yale.edu/missionperiodicals, which aims to list all missionary periodicals published in Britain between the eighteenth century and the 1960s. See also Mackenzie's two volumes on empire and popular culture; Darton's classic history of nineteenth-century children's literature; and Castle. On Ballantyne, see especially Bristow and Kestner.

3. In the preface to the *Juvenile Missionary Magazine*, a continuation of the *Juvenile Magazine*, the editor claimed, "The Magazine has achieved a sale beyond

expectation. If demand be an index of approval, *two hundred thousand votes* are in its favour" (1 [June–Dec., 1844]: vii). The London Missionary Society "produced over one million juvenile magazines per year by 1850" (Prochaska 112).

4. For a handy list of such missionary associations see "Missions," *Encyclopedia Britannica* (1888). For a contemporary account of juvenile missionary associations, see Blake, *The Day of Small Things*. A broader historical view is provided in Wolfe, *Religion in Victorian Britain*, and by Altholz.

5. From 1866 onward with the publication of *Boys of England* and with the later addition in the 1890s of Harmsworth's *Half-Penny Marvel* and *The Union Jack*, boys (and the girls who stole their papers to read) devoured the existing alternatives to edifying evangelical literature.

6. Altholz's bibliography follows all these changes in name—the apparent accommodation to a more secular market or ethos, noted by most historians of Victorian religion in other contexts—and at the same time acknowledges that religious conceptions had already shaped the cultural geography of empire. It was no longer necessary to purvey a didacticism that had become implicit in a publishing formula. The formula for *Parley's Magazine*, for the church and missionary society organs, and for later secular mass market magazines aimed primarily at boys, including working-class boys, followed the same outline with remarkable persistence. Adventure stories became more graphic, but only the stories of children's holy dying disappeared, with other elements of the formula holding constant even into the twentieth century.

7. *Parley's Magazine for Youth* 1, no. 1 (March 16, 1833) contains these contents, and while it argues for no religious affiliation, it is notably Christian in content, including, for example, an article on Persees (Parsis) and the beginning of a serialized story on Reginald Heber, Anglican bishop of Calcutta. In discussion of the Religious Tract Society's publications, Altholz neatly typifies this publishing formula and the move from what he characterizes the dreary didacticism of the *Child's Companion* to the strategically attractive *Boy's Own* and *Girl's Own* papers; at issue in giving a more ostensibly secular tone to these later magazines was the clash between strict sabbatarianism and the RTS's felt need to reach more children than it could by continuing the stodgy and heavily moralized tracts of its earlier years (Altholz 53–55). While Altholz is undoubtedly right about the lighter tone of these later publications, I would argue that the publishing formula was so embedded in the culture that patriotism, particularly for boys, figured as a kind of spilt religion,

perhaps the more powerfully so in that heavy-handed didacticism was no longer required.

8. Such pleas for children's financial help continued through the century. The editors of the *Wesleyan Juvenile Offering*, under its new name *At Home and Abroad*, exhorted their readers in 1882: "For the purposes of this Mission work at home and abroad the General Committee depends very much upon our juvenile collectors. There are many persons who cannot make large gifts, but who would be both able and willing to give small sums. To find these out as soon as possible, and to call upon them regularly, is the work of the juvenile collector, assisted by the experience and knowledge of the secretary of the Association" (4 [1882]: 2). Details of the extraordinary financial contributions by children to missionary causes—and their importance as collectors of missionary funds—is provided by Prochaska in "Little Vessels." Indeed, children's contributions to missionary endeavors were so important that the missionary box (the forerunner of the UNICEF Halloween collection box) was personified, as was the penny it might contain. See for example Whymper, *The Autobiography of a Missionary Box*; a brief search of Worldcat turns up numerous titles invoking the missionary boxes (both the collection box itself and boxes of clothing and other materials sent to missionaries in the field) and missionary pennies. Prochaska describes the "collecting card, often beautifully engraved," which had space for names of about twenty subscribers and "could be placed conspicuously on a mantelpiece;" missionary collecting boxes were wooden and "attractively labeled" coming in different colors, and they were placed (as such boxes for good causes still are) in a variety of public places (Prochaska 110). Prochaska points out that girls raised by far the greater proportion of funds for juvenile missionary societies.

9. See for example Marmaduke Park, *Thrilling Stories of the Ocean* (Philadelphia: C. G. Henderson and Co., 1852) and William Swinton, *Swinton's First (Sixth) Reader* (American Book Co., 1882). Christopher Kent Rovee remarks on another version, published in 1811 in *The Mirror of Truth*, a game of "moral instruction" published by John Wallis's *Juvenile Repository*. Obviously, Volney Becker provided a story so graphic that it was graphically recycled. The Primitive Methodist version, however, beats the others for gore, being the only one I have found that describes the boy's dismembered but "palpitating body" hoisted to the deck. An interesting comparison here might be provided, as James McGavran suggested to me, by Felicia Hemans's "Casabianca," which can be read both "straight" as a glorification of duty

and ironically as an indictment of the needless death entailed by masculinist war. In contrast to Hemans's boy on the burning deck, Volney Becker is presented as an unambiguous hero.

10. Petroschka 113.

WORKS CITED

Altholz, Josef L. *The Religious Press in Britain, 1760–1900*. Contributions to the Study of Religion, 22. Ed. Henry Warner Bowden. New York: Greenwood, 1989.

Armstrong, Nancy. *Desire and Domestic Fiction: A Political History of the Novel*. New York: Oxford UP, 1987.

Ballantyne, Robert Michael [R. M.]. *Coral Island: A Tale of the Pacific Ocean*. London: Nelson, 1867.

Blake, Joseph. *The Day of Small Things, or a Plain Guide to the Formation of Juvenile Home and Foreign Missionary Associations*. Sheffield, UK: W. Townsend, 1865.

Bristow, Joseph. *Empire Boys: Adventures in a Man's World*. Reading Popular Fiction Series. Hammersmith, London: Harper Collins Academic, 1991.

Castle, Kathryn. *Britannia's Children: Reading Colonialism through Children's Books and Magazines*. Manchester, UK: Manchester UP, 1996.

Darton, F. J. Harvey. *Children's Books in England: Five Centuries of Social Life*. Cambridge: Cambridge UP, 1958.

Demers, Patricia. "Mrs. Sherwood and Hesba Stretton: The Letter and the Spirit of Evangelical Writing of and for Children." In *Romanticism and Children's Literature in Nineteenth-Century England*. Ed. James Holt McGavran, Jr. Athens: U of Georgia P, 1991. 129–49.

Kestner, Joseph. *Masculinities in British Adventure Fiction, 1880–1915*. Burlington, VT: Ashgate, 2010.

Mackenzie, John M., ed. *Imperialism and Popular Culture*. Studies in Imperialism. Manchester, UK: Manchester UP, 1986.

———. *Propaganda and Empire: The Manipulation of British Public Opinion, 1880–1960*. Studies in Imperialism. Manchester, UK: Manchester UP, 1984.

Makdisi, Saree. *William Blake and the Impossible History of the 1790s*. Chicago: U of Chicago, 2003.

Park, Marmaduke. *Thrilling Stories of the Ocean*. Philadelphia: C. G. Henderson, 1852.

Prochaska, F. K. "Little Vessels: Children in the Nineteenth-Century Missionary Movement." *Journal of Imperial and Commonwealth History* 6 (1978): 103–18.

Rovee, Christopher Kent. *Imagining the Gallery: The Social Body of British Romanticism*. Palo Alto, CA: Stanford UP, 2006.

Swinton, William. *Swinton's First (-Sixth) Reader*. New York: American Book Co., 1882.

Whymper, Annette. *Autobiography of a Missionary Box*. London: Religious Tract Society, 1896.

Wolfe, John, ed. *Religion in Victorian Britain*. Vol. 5 *Culture and Empire*. Manchester, UK: Manchester UP, 1988.

JOCHEN PETZOLD

→ The End Was Not Ignoble?

Bird-Nesting between Cruelty, Manliness, and Science
Education in British Children's Periodicals, 1850–1900

At first sight, the topic of "bird-nesting"—a term that can refer to the search for birds' nests, the removal of eggs or young birds from a nest, or the taking of a whole nest with or without eggs or birds—as presented in children's literature may seem marginal, even obscure. Yet references to it abound in children's magazines in the second half of the nineteenth century. This essay is based on more than seventy articles that primarily deal with bird-nesting, and there are many more passing references to the practice in stories printed in these magazines. Thus, the available evidence suggests that as a practice bird-nesting was widespread through much of the nineteenth century, growing in cultural and medial importance as the century progressed.[1] Furthermore, closer analysis will reveal that bird-nesting provides an interesting focal point for the study of childhood, since it ties in with various debates about the nature of childhood, the proper behavior of children, and their education. And while it may seem marginal, it is in fact a topic with a literary tradition reaching back at least to the late seventeenth century, when the first-person narrator of John Dunton's *A Voyage Round the World* (1691) tells his readers that he will not trouble them "with *every Expedition* I made a *Nutting*, or *Birds-nesting*" (59, emphasis in the original).

While few readers today will have heard of Dunton or his text, not all references to bird-nesting are as remote. Arguably the most famous literary representation occurs in the first book of William Wordsworth's *The Prelude* ([1805] ll. 336–50, in Wordsworth 20–22):

> [. . .] was I a plunderer then
> In the high places, on the lonesome peaks
> Where'er, among the mountains and the winds,
> The Mother Bird had built her lodge. Though mean
> My object, and inglorious, yet the end
> Was not ignoble. Oh! when I have hung
> Above the raven's nest, by knots of grass
> And half-inch fissures in the slippery rock
> But ill sustain'd, and almost, as it seem'd,
> Suspended by the blast which blew amain,
> Shouldering the naked crag; Oh! at that time,
> While on the perilous ridge I hung alone,
> With what strange utterance did the loud dry wind
> Blow through my ears! the sky seem'd not a sky
> Of earth, and with what motion mov'd the clouds!

What Wordsworth describes in the last lines of the excerpt is a vision of a "supernatural" nature that goes beyond normal perception, apparently induced by the imminent danger of falling and seriously injuring himself. Interestingly, in this reminiscence Wordsworth himself classifies his "object" as "mean" and "inglorious," an act of "plunder"—and yet he insists that "the end was not ignoble." The choice of the word "end" here is significant in its various levels of meaning. The phrase "the end was not ignoble" would, in most contexts, refer to the purpose of an action, the intention behind it. In the present context, however, this reading would be paradoxical, since this purpose—the taking of eggs or young birds—has already been denigrated as inglorious. Thus, the word "end" would have to refer to the actual outcome of his action, which was clearly not intended, namely the supernatural vision of nature. And yet, the more usual meaning seems to linger somewhat uneasily, as if the speaker was trying to justify an activity that he knows "should" be condemned.

In fact, when Wordsworth wrote his *Prelude*, bird-nesting had been criticized for decades, in countless texts written for young readers. *A Little Pretty
Pocket-Book* is an important case in point. Printed (and probably written)
by John Newbery in 1744, this text marks the starting point for a British
publishing industry specifically aimed at entertaining children (Thwaite
2f.), and it was reprinted repeatedly in the eighteenth century. It includes a
short poem on bird-nesting (95):

Birds-Nesting
Here two naughty Boys,
Hard-hearted in Jest,
Deprive a poor *Bird*
Of her Young and her Nest.

Moral
Thus Men, out of Joke,
(Be't spoke to their Shame)
Too often make free
With others good Name.

The poem is accompanied by a rather simple woodcut—the referent of
"Here" in the first line—depicting the two boys, one handing down a nest
from a tree, but the image is not clear enough to be self-explanatory so
that the "Moral" is necessary to make the point of moral condemnation.
While the book's subtitle claims that it is intended for "Instruction and
Amusement," this particular poem offers little in the way of amusement; it
is rather "instruction" through prohibition—and in its negative representation of bird-nesting it is certainly typical of a very large number of texts.[2]

In view of this widespread disapproval, Michael Heyman suggests that
"Wordsworth's lax attitude" toward bird-nesting displayed in *The Prelude*
"could have been viewed as scandalous" (154), but despite this reserva-
tion, Wordsworth's poem is an ideal introduction to the topic, because it
includes three key motives that turn into individual discursive fields and
that will be at the center of my discussion—though not always in the exact
sense used by Wordsworth. These motifs are the rejection of bird-nesting
on moral grounds (here condensed into the words "plunder," "mean," and

"inglorious"), that of danger and physical achievement inherent in the activity, and finally the idea that there might be a justification to the practice that moves it to some higher plane.

Throughout the nineteenth century, juvenile magazines published a steady current of articles, stories, and poems denouncing bird-nesting, but two strong countercurrents develop during the second half of the nineteenth century: From the late 1850s onward, a number of articles present bird-nesting in a positive light either by praising it as a dangerous adventure that will prove a boy's character, or by linking it to scientific observation and the study of natural history. This triptych of approaches to bird-nesting—condemnation, approval as "adventure," and approval as "science"—represents three distinct positions in a debate that has much wider implications than the question of whether a child should or should not be allowed to take eggs from the nests of wild birds: on the one hand, it can tell us something about contrasting views of childhood; on the other, it is indicative of much broader debates on appropriate behavior of children and finally on the role of natural sciences in their education.[3]

CRUEL, CRUEL SPORT:
THE ARGUMENT AGAINST BIRD-NESTING

From the early nineteenth century onward, articles denouncing the activity of bird-nesting started to appear more or less regularly in magazines aimed at young readers, particularly in magazines with a strong religious orientation, like the *Children's Friend* (1824–1929) or the *Child's Companion* (1832–1923),[4] both issued by the Religious Tract Society. These articles utilize three arguments that can be employed independently or in combination; all three arguments are already indicated in the short poem in Newbery's *Pocket-Book*. The first strategy is to depict bird-nesting as theft ("deprive . . . of," ll. 3–4), and hence as an infraction of God's commandment "Thou shalt not steal." The second argument hinges on the conviction that bird-nesting is cruel, alluded to in Newbery's poem when the bird is described as "poor" (l. 2). The third line of argument does not focus on the action as such, but on the perpetrator's character—which can, of course, be inferred from the wrongness of the action. Hence, the two boys in the poem are called "naughty" (l. 1).

By far, the most common strategy of these anti-bird-nesting pieces is to appeal to the readers' sympathies for the "poor birds" and to denigrate bird-nesting as cruel. In order to do so, the birds are personified and endowed with feelings akin to those of humans. Once the birds' capacity for feeling is established—or, more frequently, simply taking this for granted—there are two potential objects for the children's sympathies: the parent birds and the young ones. Sympathy with the young birds is frequently called for, and one common strategy is to link the birds to the children and to invite them to imagine the plight of the birds. For example, the image of shared captivity is used very drastically in "The Bird Robbers," a short story published in *Peter Parley's Annual* of 1867. In this story, three friends go bird-nesting in their youth; they later become soldiers, are captured, and imprisoned:

> Then it was, while in this most pitiable condition, that they thought of the bird-nests they had robbed and destroyed, and especially of the manner in which they had cruelly caged and tormented the young birds: [. . .]. They were now in a cage themselves, and knew something of the sufferings of poor little birds, and their hearts smote them for their cruelty, and they thought of their wickedness till they were nearly mad with remorse and horror. (73f.)

In the story itself the narrator does not explicitly create a causal link between bird-nesting and their "sad fate" (74), but the presentation of a chain of events implies that things happen *because* of their thoughtless cruelty as children. Furthermore, the piece ends with an explicit moral, which reinforces this link: the narrator states that the story of the bird robbers "ought to be a warning to all little boys who are so cruel as to rob birds of their young, or keep them in cages for their sport—a cruel amusement" (74).

This strategy of inviting children to imagine themselves as captives has a highly influential precedent in Ann Taylor's poem "The Bird's Nest," the second poem in Ann and Jane Taylor's *Original Poems for Infant Minds*. The collection was first published (anonymously) in 1804–1805, was already in its twelfth edition in 1812, and was popular throughout the century. The poem starts by suggesting a bird-nesting expedition, but then the speaker objects that it "would be cruel and bad, / To take their poor nestlings away;" (15, ll. 16–17),[5] emphasizing the point by inviting the child to imagine the following:

> Suppose some great creature, a dozen yards high,
>   Should stalk up at night to your bed;
> And out of the window along with you fly,
> Nor stop while you bid your dear parents good bye,
>   Nor care for a word that you said: (15, ll. 21–25)

This striking image of the giant taking the reader away is used in a number of articles during the nineteenth century, and it is repeated almost 100 years later in the poem "Bird-Nesting," printed in *The Child's Companion* in 1900:

> Now how would you like a big giant to come
> When you were in bed, and with "Fe, fa, fo, fum!"
> Take hold of you tight with his cruel big hands,
> And then march you off to strange people and lands, (62, ll. 5–8)

The context of the pious *Child's Companion* and the explicit moral at the end, "Then do unto others as you'd be done by" (l. 20), leave no doubt that this poem is intended as a serious warning against the cruelty of bird-nesting. However, the poem also illustrates a potential problem with the strategy of personification and specifically the giant-comparison: the comparison holds only limited power of conviction. Even the language used betrays this problem: the giant's speech is nonsensical and funny when he snatches the child with a "Fe, fa, fo, fum!" and it seems unlikely that the poem in itself would do much to convince bird-nesters of the "error of their ways."

Nonetheless, the charge of cruelty is the single most common attribute used to denounce the practice of bird-nesting. By comparison, the argument that bird-nesting is a form of theft is used much less frequently. Except in those cases where the owner of the land had a vested interest in the birds—primarily in cases involving game birds (grouse, pheasant, and partridge) whose eggs were actually protected in England (but not Scotland) by the Game Act of 1831 (447, sec. 24)—the argument again hinges on the personification of the birds. Only if they are seen as the legal owners of the nest and its contents does the charge of "theft" make sense.

One story that denounces bird-nesting as theft is "The Young Robbers," which appeared in *The Children's Treasury* in 1873. The protagonist of the story is a boy "who had earned the name of lazy Dick" (52), who is arrested while bird-nesting and (wrongly) accused of stealing fruit from an orchard. Luckily, the master of the college intervenes, but the boy does not escape punishment and the teacher explains: "A boy who would steal a bird's nest was as much a robber as one who would rob an orchard of its fruit" (53). The story actually ends happily when Dick changes for the better, but not quite trusting the readers to learn by positive example alone, the author reinforces the moral with implicit threats: "Every boy who can rob a bird's nest must be cruel and hard-hearted, and, unless his heart be changed, will certainly grow up a bad and wicked man. The pretty songsters are man's best friends, and he who would hurt them must be an enemy to his own interest, and an enemy to God, who made them and pronounced them to be good" (53f.). The moral employs strong words: the boy is indirectly called "an enemy to God." Today, this may well seem excessive, but it is hardly exceptional by nineteenth-century standards. In many stories, bird-nesters come to a bad end, either being crippled through an accident, or because bird-nesting is described as a stepping stone on their personal road to immorality.

This last point ties in with the strategy of presenting bird-nesting as one aspect of a bad or sinful character. This view received support from John Locke's *Some Thoughts on Education* (1693), one of the most influential treatises on education in the eighteenth and early nineteenth centuries (Richardson 44) that was still reprinted regularly in the Victorian period. In this text, Locke connects cruel behavior of children toward animals to potential cruelty of adults toward men, and he suggests that the behavior of children toward animals should be monitored and controlled:

> One thing I have frequently observ'd in Children, that when they have got Possession of any poor Creature, they are apt to use it ill: They often torment, and treat very roughly young Birds, Butterflies, and such other poor Animals, which fall into their Hands, and that with a seeming kind of Pleasure. This I think should be watched in them, and if they incline to any such *Cruelty*; they should be taught the contrary Usage. For the custom of tormenting and killing of Beasts will, by Degrees, harden

their Minds even towards Men; and they who delight in the Suffering and Destruction of inferior Creatures, will not be apt to be very compassionate or benign to those of their own kind. (100f.)

These sentiments can be easily applied to the topic of bird-nesting. For example, the moral of "The Young Robbers," quoted above, sketches a road from a child's cruelty toward animals to becoming "a bad and wicked man" (53), and the words of Locke are most directly echoed in "Cruelty and Cowardice of Bird-nesting" that appeared in The Children's Friend (1876): "A hard-hearted boy never becomes a brave, a great, a generous, or a happy man; and the youthful tormentor of animals almost invariably grows up to be the hated and feared oppressor, or the degraded and spiritless slave of his fellow-men" (111).

More generally speaking, bird-nesters are frequently described as indolent—they often abstain from school in order to follow their passion—and bird-nesting is often one sign for a more profound streak of cruelty in their characters, a cruelty that will surface in bullying other boys (e.g., "Bird's-Nesting," "The Young Peacemaker").

The tainted character of many bird-nesters suggests that these are typical examples of an Augustinian view on childhood. In this "traditional Christian view" (Stone 225), even newborn babies are marked by original sin, living in a "fallen" state that needs to be redeemed through baptism. Texts in this tradition are explicit in their moralizing and absolute in their convictions, supposing that children need to be controlled and guided by a firm hand. However, quite a number of short stories from the magazines also show signs of a variant to this view, one in which the child is not merely the passive recipient of moral instruction but becomes the focal point of the description of a moral development—which is presented as a positive example intended for bettering others. As Gillian Avery points out,

[a]nalysis of character is a very good medium for improving moral and religious sense, and this was the aim of Miss Sewell and her contemporaries. For them it was no longer enough to scratch the surface as the Georgians had done and seek merely to improve behaviour. They showed children struggling with their consciences, resisting sin, giving way to it, suffering terrifying pangs of remorse. (66)

We have already seen how "lazy Dick" is reformed and how the protagonists of "The Bird Robbers" are smitten with belated remorse. Particularly the latter story approaches an internal presentation of their moral agonies, but their repentance comes too late. There are, however, numerous stories in which the protagonists vow to change their ways and to abstain from bird-nesting in the future. A case in point is G. Russell's "A Few Thoughts about Birds, Their Nests and Their Robbers" (1880), a first-person narrative that retrospectively follows its narrator through the stages of sinning, repenting, and "forsak[ing] the paths of sin" (83):

> In this wicked pursuit of cruelly stealing the property of the birds I continued, [. . .] until, on one occasion, [. . .] I caught sight of a thrush upon its nest. [. . .] I stepped into the hedge, and took the bird up, but could not touch the eggs. My convictions became so powerful that the eye of God was upon me, and that my wickedness was seen by him, that I had not carried the bird many steps before I felt bound to cast it into the hedge out of my sight, forsake the hedge, and make my way home, trembling and fearing lest God should deal with me as I had dealt with the bird, and make me to reap as I had sown. (82f.)

Thus, while some stories or poems simply state that bird-nesting is wrong and should be abandoned, most pieces from the last forty years of the nineteenth century try to elicit their readers' sympathies and awaken (or strengthen) their consciences.

In this aim, girls can take on a specific function as a positive moral influence on bird-nesting boys.[6] While Lucy in *Fabulous Histories* is doubtful of her power to change her brother for the better (cf. 77), the female protagonist in the short story "Bird's-Nesting" that appeared in *Little Wide-Awake* (1883) clearly has such a positive influence. When a girl surprises her brother at bird-nesting, she is "distressed" but promises not to tell their parents and instead makes him "give her his word of honour not to take a nest again" (135). It is significant that the sister does not resort to an external authority—telling the parents would have been considered inappropriate behavior in the context of a school-story—but rather manages to "convert" her brother through her distress.

Generally speaking, while most of the children portrayed in texts criticizing bird-nesting are clearly not depicted as small angels, most of the perpetrators are also not naturally bad and beyond redemption. Rather, most of these stories work with positive examples, and bird-nesting boys are shown to change for the better.

BOYS WILL BE BOYS: BIRD-NESTING AS ADVENTURE

Despite the strong current of anti-bird-nesting literature reaching back to the eighteenth century, from the late 1850s onward some juvenile magazines began to run pieces that portray the practice in a positive light: as an adventurous and character-building exercise for boys, where the activity is combined with character traits that are said to be either natural or implied to be desirable in (young) men.

For example, the article "Birds'-nesting in Earnest," published in *Kind Words* (1868), starts by presenting it as a *natural* phenomenon: "It seems quite a natural thing for boys to hunt for birds' nests, does it not? They take to it as naturally as young ducks to the water" (180). By comparing bird-nesting boys with young animals following their instincts, the author removes the issue from the realm of moral judgement and censure. This image of the child is not that of fallen man within fallen nature; rather, it is reminiscent of Wordsworth's image of his younger self in *The Prelude* and much closer to the childhood concept of Jean-Jacques Rousseau, whose *Émile* (1762, trans. 1765) proposed a course of education in nature and through nature. The text goes on to suggest a reason for the boys' predisposition to bird-nesting,

> though the nesters are perhaps not aware of it. It has all the *uncertainty* of real sport, and that is always a pleasant thing. You never know what will turn up next, or what it will prove to be [. . .] your eyes, and ears, and legs, and arms, are exercised in the open air, your lungs are helped to do their work well, and your young blood goes bounding through every artery and vein, till you feel so hungry that a hunch of bread tastes as good as the richest cake in Squire Matthew's pantry. (180)

If the bird-nesters are not consciously aware of this "reason," this is another indication of how "natural" the activity is. Bird-nesting is portrayed as a vigorous and healthy exercise, apt to make you appreciate the simple pleasures in life—a version of the "muscular Christianity" that had been popularized through Thomas Hughes's *Tom Brown's Schooldays* (1857) and an idea that is also reminiscent of Wordsworth, namely of his focus on low and rustic life in the *Lyrical Ballads*.

The echo of the bird-nesting experience in *The Prelude* is even stronger in stories that highlight the dangerous aspect of reaching nests, like the Reverend J. C. Atkinson's "Hawk Scar; A Bird's Nesting Adventure," published in *Every Boy's Magazine* (1862). The first-person narrator of this story recounts a near-fatal accident during a bird-nesting trip: "All that I seemed to feel was that death lay below me. [. . .] Here was a pretty fix to be in. A lame leg, a game ankle, my nerves shaken, and a narrow and not very even ledge of fourteen or fifteen feet in length to walk along, and then a precipice to descend before I could be safe" (92f.). The situation reads like an exaggerated version of the bird-nesting scene in Wordsworth's *Prelude*: both texts describe an intense experience that is a physical as well as a mental challenge. In Wordsworth's recollection, it leads to a heightened sensitivity and a supernatural perception of nature that singles him out as an artist; in Atkinson's story, it is a test of character that proves the "pluck" and "manliness" of the narrator. In both cases, bird-nesting is a catalyst that brings out the protagonists' hidden strengths. Thus, pieces that describe bird-nesting as a dangerous adventure respond, as it were, to the accusation that bird-nesters are cowards or bullies (while ignoring the issues of cruelty and theft). But this is not made explicit; rather, articles emphasizing the adventurous aspect of bird-nesting present it as a "natural" occurrence that is not questioned or justified.

Even if bird-nesting is described as illegal—and the legal protection of birds had been an issue throughout the second half of the nineteenth century, leading to a number of individual acts[7]—this aspect can be presented as an additional challenge. A case in point is "How We Took the Osprey's Nest" that appeared anonymously in *The Boy's Own Paper* in 1894. In this story, sentries have to be dodged and there is clearly an element of pride in "having gotten away with it" when the narrator relates: "they never found out who the delinquents were" (458). This story is also significant because it shows young men, rather than boys, as active bird-nesters, indicating that the qualities ascribed to it are indeed "manly" and not merely "boyish."

These stories of bird-nesting adventures also represent a minor strand in a fast-growing body of texts that encourages boys to an active life that might occasionally go beyond what would be acceptable behavior in "normal circumstances"; a literature of adventure, often set in foreign countries, that celebrated "manly" qualities and that taught "dash, pluck, and lion-heartedness, not obedience, duty, and piety" (Green 220). In the analysis of Martin Green, "the adventure tales that formed the light reading of Englishmen for two hundred years and more after *Robinson Crusoe* were, in fact, the energizing myth of English imperialism" (3). And while the bird-nesting stories do not usually draw explicit connections to the British Empire, they clearly address the same audience, and they endorse the same set of character qualities: like colonial adventurers, bird-nesters are presented as brave and daring heroes.

In this context of hero-worship, it is not surprising that passing references to bird-nesting can be found in short biographies of famous men—men like Vice-Admiral Horatio Lord Nelson ("Nelson"); the businessman Colonel John North, known as the "Nitrate King" ("The Secret of Success"); Major-General Sir Henry Havelock, hero of the Indian rebellion ("Some Boys Who Became Famous"); or the civil engineer George Stephenson, known as the "Father of Railways" ("George Stephenson"). While articles condemning bird-nesting usually describe it as a character fault indicative of a more profound lack of morality, the activity is here presented as an attribute of "great men" whose integrity is beyond dispute; and in keeping with the notion of adventure and empire, two of those four men are military heroes and a third made his fortune in South America.

Of course, the image of the (male) child changes in accordance with this redefinition of bird-nesting—as indicated by F. C. Thompson's poem "A Half Holiday," included in *Our Young Folks Weekly Budget* (1872):

Some are for bird-nesting out in the wood
(Boys will be boys, and we're none of us good);
Mischievous urchins! Climbing the trees.
Look at young Johnny, there, up to his knees
In brier-bush and nettles! He winces with pain;
But he knows there's a nest in the thicket to gain.

> Then there's Jack in the dell—why, he cares not a pin
>
> For the scratches he gets, or the mess he is in. (175, ll. 13–20)

Endurance of pain, hardiness, and a disregard for outward appearance are here presented as very positive and desirable qualities. Boys are not expected to behave as little angels and neither is their stipulated "sinfulness" seen as imperilling their soul; rather, they are expected to break certain rules in their natural pursuit of active manliness, and they are not threatened with the wrath of God, as in much of the anti-bird-nesting literature.

FORMING A COLLECTION: BIRD-NESTING AS SCIENCE

If the literature condemning bird-nesting draws on Augustine and Locke, and the bird-nesting adventures can be described as a minor current in the rising flood of adventure fiction, the texts that start defending the pastime on "scientific" grounds need to be contextualized in the much wider debate on the role science should play in the education of children. This is a debate that had gained momentum in the 1850s and that continued throughout the second half of the century. In 1864, the Clarendon Commission investigating the public schools reported that "natural science with slight exceptions is practically excluded from the education of the higher classes in England" and pronounced the conviction that "the introduction of the elements of natural science into the regular course of study is desirable" ("Report," 32). In fact, at the time of the commission's report things had already begun to change. Of the nine public schools examined, Rugby was most progressive in this respect: science had been added to the curriculum in the late 1850s (cf. Wilson), and other schools followed suit over the next decade (cf. Huxley 113). Thus, from the 1870s onward, many male pupils from an affluent background would have received at least a smattering of science education—while natural science would have been virtually absent from the education of well-to-do girls, who were usually home-schooled (Birch 58ff.). Lower down the social scale, after the Endowed Schools Act of 1869, the Endowed Schools Commission received dozens of management schemes that included natural science in their curricula. These changes to curricula notwithstanding, Gordon Roderick and Michael Stephens caution that "the cause of science probably suffered as much from indifferent teaching as from its absolute exclusion from the schools" (34), and it seems fair to conclude that throughout the nineteenth century, most pupils would not have received a systematic introduction to the natural sciences, or where they did, this introduction would have been almost purely theoretical.

If this assessment is correct, educators did not take the "natural" interests of their pupils into consideration when devising curricula or planning their lessons. In 1867, J. M. Wilson, assistant master at Rugby, acknowledged that "most boys show a degree of interest in their scientific work which is unmistakeably greater than in any other study" (244). This observation is an indication that scientific topics were of interest, particularly to boys; and while educators failed to act on this observation, publishers recognized that this interest could be exploited economically. Consequently, the debate on the role of science in education is accompanied by developments in the growing market of periodicals for young readers.

While religious magazines like the *Children's Friend* or the *Child's Companion* mentioned above continued publication in the second half of the nineteenth century and new titles were added continuously, they were augmented—and frequently outsold—by commercial publications (cf. Drotner, Findlay). The market was also increasingly subdivided into various fields: some magazines, like *Little Folks* (1875–1933) or *Little Wide-Awake* (1875–1899), were aimed at young children of both sexes, while other magazines clearly targeted a somewhat older readership who might buy the papers themselves, and many of those magazines were explicitly defined through gender references in their titles. These magazines offered an eclectic mixture of "Fact, Fiction, History, and Adventure," as the subtitle of the *Boy's Own Magazine* pronounced, and provided "Recreation and Instruction" as the subtitle to *Young England* declared. Articles that at least touch on natural science or deliberately offer information on science topics are frequent, and Diana Dixon concludes that "Children's magazines became an important vehicle for the popularisation of science in England from the 1850s onwards" (228). Thus, at a time when natural science would not have featured prominently in many school curricula, many juvenile magazines, particularly those aimed at boys, offered articles on such diverse topics as geology, astronomy, botany, zoology, physics, and chemistry. Furthermore, many of the articles on scientific topics tried to present them in an accessible manner that emphasized practical experience. Particularly the magazines aimed at boys offered instructions for experiments in physics or chemistry or even advised on the proper methods of taxidermy. In Dixon's analysis, what "emerges from all the boys' periodicals' treatment of science is that it is to be enjoyed" (234).

It is in this context that bird-nesting is presented in a completely new perspective, as a scientific activity that is to be encouraged rather than condemned. In the process, the term bird-nesting is again redefined. The Reverend J. G. Wood—a prolific writer of articles on natural history in a number of magazines—made this redefinition very explicit in an article called "Birds' Eggs and Egg Collecting" that appeared in the *Boy's Own Paper* in 1880:

> To begin, many persons have asked, [. . .] how I could advocate the cruel amusement of Bird-nesting. Heart-rending letters have been copiously showered upon me depicting the agonies suffered by birds when deprived of their young, and comparing me to a variety of historical personages. [. . .] The well meaning writers of these letters (which I never answer) and I attach two different meanings to the term "bird-nesting." They fancy that it signifies the destruction of every nest that can be found, the theft of all the eggs, and either the robbery or murder of the young. [. . .] My idea is totally different. Just as the genuine entomologist is the best friend of the insects, never killing even a noisome insect without just cause, so is the genuine ornithologist the best friend of the birds, [. . .]. (478)

Wood skillfully manipulates his readers' sympathies by first presenting himself as the victim of unfair accusations. He then presents an exaggerated version of his opponents' interpretation of the term "bird-nesting" in which it is rendered as wantonly destructive and utterly senseless. He suggests entomology and the killing of "a noisome insect" as a comparison, and by introducing the concept of a "just cause," Wood counters the accusation of wantonness. However, his justification remains oddly vague. The reader can only assume that the scientific end is such a "just cause," warranting the killing of an insect, or the collecting of eggs.

More generally speaking, in order to be effective as a defense of the former "sport," the proponents of "scientific" bird-nesting have to counter the accusation of cruelty; and they have to demonstrate that bird-nesting is, in fact, a scientific activity. The first part is achieved by regularly instructing their readers *not* to interfere with nests once young birds have hatched, and *not* to take all the eggs: poultry farming is frequently cited as proof that birds will not miss individual eggs and will continue laying provided some are left in the nest (e.g., "Birds' Eggs and Egg Collecting"). Under these circumstances, even a magazine like *Kind Words*, asking its readers to "practice kind *deeds* even though it may be at the cost of a little self denial," could condone bird-nesting: "you may make a capital collection of birds' eggs without mischief or cruelty" ("Birds'-nesting in Earnest," 180). As in this quote, the second part in the defense strategy usually consists in references to the "collection" formed by the bird-nesting boy, who frequently features as a "naturalist." Thus, in the "Chapters for Young Naturalists" in *Chatterbox* (1871), Henry Ullyett gives very detailed advice on forming a scientific collection: After reminding his readers that they should not aim for mere quantity but quality in terms of species variety, the author instructs his readers that the eggs "should be carefully mounted, with gum or glue, on a card. On this card should be written the name of the bird to which the egg belongs, both its scientific and its common name" and he continues by explaining the classificatory principle behind scientific names (87f.).

In these articles, the activity of bird-nesting has undergone a profound redefinition that transforms wanton cruelty into the pursuit of scientific knowledge. Significantly, this change in the rules of discourse goes beyond the articles that appeared in magazines for young readers and informs the representation of bird-nesting more generally. Thus, the 1880s and 90s also saw the publication of a number of books on the subject, books recommending the collection of eggs to "every young person desirous of some occupation for improving both his mind and body" (Bath "preface" n.p.), catering for "the needs of the intelligent schoolboy" (Newman/Christy ix) and "not intended to encourage the useless collecting of bird's eggs from a mere bric-à-brac motive, but to aid the youthful naturalist in the study of one of the most interesting phases of bird life" (Kearton "preface" n.p.).

Despite its wide appeal, this conception of bird-nesting and its implicit assumptions about the scientific motivation of bird-nesters had its critics. At the close of the century, the *Boy's Own Paper*—which had printed numerous articles either hailing bird-nesting as an adventure or as a scientific activity—included Linda Gardiner's "The Bird World" (1900), a piece condemning the pseudo-science of self-ascribed naturalists: "not one-tenth or one-fiftieth of the 'collectors' know anything of the sciences of ornithology and oology" (311). However, the vast majority of articles that discussed bird-nesting in terms of its scientific potential did so favorably, and even Arachne in the "Conversations on the Band of Mercy," an article critical of bird-nesting, concedes that she "would not prevent a boy from collecting eggs in an intelligent way, and naming them" (482).[8]

This scientific defense of bird-nesting presents yet another concept of childhood. Whereas those stories emphasizing the adventurous aspect of the pastime stress "manly" qualities like bravery and perseverance, the child is here presented as a rational being who is driven by intellectual curiosity. And while the breaking of rules is part of the fun in many bird-nesting adventures, the strict adherence to scientific procedure is a requisite for scientific bird-nesting. If the idea behind the adventurous boy is the formation of those character traits deemed necessary for success in a violent man's world and it is seen as a state through which the boy progresses in adolescence, the child in the scientific stories is treated almost like an adult, and the concept of "fun" is much more explicitly harnessed to utility.

CONCLUSION

As we have seen, over the course of the second half of the nineteenth century—and particularly in its last three decades—the discourse on bird-nesting develops into three strands which represent three distinct concepts of bird-nesters. The Lockean view that a child's cruelty toward animals is likely to develop into an adult's cruelty toward his fellow men is reiterated in countless stories and poems endeavoring to teach kindness to animals to their young clientele—and bird-nesting is a common target of their critique. Starting in the late 1850s, this discourse is augmented, more or less simultaneously, by the two pro-bird-nesting strands discussed above: one glorifying the adventurous aspect of the pastime, the other recasting it as a (proto-)scientific activity. Both discourses also change their implicit concepts of childhood to one that is closer to the natural innocence of the child proposed by Rousseau. But while the adventure strand emphasizes experience and strong emotion (and the overcoming of these emotions), the science strand focuses on the rational and systematic ordering of nature. While the former seems Wordsworthian in the intensity of experience it portrays, the latter moves beyond experience to rationalization—a course Wordsworth had explicitly rejected in The Prelude.[9] However, the two strands are clearly connected, since many adventure stories legitimize the bird-nesting adventure with reference to a "collection," and since articles on scientific bird-nesting also talk about the fun and excitement of the activity. They are also linked by the concept of utility, although neither reduces bird-nesting to a utilitarian activity in the sense of immediate monetary usefulness. Rather, bird-nesting is described as "useful" in a more abstract sense—as an aid to building "manly" character in the one case, as an aid to building a scientific mindset in the other.

While the two more recent discourses of bird-nesting are thus interrelated and clearly distinct from the earlier discourse of cruelty, all three discourses share a strong gender bias: bird-nesting is almost exclusively described as an activity carried out by boys. And while girls sometimes have a specific function as moral influence in condemnations of bird-nesting, they disappear almost completely from depictions of adventurous or scientific bird-nesting. This can be taken as a symptom of the changing landscape of the literary market for young readers (cf. MacKenzie 202f.), and it is indicative of the market's dependence on the gender roles of Victorian society: the market had changed, because society clearly distinguished between boys and girls in questions of appropriate behavior and conduct, making it possible and profitable to target publications at particular audiences. Thus, the gender division displayed in articles on bird-nesting highlights the more fundamental gender bias of Victorian concepts of childhood that would put activities like climbing trees and concepts like "adventure," "bravery," or "science" firmly in the realm of boys, whereas girls—if they feature at all—are presented as a good moral influence, a version of the "angel in the house" they were supposed to turn into as women.

NOTES

Research for this paper was conducted as part of the Marie Curie Intra-European Fellowship "Science in Magazines," funded by the European Union (FP7), and supported by the Institute for Advanced Studies in the Humanities at the University of Edinburgh.

1. A search for bird-nesting and its spelling variants in the online database "Nineteenth Century British Library Newspapers" (CENGAGE learning) produces 584 hits, seventy-two percent of which appeared in the last three decades of the century.

2. Another influential text that criticizes bird-nesting is Sarah Trimmer's *Fabulous Histories Designed for the Instruction of Children, Respecting their Treatment of Animals* (a.k.a. *The History of the Robins*) first published in 1786 and reprinted throughout the nineteenth century.

3. The fact that bird-nesting also illustrates the importance of gender in Victorian concepts of childhood can only be touched on in the space of this paper.

4. The publication dates of the magazines are taken from *The Waterloo Directory*, which also provides additional information on the scope of the magazines. In those (frequent) cases where the title of a magazine changes during its publication span, I have used the appropriate name for the period discussed, which usually is also the name under which the magazine is best known today.

5. The text here quoted is that reprinted from the second edition onward. There are a number of differences between the first and subsequent editions. Most interestingly, the word "wicked" is changed to "cruel" (l. 16), anticipating the line of argument against bird-nesting that predominates in the nineteenth century.

6. Admittedly, there are also boys who exert a good influence on bird-nesters, like Lewis, the "Young Peacemaker" in the eponymous story from the *Sunday School Hive* (1877).

7. I.e. the Sea Bird Preservation Act of 1869, the Wild Birds Protection Act of 1872, the Wild Fowl Preservation Act of 1876, and the Wild Birds Protection Acts of 1880 and 1881 (cf. Newman).

8. The "Band of Mercy" was a newly formed humane society for children and part of the RSPCA (cf. Fairholme 165–68).

9. In *The Prelude* of 1805, Wordsworth warns of a scientific rationality which uses "logic and minute analysis" (*Prelude* [1805] bk. 11 l. 126, in *Prelude* 436) to scrutinize nature; in 1850 he speaks of a "mind so far / -Perverted" to scan "the visible Universe [. . .] with microscopic view" (*Prelude* [1850] bk. 12 l. 88–91, in *Prelude* 437).

Articles in Magazines

Since most articles appeared anonymously, with abbreviated names or under pseudonym, the magazine articles referred to or quoted in the text are listed here by title. All articles were accessed through the database "Nineteenth Century UK Periodicals Online" (GALE CENGAGE Learning) and each entry is followed by the appropriate Gale Document Number (GDN).

"A Few Thoughts about Birds, their Nests and their Robbers." G. Russell. *The Friendly Companion* 64 (01.04.1880): 82–84. [GDN: DX1901668679]

"A Half Holiday." By F. C. Thompson. *Our Young Folks Weekly Budget of Tales, News, Sketches, Fun, Puzzles, Riddles &c.* 75 (01.06.1872): 175. [GDN: DX1901153263]

"Bird-Nesting." *The Child's Companion* (1900): 62. [GDN: DX1901657605]

"Bird's-Nesting." *Little Wide-Awake* (1885): 135. [GDN: DX1901519794]

"Birds' Eggs and Egg Collecting." By Rev. J. G. Wood. *The Boy's Own Paper* 2:67 (24.04.1880): 478–79. [GDN: DX1901396120]

"Birds'-nesting in Earnest." By Cousin William. *Kind Words* 127 (04.06.1868): 180–81. [GDN: DX1901869465]

"Chapters for Young Naturalists." By Henry Ullyett. *Chatterbox* 11 (09.02.1871): 87–88. [GDN: DX1901314508]

"Conversations on the Band of Mercy." *The Monthly Packet* 29 (01.05.1883): 482–85. [GDN: DX1902025737]

"Cruelty and Cowardice of Bird-nesting." *The Children's Friend* 187 (01.07.1876): 110–11. [GDN: DX1902090823]

"George Stephenson." By "Cousin Alfred." *Kind Words* (01.05.1874): 157-58. [GDN: DX1901497883]

"Hawk Scar; A Bird's Nesting Adventure." By Rev. J. C. Atkinson. *Every Boy's Magazine* 2 (01.03.1862): 85–94. [GDN: DX1901733149]

"How We Took the Osprey's Nest." *The Boy's Own Paper* 16:797 (21.04.1894): 457–58. [GDN: DX1901391408]

"Nelson." *Chatterbox* 32 (1899): 255. [GDN: DX1901313809]

"Some Boys Who Became Famous." *The Boy's Own Paper* 2:69 (08.05.1880): 504–07. [GDN: DX1901396144]

"The Bird Robbers." *Peter Parley's Annual* 27 (1867): 69–74. [GDN: DX1901718724]

"The Bird World." By Linda Gardiner. *The Boy's Own Paper* 22:1101 (17.02.1900): 310–12. [GDN: DX1901390545]

"The Secret of Success." By A. C. Harmsworth. *Young Folks Paper* 948 (26.01.1889): 54. [GDN: DX1901060747]

"The Young Peacemaker." *Sunday School Hive* 10 (01.10.1877): 149–50. [GDN: DX19001993024]

"The Young Robbers." By F. T. G. *The Children's Treasury* 5 (01.05.1873): 52–54. [GDN: DX1901177449]

Other Sources

Avery, Gillian. *Nineteenth Century Children: Heroes and Heroines in English Children's Stories 1780–1900*. London: Hodder and Stoughton, 1965.

Bath, Harcourt. *The Young Collector's Handbook of British Birds, and Their Nests and Eggs. With a chapter on collecting and preserving birds*, by Bowdler Sharpe. London: Swan Sonnenschein, 1888.

Birch, Dinah. *Our Victorian Education*. Oxford: Blackwell, 2008.

Dixon, Diana. "Children's Magazines and Science in the Nineteenth Century." *Victorian Periodicals Review* 34 (2001): 228–38.

Drotner, Kirsten. *English Children and Their Magazines, 1751–1945*. New Haven and London: Yale UP, 1988.

Dunton, John. *A Voyage Round the World*. London: Printed for Richard Newcome, [1691]. *Early English Books Online*. Durable URL of relevant page: <http://gateway.proquest.com/openurl?ctx_ver=Z39.88-2003&res_id=xri:eebo&rft_id=xri:eebo:image:62151:47>

Fairholme, Edward, and Wellesley Pain. *A Century of Work for Animals: The History of the R.S.P.C.A., 1824–1924*. London: John Murray, 1924.

Findlay, Rosie. "Small Print: The Golden Age of Children's Periodicals in Great Britain." *Cahiers Victoriens et Édouardiens* 55 (2002): 53–69.

"Game Act." ["An act to amend the Laws in England relative to Game," Cap. 32 1° and 2° Gulielmi IV, 1831] *The Statutes of the United Kingdom of Great Britain and Ireland*, Vol. 12, 1829, 11 George IV. To 1832, 2 and 3 William IV. London, 1832. 442–51.

Green, Martin. *Dreams of Adventure, Deeds of Empire*. London: Routledge, 1980.

Heyman, Michael. "Isles of Boshen: Edward Lear's Literary Nonsense in Context."

Ph.D. thesis, University of Glasgow, 1999. Electronic resource, University of Glasgow. <http://hdl.handle.net/1905/330> (viewed 28.09.2009).

Huxley, Thomas Henry. "Scientific Education: Notes of an After-Dinner Speech." [1869]. *Science and Education. Essays.* By T. H. Huxley. Collected Essays, Vol. 3. London: Macmillan, 1893. 111–33.

Kearton, Richard. *Birds' Nests, Eggs and Egg-Collecting.* Ill. with 22 colour plates. Rev. and enlarged. [1890]. London: Cassell, 1896.

Locke, John. *Some Thoughts Concerning Education.* Introd. Rev. R. H. Quick. Cambridge: Cambridge UP, 1902.

MacKenzie, John. *Propaganda and Empire: The Manipulation of British Public Opinion, 1880–1960.* Manchester, UK: Manchester UP, 1984.

Newbery, John. *A Little Pretty Pocket-Book, Intended for the Instruction and Amusement of Little Master Tommy, and Pretty Miss Polly.* [1744]. Facsimile of the edition London 1767. Ed. and introd. M. F. Thwaite. London: Oxford UP, 1966.

Newman, Edward. *Birdsnesting and Bird-skinning: A Complete Description of the Nests and Eggs of Birds Which Breed in Britain.* London: Fisher Unwin, 1888.

"Report of Her Majesty's Commissioners Appointed to Inquire into the Revenues and Management of Certain Colleges and Schools, and the Studies Pursued and Instruction Given Therein; with an Appendix and Evidence." [1864]. Vol. I. *Command Papers; Reports of Commissioners,* paper nr. 3288, vol. XX.1 and XXI.1. House of Commons Parliamentary Papers. Durable URL: <http://gateway.proquest .com/openurl?url_ver=Z39.88-2004&res_dat=xri:hcpp&rft_dat=xri:hcpp:rec :1864-040141>. Viewed 12.10.2009.

Richardson, Alan. *Literature, Education, and Romanticism: Reading as Social Practice, 1780–1832.* Cambridge: Cambridge UP, 1994.

Roderick, Gordon, and Michael Stephens. *Scientific and Technical Education in Nineteenth-Century England. A Symposium.* Newton Abbot: David and Charles, 1972.

Stone, Lawrence. *The Family, Sex and Marriage: In England 1500–1800.* Abridged ed. Harmondsworth: Penguin, 1979.

Taylor, Ann, Jane Taylor, et al. *Original Poems for Infant Minds.* By several young persons. Vol. 1. New and rev. ed. London: Arthur Hall, 1854.

Thwaite, M. F. "John Newbery and his first book for children." *A Little Pretty Pocket-Book* [1767]. By John Newbery. Facsimile ed. London: Oxford UP, 1966. 1–49.

Waterloo Directory of English Newspapers and Periodicals, 1800–1900. Series 2. Waterloo, Ont.: North Waterloo Academic Press, 2003.

Wilson, J. M. "On Teaching Natural Science in Schools." *Essays on a Liberal Education.* Ed. F. W. Farrar. London: Macmillan, 1867. 241–91.

Wordsworth, William. *The Prelude, or: Growth of a Poet's Mind.* Ed. Ernest de Selincourt. Oxford: Clarendon, 1959.

RICHARD FLYNN

✎ My Folk Revival

Childhood, Politics, and Popular Music

> Behold a race of young ones like to those
> With whom I herded—easily, indeed,
> We might have fed upon a fatter soil
> Of Arts and Letters, but be that forgiven—
> A race of real children, not too wise,
> Too learned, or too good, but wanton, fresh,
> And bandied up and down by love and hate;
> Fierce, moody, patient, venturous, modest, shy,
> Mad at their sports like withered leaves in winds;
> Though doing wrong and suffering, and full oft
> Bending beneath our life's mysterious weight
> Of pain and fear, yet still in happiness
> Not yielding to the happiest upon earth.
> —Wordsworth, 1805 *Prelude, Book V*, lines 433–45

OVERTURE

In the summer of 2010, my wife, Becky Kennerly, and I drove to Hollins University, near Roanoke, Virginia, where I was delivering a lecture about Randall Jarrell's children's story *The Bat-Poet* (1964) to students and faculty in the Hollins children's literature program. As a senior professor specializing in children's literature and poetry at Georgia Southern University, I enjoy the opportunity to travel, especially to invited talks. Furthermore, in the aftermath of a rewarding but time-consuming period editing the *Children's Literature Association Quarterly* for five and a half years, I was particularly pleased to be reengaged with my own scholarship on children's poetry and on the idea of childhood in poets who write about childhood for adults. I looked forward to this particular trip, because it would give me the opportunity to visit with my dear friend and former student, Joseph Thomas, who was teaching the summer course in children's poetry, and because I was to meet for the first time in thirty-eight years my first love, Linda.

I was nervous about this meeting. Linda had found me through Facebook on New Year's Eve 2009, and for both of us it seemed that, in the words of Bob Dylan, "the past was close behind." Linda has been married for over thirty years to a professor, and they have two grown children. I have been married and divorced, remarried and widowed, and now happily remarried, with one lovely grown son from my first marriage and, in 2010, a lovely new daughter-in-law. Linda and I broke up in 1972.

I brought my guitar with me, as I always do when I travel by car. Music is still a vital part of my life—I play with two of my buddies in a trio called Mid-Life Crisis. In any event, the first evening we arrived in Virginia, Becky and I sat on the porch with Linda, her husband, Bill, and her son Nick, all of us singing and playing Country Joe MacDonald's "I Feel Like I'm Fixin' to Die Rag."

I also played some blues on slide guitar, something I have done more often since I accidentally injured my fretting hand on the exposed blade of a blender in my parents' kitchen in the fall of 1971 when I was sixteen.

FAIR SEEDTIME

In "Memories of West Street and Lepke," from *Life Studies*, the book which signaled the advent of "confessional" poetry and contemporary confessional culture, Robert Lowell recalls his time as "a fire-breathing Catholic C.O." (85) and asks, alluding to the beginning of Wordsworth's *Prelude*, "Ought I to regret my seedtime?" Let me state here at the outset that I don't regret mine, but I also wish to guard against idealizing it. Judith Plotz shows in her study *Romanticism and the Vocation of Childhood* how a preoccupation with what she calls the "Essential Child" becomes, in the nineteenth century, a non-threatening means of commitment to social hope without the need of a political and social transformation. The Romantic child, like the Romantic imagination, is placed beyond the shocks of history. Sometimes produced through retrospective reclamation of the self embalmed within, sometimes constructed as a sequestered pastoral solitary, the Romantic child serves as a buffer against the vicissitudes of the public sphere. (39)

In addition, in *The Hidden Adult: Defining Children's Literature*, Perry Nodelman speculates that children's texts invite child readers to "share the nostalgia" of the adults "driven" by their own nostalgia to write for children. Children's texts, he argues, invite children "curiously, to view their own current childhoods nostalgically": "In a sense [children's fiction] invites child readers to develop a double consciousness[1]—to be both delightfully childlike, and separate from that childlikeness, viewing and understanding it from an adult perspective" (46).

This essay is, I hope, an exercise in critical nostalgia.[2] In a poetic or prose memoir, in which an adult reconstructs a child self, avoiding nostalgia is impossible. And if, as Nodelman argues, child readers enact nostalgia for their childhoods at the moment they enter into the children's writer's fictional universe, in the act of reading, perhaps nostalgia is inevitable. But it seems just as likely to me that double consciousness can be a positive attribute fostering an awareness at work (or at play) in the artistic creations of young people themselves: I see it in the poems and songs I wrote as a youngster and also in the folk songs and later the rock songs on which I raised myself to adulthood.

And while, as children, we created a kind of urban pastoral, our private refuge was always implicated in the public sphere: we sought to save a world or build a new one to replace the one that appeared to be falling apart all around us. By the time I was fifteen, the songs and poems I was writing often turned out to be laments about the end of summer and the loss of youth, such as my song, "Seasons":

Green leaves fade
We're growing older every day
Winter's on its way
Summer sun has gone away

Not that my songs were purely nostalgic. Summer also represented the freedom to run barefoot on the streets, freedom from parental supervision. As I immersed myself in music, the increasing number of paying gigs I was getting at coffeehouses and private parties also helped give me at least the illusion of independence.

But the nostalgia I felt for my own youth was also apparent in the songs composed by others that I would perform in my coffeehouse sets: Joni Mitchell's "The Circle Game" or "Both Sides, Now;" John Lennon's "In My Life" (which I first learned off a Judy Collins record); Sandy Denny's "Who Knows Where the Time Goes" (also learned via Judy Collins); the introspective lullaby, James Taylor's "Sweet Baby James;" as well as countless other melancholy ballads. "The Circle Game" is a case in point. Joni Mitchell composed the song as a hopeful, forward-looking response to her friend Neil Young's lament at the passing of his teen years: "Sugar Mountain" ("You can't be twenty on Sugar Mountain / Though you're thinking that you're leaving there too soon"). I learned "The Circle Game" off Ian and Sylvia's record *So Much for Dreaming* (1966—the earliest recording of the song) and played it for my mother, who wept upon hearing it, but insisted that I play the song repeatedly. The song invokes nostalgia for lost youth while criticizing it at the same time. And as the chorus indicates, the song's hopefulness is tinged with a kind of fatalism:

> And the seasons they go round and round
> And the painted ponies go up and down
> We're captive on the carousel of time
> We can't return we can only look
> Behind from where we came
> And go round and round and round
> In the circle game.[3]

Undoubtedly, at age eleven or twelve, the song told me there was something of value in the childhood I was leaving behind. Perhaps that's what attracted me to the song in the first place. But like the "child [who] moved ten times round the seasons" I would not long be appeased by "words like when you're older." Seeing my mother's emotional frailty on display provoked complex feelings in me that scared me, feelings that, while I may understand them in retrospect, are now colored by my knowledge of the toll my mother's chronic mental illness would take on our family.

But emphasizing these melancholy introspective songs tells only part of the story. Also in my repertoire was the post-Chicago political anger and bitterness of Phil Ochs's "Pretty Smart on My Part" and "I Kill Therefore I Am." There was "When the Music's Over" by the Doors. There were Hendrix, Joplin, electric blues (J. B. Hutto and the Hawks), and trips to the jazz club on New York Avenue where I saw Mc Coy Tyner and Sun Ra. There were the songs of Neil Young and Dylan's surrealism—I sang "Visions of Johanna," uneasily reminded that my mother's name was Joanne. And in the band I joined, I felt the rage of the Stones's "Street-Fighting Man." More comical, from my present perspective, was that band's version of "Stray Cat Blues." (It is amusing to remember a bunch of fifteen- and sixteen-year-old boys singing, "Well I can see that you're just fifteen years old / But I don't want your i.d."). But there was much more than melancholy, anger, and swagger in our merry band of teenagers: there was play and street theater and truly expanded awareness of the possibilities we sought out in urban gambols, public parks, and trips to rural Maryland or (almost-heaven) West Virginia.

WE SHALL OVERCOME, FOLK MUSIC CELEBRITIES, AND "THOSE KIDS"

Murray Lerner's movie *Festival!*, which documents the Newport Folk Festival between 1963 and 1966, deftly juxtaposes the diverse performances and utopian nature of the 1963 festival in which popular stars like Peter, Paul, and Mary, Joan Baez, Bob Dylan, Odetta, and Buffy Sainte-Marie played alongside the Georgia Sea Island Singers, Staples Singers, Freedom Singers, recently rediscovered bluesmen such as Son House, Mississippi Fred McDowell, and Mississippi John Hurt, and activists like Fannie Lou Hamer with the celebrity-worship of Dylan and Baez at the 1964 festival.[4] In a revealing moment, a twenty-three-year-old Baez comments on the youngsters at the 1964 festival where she and Bob Dylan were the reigning king and queen of folk:

With kids, I like kids, you know . . . it's just, idolatry's a little weird, that's all because it doesn't mean anything. If it's . . . I don't think it hurts anybody, I mean, It it's . . . I don't think it hurts those kids, what they're doing. And the fact that they ask for things like "We Shall Overcome" and they know what it's about, most of them. The ones who ask know what it's about. I think that's wonderful, you know, and I don't care if they act like a bunch of monkeys like that. . . 'cause you know they're sweet. When grown-ups do it, it's a little silly. These kids are free and the boys have long hair and the girls have long hair and there's a freedom, you know, like uh, I'd like it if a lot of them took a bath more often, but um, I love the way they look. . . . There's got to be an alternative to whatever ways of life that is offered to them, you know, I mean Democrat, Republican . . . [sigh] you know, uh, and I would like to offer some kind of alternative, somehow, you know, or help. All the words all the important things like truth—truth and love are just buried in this society, you know, they're buried and laughed at and giggled at and, uh, if people don't get back to them somehow then there's no sense living, I don't think.

Lerner's film features the now iconic moment at the Newport Folk Festival, July 28, 1963, when Dylan, Pete Seeger, The SNCC Freedom Singers, Joan Baez, and Peter, Paul, and Mary sang Dylan's "Blowin' in the Wind." There is Dave Gahr's famous photograph and a recording, but not, as far as I know, film footage of their encore a capella performance of "We Shall Overcome," when they were joined by Theodore Bikel, who later described the moment to David Hadju as "the apogee of the folk movement. . . . There was no point more suffused with hope for the future" (*Positively* 166).[5]

Now, I do have a sense of humor, and I enjoyed Christopher Guest's *A Mighty Wind*, a hilarious parody of the sort of folk music nostalgia shows aired on PBS. Tune in during fund-raising time and you'll see a veritable parade of old folkies—most of them second string at best. But as David Hadju notes in his *New York Times* review, "the greatest disappointment of 'A Mighty Wind' is the inexplicable absence of any hint of politics. For all the faux historical footage and memorabilia from the 60s, and for all the reminiscing by the reunited groups, we don't see a moment of protest or debate." Likewise, on folk music nostalgia shows, you'll rarely encounter topical songs other than Barry McGuire (in biker regalia) doing "Eve of Destruction"—which doesn't count. While Bob Dylan wrote and performed specific topical songs such as "Only a Pawn in Their Game" and "The Lonesome Death of Hattie Carroll," his more generalized protest work, such as "Blowin' in the Wind" and "The Times They Are A'Changin'"—and often not even that—is what gets featured in Public Television's geriatric hootenannies.[6] While "Blowin' in the Wind" survives because of its more universal appeal, it is that same universality that quickly allowed it to become palatable to the mainstream, even at the height of the so-called generation gap. By the time Lerner's *Festival!* was released in 1967, the song seemed quaint and domesticated next to LBJ's escalation of the war and the advent of the Summer of Love.[7] By the 1969–70 school year, "Blowin' in the Wind" would prove no more threatening than "Kumbaya"; I would regularly perform the song with my friend Philip and others in chapel in the Little Sanctuary at St. Albans School and at the Sunday guitar mass in St. Joseph's Chapel at the National Cathedral. In chapel, we'd also perform "The Times They Are A'Changin,'" but the headmaster deemed unacceptable the verse "Come mothers and fathers throughout the land / And don't criticize what you can't understand / Your sons and your daughters are beyond your command." When we sang it initially we had delivered the verse both *piano* and with pathos, in keeping with Mary Travers's performance. The next time we played it, we defied the censorship order: not only did we *not* omit the offensive verse, but we delivered it *fortissimo*, with a snarl worthy of Dylan himself.

THE KINGSTON TRIO, 1960–1963

A confession: My folk revival didn't begin with Pete Seeger or Joan Baez or Bob Dylan or even Peter, Paul, and Mary. It began with the Kingston Trio. My first memory of politics was the 1960 presidential election—I was five and proclaimed my preference for Kennedy to the chagrin of my Republican parents. While my first folk music memories involve being sung to at bedtime—my father was fond of "The Wreck of the Old '97"—finding the debut album *The Kingston Trio* in the family record collection hooked me on folk music for life. My parents thought the Trio was a safe choice and even took me to see them at Mr. Kelly's in Chicago when I was about six or seven. I'd frequently sing along to their records, playing badminton racket guitar. I'd enlist my younger brother and sister as trio members.

In his history of the folk revival, *Rainbow Quest*, Ronald Cohen notes that the Trio had "the perfect combination of charm, wealth, security, and modesty. 'Rockless, roll-less and rich,' *Time* proclaimed." In the late fifties, "The Kingston Trio emerged as moral gatekeepers at an optimal time. Rock and roll's upsurge during the mid-1950s had shaken adult society's aesthetic and moral foundations, leading to escalating recriminations, censorship, and soul searching. Could middle-class culture survive? Were young people out of control?" (133). Despite their commercial slickness, however, the Trio's influence extended beyond their gatekeeper role. Warren Bareiss argues that they both demonstrated the commercial potential of folk music and were able to "carve a middle brow niche between Cold War conservatism and a nascent countercultural movement rooted largely in 1950s San Francisco" (9). While they were often attacked by folk purists for their lack of "authenticity," they were also influential models for a later generation of singer-songwriters and even for roots artists like Doc Watson, who credited them with "point[ing] our noses in the right direction, even the traditional performers" (qtd. in Cohen 133). In *Which Side Are You On?* Dick Weissman, former member of the pop-folk group the Journeymen (along with John Phillips and Scott McKenzie) defines the "pop-folk revival" as the period between 1955 and 1964, beginning with the Carnegie Hall reunion concert of the Weavers who had been blacklisted in 1951 and ending with the Beatles' arrival in the United States. It was the pop version of the folk revival that first captivated me.

Some pop-folk groups such as the New Christy Minstrels purveyed an ideologically compromised mythology in which whitewashed and white middle-class versions of ethnic folk heroes such as John Henry or fakeloric heroes such as Joe Magarac were meant to bolster Cold War patriotism. But the apparent conservatism of the Minstrels' *Land of Giants* (1964), which carried an endorsement from former President Eisenhower on the back of the record jacket, also hinted at ways in which "outlaw" mentality would enter the unconscious of young fans.[8] Clean-cut campus acts like the Chad Mitchell Trio introduced me and undoubtedly other impressionable youngsters to the topical satire of the "John Birch Society" and "Barry's Boys" (Goldwater, that is) as well as to the work of Phil Ochs, Tom Paxton, and others. And for burgeoning musicians like me, we would follow side-men like Jim (later Roger) McGuinn (accompanist to Judy Collins, Chad Mitchell Trio, and others) into the folk-rock future when he formed the Byrds. The "Jet Age" folk-rock sound of Jefferson Airplane transformed, in my adolescence, into the clarion call of "We Can Be Together": "We are obscene lawless hideous dangerous dirty violent—and young."

Cohen's history quotes folksinger Frank Hamilton's assessment of the folk scene in 1950s Greenwich Village: "The kids around Washington Square had a Rousseauian view of folksingers. We were all kind of wide-eyed. We were the prisoners of the big city and we romanticized the freedom and virtue of country life" (7.) Such romantic notions could be applied more than a decade later to the so-called "electric children" of my generation. (I was born in January of 1955, at the tail end of the first cohort of baby boomers.) We were weaned on the folk revival, later to become romantics of revolution, and, when it all came crashing down, moved to despair. In the words of Joni Mitchell, the peace movement, in which we were so heavily invested, seemed like "just a dream some of us had."

LITTLE BOXES, 1963–1968

In August 1963, after my family moved from Wilmette, Illinois, to Washington, D.C., I was only dimly aware of the events on the Mall on August 28, 1963, from the vantage point of our upper-Northwest Friendship Heights neighborhood. But that fall, deeply disappointed by my authoritarian third grade teacher but overjoyed to be taking the guitar lessons I had been promised to ease the pain of the move, my sense of social justice was quickly awakening. I won't pretend to have the vivid recall necessary to reconstruct the events in detail, but that fall, my mother and I arrived for my lesson at the Music and Arts Center in Bethesda to find my guitar teacher in tears as he told us that President Kennedy had been killed.

That Christmas, I requested and was given records that would begin to change my life: Peter, Paul, and Mary's *In the Wind* and *The Freewheelin' Bob Dylan*. Depicted on the back cover, in a photograph of them playing at the Washington Monument during the March on Washington, Peter, Paul, and Mary were romantic, celebrity folk heroes to me. While it took some time for Dylan's rougher version of his anthem "Blowin' in the Wind" to supplant the trio's radio hit version, the photo of Dylan and Suze Rotolo arm in arm on the Village streets on the cover was immediately iconic. I became a subscriber to Sing Out! As my technical facility on the guitar grew, I became a somewhat precocious musical prodigy, performing Malvina Reynolds's "Little Boxes" at a recital—because my teacher was delighted by my exaggerated diction on "business ECK-ecutives."

Although I had escaped living in a ticky-tacky house, I understood "Little Boxes" intimately, even at the age of eight or nine. Folk songs, even in their most compromised versions, promised avenues of empowerment for me as a child and filled me as well as countless others of my immediate generation with the utopian longing that we might escape or even transcend the boxes prescribed by Cold War family values. Five years later, I would be consumed by tears of rage at thirteen, when, from the uneasy safety of my largely white and privileged neighborhood, I saw the night sky ablaze after the assassination of Martin Luther King, Jr. I grew to be both politically aware and active after that, marching the following June in the Poor People's March on Solidarity Day past the Resurrection City tents that lined the length of the Mall.

I became increasingly proficient as a young folksinger myself, and music became the single most powerful force for me as I negotiated between two worlds: my parents' world of Washington privilege and my much more important community of fellow children sporting in the streets of the nation's capitol; decidedly, as far as we saw it, we were the race of real children.

COFFEEHOUSE DAYS, 1968–1972

I began attending St. Albans School for Boys in the fall of 1968, against my wishes. Increasingly unhappy at school and unhappy at home, I took refuge not only in my music, but also, like many other young people at the time, in one of the adult-sanctioned gathering places for youth. On the grounds of the National Cathedral, though separate from the Cathedral and the girls' and boys' schools, the St. Albans Parish Church had started the Pipeline Community Center, which featured a Friday night coffeehouse. I began playing in public there, first with some older friends I had met there, and later as a solo act and with various bands. Although I continued to resist St. Albans School, this church and indeed the entire Cathedral close became the center of my social life. D.C. area indie folk-rocker Alice Despard, who also frequented the Friday night coffeehouse, describes it as one of the many "places in D.C. for the young hippies to congregate and hang out."

In addition to the lax enforcement of D.C.'s eighteen-year-old drinking age (for beer and wine only) and the growing availability of marijuana and psychedelics, there were simply vast numbers of teenagers with disposable income and a lot of freedom, but few places for them to congregate. This was in the days before shopping malls (at least not any accessible to kids without cars) and long before the construction of the Metro. There were D.C. transit buses that ran fairly infrequently, but our normal mode of transportation was the thumb. Aside from a number of church halls and basements, there also sprang up such venues as the Emergency in Georgetown (which lasted from 1969–1971),[9] an alcohol-free club that featured local bands and national acts, and Fort Reno Park (a short walk from my home) as well as P Street Beach—both had summer concert series.

Between St. Albans Church and St. Albans School was the Peace Cross, to me the most sacred place on the Cathedral close. In the 1970 edition of *The Albanian* (St. Albans yearbook) there is a picture of me playing guitar at the Cross as part of the October 15, 1969, Moratorium Day demonstrations I helped organize. One advantage of attending a religious school was that, at this time, the priests were sympathetic—and they, too, were growing increasingly dissatisfied with the war. The St. Albans School chaplain, Craig Eder (who passed away in 2009 at the age of ninety), was particularly kind to me. And even at the staid Cathedral schools, our activism was at least tolerated. In the 1969–70 school year, it was the students from National Cathedral School for Girls who really took the lead in the antiwar movement. I still possess a fading ditto copy of a student-produced paper—I've lost the first page, but I recall it was titled *Mithrandir*—that came out just after the Kent State shootings. My impassioned essay titled "Cambodia: The Final Blow" led off the issue, followed by a rebuttal, "Rationale of U.S. Involvement in Cambodia," written by Hank Haldeman (son of H. R. "Bob," later of Watergate fame).

During the spring and summer of 1970, I experienced a heady combination of commitment and creativity. That summer, wanting to keep me occupied, my father allowed me to enroll in a summer theater program at my school, taught by cast members from the Arena Stage. So I spent nearly all my time that summer on the campus of a school I hated during the year, which had transformed itself into a young preppy-hippie paradise.

I gravitated to the Peace Cross daily. I'd sit there, barefoot, playing guitar, not for an audience, but for myself. One day that summer I sat playing, waiting for a girl I knew to stop by with a friend of hers. That friend was Linda, my first love. For the next two years, she and I, and a circle of close friends, created what we thought of as an alternate family—a tribe of lost boys and girls—who tried to give each other the love and nurture we weren't receiving from our damaged families. Linda's parents were divorced (my own parents would split up in 1974, much to their children's relief), and she lived in a garden apartment in McLean Gardens (off Wisconsin Avenue near Sidwell Friends) with her mother. She was nearly as tall as I was and almost two years older. She attended (public) Woodrow Wilson High School and she had a powerful sense of humor and a powerful intensity. She was an artist—I still have a papier-mâché sculpture she made of me playing guitar on a stool that makes me think of Joni Mitchell's "For the Roses" whenever I see it: "Remember the days when you used to sit and / make up your tunes for love and / pour your simple sorrow / to the sound hole and your knee."

Stuck as I am with my adult perspective, I have perhaps smoothed over the fact that when we were lost children, we didn't always idealize our own lostness. Linda dropped out of school for a time to work as a STAT lab technician trainee at Walter Reed—living with our family, and, ostensibly, sharing a room with my sister. Our entire house was in utter chaos as neither of my parents had the emotional wherewithal to help us. After Linda had moved out of our house to live with her father so that she could finish high school in Alexandria, I was talking to her on the phone and I distractedly tried to remove the exposed blade of the blender, which had been left on the machine without the blender bowl. Somehow I flicked the switch and blood from my left hand flew all over the kitchen. Any right-handed guitar player will understand my shock. I was terrified that I'd never play again. While I did play soon after and continue to play today, my left hand has never been the same. After the injury healed, I underwent an operation to repair the nerve damage to my thumb. An overdose of the anesthetic administered during that operation sent me into manic overdrive. I didn't sleep for seven days.

Shortly after my seventeenth birthday I ended up spending the second semester of my junior year confined to a psychiatric ward, misdiagnosed as schizophrenic, and pumped full of the same Thorazine that had destroyed my mother. It would take me years to overcome this. I got out in the summer of 1972, having been granted a release on the condition that I must not live with my parents. I lived during the summer at a psychiatric halfway house before moving into the dorms at St. Albans to repeat my junior year. That year was a disaster, and I was not invited back. The drugs I was forced to take had made me one of the walking dead. And Linda, who had to save herself, broke up with me, bringing to an end the lost world of our substitute family of lost children.

CODA

I've always loved that bittersweet moment at the end of "Tiger, Tiger" in Kipling's *Jungle Books*, where he tells the reader that Mowgli "was not always alone, because, he became a man and married. But that," Kipling reassures the reader, "is a story for grown-ups" (72). Like most academics, I get older, while most of my students stay the same age. The eighteen- to twenty-three-year-olds who are supposedly adults seem to me to claim less agency than we did when we were their age. It is commonplace that we live in an age not of helicopter parents, but of Velcro parents. Childhood is now, it seems to me, constructed in reaction to what is perceived as a more dangerous world (I have my doubts that this is so) and also, perhaps, in reaction to the standard neo-conservative cautionary tale that presents the youth movements of the baby boom as exhibit A.

Responding to a draft of this essay, Linda reminded me of what I meant to her all those years ago, reminded me that I had encouraged her pursuing her talent for drawing, and reflected on our circle of friends as "vibrant seekers" with "passionate interests in drama, politics, and the spiritual, along with the common bond of a shared love of music." Moreover, she wrote that despite the passage of thirty-eight years since we had last been in touch, and even though both of us had been through many life changes, she felt that today "we still shared the same enthusiasm for artistic endeavors, and our political, social, and cultural points of view were still in tune." She also reminded me of her desperate attempts to intercede with my parents, pleading with them to take me off the soul-killing tranquilizers, and that she finally had to let me go "because they were killing you and I couldn't stand to watch it anymore."

In the course of researching this essay, I came across a YouTube video of Peter, Paul, and Mary, briefly reunited shortly after their initial breakup. The video is from the April 24, 1971, demonstration at the Washington Monument kicking off the May Day demonstrations. Linda and I participated in that demonstration and in many of the other events during this time, including giving aid and comfort (and food and money) to the Vietnam Vets against the War when we visited their encampment on the Mall. The demonstration took place the day after John Kerry's historic testimony before the Senate Foreign Relations Committee. In the video, Mary forgets the words to "Blowin' in the Wind," but the group recovers the song for her. Later in the video, joined by John Denver, they sing John Lennon's "Give Peace a Chance." I feel embarrassed for them as I watch it, almost as if I were watching one of those public television nostalgia shows. The promise of their earlier freshness seems somewhat dimmed, and the trio seems out of place in light of my later knowledge of how the movement became torn and frayed. The culmination of the May Day festivities was a host of illegal arrests and the calculated demonization of the antiwar movement by Nixon, his henchmen, and the press.

I am under no illusions that the culture of my own youth was any less commodified or compromised than the youth culture of today, but I refuse to see it as either meaningless or futile. Just as today's children claim agency and create their own culture out of highly commodified forms, I believe that my attention to the intersection of music, politics, childhood, and adolescence in my own life is not uncritically nostalgic. And so I dare to hope that increased awareness of our own doubleness as adults concerned with children's literature and culture may help us pay attention to the workings of double consciousness in children. Rather than dismissing our ability to explore the worlds of children and childhoods, past and present, as mere romantic fantasy, we should try hard to attend to their music. And, tempering my tendency to view my own lost world with somewhat of a sad perplexity, I still believe in working to make a world in which a new music of humanity may be heard.

NOTES

This essay is dedicated to the memory of my beloved friend, colleague, and former student, David Starnes (1943–2007), who encouraged me in our many wonderful discussions about music and our listening sessions "to write that all down."

1. Nodelman is fully aware that the double consciousness he speaks of cannot be exactly analogous to Du Bois's concept of racial double consciousness, described in *The Souls of Black Folk* (1903).

2. What I am aiming for is something approaching what Svetlana Boym describes as "reflective nostalgia," which she distinguishes from "restorative nostalgia":

> Restorative nostalgia evokes national past and future; reflective nostalgia is more about individual and cultural memory. . . . Nostalgia of the first type gravitates toward collective pictorial symbols and oral culture. Nostalgia of the second type is more oriented toward an individual narrative that savors details and memorial signs, perpetually deferring homecoming itself. If restorative nostalgia ends up reconstructing emblems and rituals of home and homeland in an attempt to conquer and spatialize time, reflective nostalgia cherishes shattered fragments of memory and temporalizes space. Restorative nostalgia takes itself dead seriously. Reflective nostalgia, on the other hand, can be ironic and humorous. It reveals that longing and critical thinking are not opposed to one another, as affective memories do not absolve one from compassion, judgment, or critical reflection. (49–50)

3. For lyrics, videos, and a veritable research library on all things related to Joni Mitchell, visit her official Web site: http://jonimitchell.com.

4. Lerner's film *The Other Side of the Mirror* is another useful source that focuses primarily on Dylan.

5. Robert Cantwell reads this "as a moment in which, like a celestial syzygy, many independent forces of tradition, ideology, and culture, wandering at large in time, some of them in historical deep space and others only transient displays in the contemporary cultural atmosphere, briefly converge to reveal the truth of our collective life" (351). Craig Werner notes, "Like so many images from the sixties, the image tells only part of the story" (53).

6. At the August 28, 1963, March on Washington, Dylan sang "When the Ship Comes In" and "Only a Pawn in Their Game." It was Peter, Paul, and Mary who sang "Blowin' in the Wind." Released in June of 1963 (the month of Medgar Evers's murder), Peter, Paul, and Mary's hit version was still on the charts at the time of the march. Dylan's version was released on *The Freewheelin' Bob Dylan* in May, but wasn't released as a single until August.

7. Werner writes: "Although 'Blowin' in the Wind' inspired real political activity, its lyrics carried an undertone of romantic passivity that contrasted with the increasingly aggressive approach of the black movement" (52). While he has a point, I prefer Aldon Nielsen's more nuanced explanation of the contrast between what Dylan later called his "finger-pointing songs" and the "higher level of metaphoricity" in songs like "Chimes of Freedom" or "Blowin' in the Wind." The songs, Nielsen argues, have a "seemingly timeless quality" because of "an unending openness in the interpretation of these songs that is also found in folk materials such as 'Many Thousands Gone' and religious songs like 'Amazing Grace'" (189).

8. They certainly entered mine. In conjunction with our study of folk heroes and tall tales and in exchange for a featured role playing guitar and singing in the school production led by Mrs. Rich, my fifth grade teacher, I wrote my first song called "These Kind of Men" ("who helped to make our country strong and free"): "Joe Magarac made steel for railroad tracks / And when his mill shut down he nearly cried / Casey Jones navigated Joe's tracks / And that's the way Casey Jones died." By the way, I loved Mrs. Rich.

9. According to a brief history on the WAMA (Washington Area Music Association) Web site, The Emergency was "a mecca for young rock'n'rollers" and the first "full-time live music club that catered to the booming demographic of young America." One of the most memorable shows I saw there was the Full House lineup of Fairport Convention (which included Richard Thompson but to my dismay and surprise not Sandy Denny, who had left the group).

Bareiss, Warren. "Middlebrow Knowingness in 1950s San Francisco: The Kingston Trio, Beat Counterculture, and the Production of 'Authenticity.'" *Popular Music and Society* 33.1 (February 2010): 9–33. Print.

Boym, Svetlana. *The Future of Nostalgia*. New York: Basic Books, 2001. Print.

Cantwell, Robert. *When We Were Good: The Folk Revival*. Cambridge, MA: Harvard UP, 1996. Print.

Cohen, Ronald. *Rainbow Quest: The Folk Music Revival and American Society, 1940–1970*. Amherst and Boston: U of Massachusetts P, 2002. Print.

Despard, Alice. "The Mobile Party Unit." Blog entry on *Washington D.C. My Hometown*. 1 October 2008. Web. Accessed 16 Feb. 2011. <http://cokinosgirl.blogspot.com/2008/09/mobile-party-unit-by-alice-despard.html>

"Emergency." Web site of the Washington Area Music Association. Web. Accessed 16 Feb. 2011. <http://www.wamadc.com/wama/emergencyclub.html>

Hadju, David. "'A Mighty Wind': 'Spinal Tap' For Folkies?" *New York Times*. 13 Apr. 2003. Web.

———. *Positively 4th Street: The Lives and Times of Joan Baez, Bob Dylan, Mimi Baez Fariña, and Richard Fariña*. New York: Farrar, 2001. Print.

Kipling, Rudyard. *The Jungle Books*. New York: Signet, 1961. Print.

Lerner, Murray, dir., *Festival!* (1967) Eagle Rock Entertainment, 2005. DVD.

———. *The Other Side of the Mirror: Bob Dylan at the Newport Folk Festival*. Sony/Columbia Performance Series, 2007. DVD.

Lowell, Robert. *Life Studies*. New York: Farrar, 1959. Print.

Nielsen, Aldon Lynn. "Crow Jane Approximately: Bob Dylan's Black Masque." *Highway 61 Revisited: Bob Dylan's Road from Minnesota to the World*. Ed. Colleen J. Sheehy and Thomas Swiss. Minneapolis: U of Minnesota P, 2009. 186–96. Print.

Nodelman, Perry. *The Hidden Adult: Defining Children's Literature*. Baltimore: Johns Hopkins UP, 2008. Print.

"Peter, Paul, and Mary-Washington Peace March [April 24] 1971." YouTube Video. Web. Accessed 13 Mar. 2011. <http://www.youtube.com/watch?v=q8U6Oh9uSY8>

Plotz, Judith. *Romanticism and the Vocation of Childhood*. New York: Palgrave, 2001. Print.

Weissman, Dick. *Which Side Are You On?: An Inside History of the Folk Music Revival in America*. New York: Continuum, 2006. Print.

Werner, Craig. *A Change is Gonna Come: Music, Race, and the Soul of America*. Ann Arbor: U of Michigan P, 2006. Print.

Wordsworth, William. *The Prelude, 1799, 1805, 1850*. Ed. Jonathan Wordsworth, M. H. Abrams, and Stephen Gill. New York: Norton, 1979. Print.

CLAUDIA MILLS

⤳ Rousseau Redux

Romantic Re-Visions of Nature and Freedom in Recent Children's Literature about Homeschooling

"Everything is good as it leaves the hands of the Author of things; everything degenerates in the hands of man" (37). With this famous opening line of *Émile*, Jean-Jacques Rousseau delivered what is arguably the most famous statement of the creed of childhood innocence, that children are naturally good and are corrupted only through improper education at the hands of inept parents and imperfect social institutions. Published in 1762, *Émile* presents Rousseau's educational program for rearing a child who can escape societal corruption, insofar as this is humanly possible, a child who is educated to be man before he is educated to be citizen. Rousseau's prescriptions for this fictitious child's comprehensive rearing are enormously detailed, from recommendations for maternal breastfeeding and against infant swaddling, to elaborate preparations for Émile's choice of his ideal mate. Supervised throughout his education by a wise and cannily manipulative tutor, Émile is to be educated in harmony with nature, following the impulse of his own childish curiosity rather than overt adult imperatives, subjected only to the natural consequences of his own poor choices rather than made to bend to the dictatorial will of others (although these seemingly natural consequences are often arranged through the machinations of Émile's tutor). Allowed to be a child during the protected space of childhood, Émile will then grow to be a man who is able to be as free in society as any man can be, simultaneously both "savage" and "citizen."

Despite its vigilant condemnation by the church and Rousseau's subsequent persecution for its more inflammatory doctrines (particularly concerning Émile's delayed and rationally grounded religious instruction), *Émile* proved to be enormously influential both in Rousseau's own time and, I will argue here, in our own. The second half of the eighteenth century witnessed a fad for raising children "à la Jean-Jacques," with decidedly mixed results. While "a certain number of notable figures did emerge from this progressive experiment, for instance the physicist Ampère, who gave his name to the ampere, and the liberator Bolívar, who gave his name to Bolivia" (Damrosch 345), a certain number of disasters emerged as well. Eighteenth-century children's author Thomas Day "legendarily attempted to follow Rousseau's teachings in life, making two attempts, both failures, to guide a young preteen girl along Rousseauvian lines in order to make her into a suitable wife for him and dying as the result of an attempt to bring Rousseauvian principles to an apparently unimpressed young horse" (Stevenson 190).

Perhaps even greater than his influence, for good or for ill, on childrearing practices has been Rousseau's influence on children's literature. Although Rousseau did not permit Émile to learn to read until his teen years, and limited him initially to only one book, Defoe's *Robinson Crusoe*, the influence of Rousseau's concept of childhood and of his prescriptions for children's education was felt throughout children's literature as it emerged as its own distinctive field of literary endeavor, mirroring Rousseau's treatment of childhood as its own distinctive stage of life. In her book-length study of Rousseau's impact on eighteenth-century children's literature, Sylvia W. Patterson writes that "Almost all histories of children's literature in England mention the impact of the writings of Jean-Jacques Rousseau, especially *Émile*," published "at a time when children's literature was in its infancy" (7). Patterson catalogs some of the most common features of Rousseau's *Émile* adapted by other writers such as Thomas Day (*The History of Sandford and Merton* - 1783), Maria Edgeworth (*Moral Tales* - 1800), and Mary Wollstonecraft (*Original Stories from Real Life* - 1788). Here readers can see such Rousseauvian inspirations as: the presence of a model, "all-knowing and ever present" tutor; the presentation of totally good child characters (contrasted to those corrupted by wealth or position); children who learn from (deliberately staged) experience rather than through adult moralizing or punishment, or only from punishment that "fits the crime" as a seemingly natural consequence of the problematic behavior; children who learn what they want to learn through their own natural curiosity; children who learn extensively about the natural world, led by their love of nature.

John Rowe Townsend distills Rousseau's influence on early children's literature in this way: "Rousseau was all for naturalness and simplicity, the language of the heart, the ideal of the Noble Savage. Where better to find and cherish an unspoiled nature than in the child?" (24). Although Townsend points out that children's authors of Rousseau's time "conveniently forgot Rousseau's ban on books," they delivered tales that taught "the goodness of what is simple and natural, and the viciousness of wealth" (25), as well as the importance of what is useful as opposed to what is frivolous. This is, for example, a lesson young Rosamond learns to her sorrow in Maria Edgeworth's best-known story, "The Purple Jar," in which Rosamond begs her mother to buy a beautiful purple jar instead of useful shoes, only to discover that the jar's beautiful purple hue derives from an unpleasant-smelling purple liquid inside; the beautiful purple jar is really neither beautiful nor even purple (Townsend 25–26).

It is possible to trace Rousseau's influence through nineteenth- and twentieth-century children's literature as well, although at this point some of his ideas were disseminated widely enough throughout literary and popular culture that they were no longer linked explicitly with his name. Rousseau's insistence on the natural innocence of the child, his rejection of original sin in favor of the original goodness of the child until corrupted by society, arguably inspired the long-popular trope of the redemptive child who transforms unhappy and embittered adults: Heidi, Little Lord Fauntleroy, Anne of Green Gables, Rebecca of Sunnybrook Farm, Pollyanna, to name only a few. These stories, however, did not offer a specifically Rousseauvian program of independent education for their young heroes and heroines. And as the twentieth century progressed, stories of redemptive children gave way to the problem novel focused on children damaged by familial alcoholism, divorce, and abuse, who are forced to assume adult responsibilities in the face of parental abdication of these responsibilities.

Rousseau's romantic legacy, and its implications for the ideal education of uncorrupted children, reappears strikingly, however, in several recent, critically acclaimed children's books that have in common their focus on homeschooling. In these books, as in Émile, some major child character is educated at home, not as a rejection of secular culture by the religious right (as is most common in current actual patterns of homeschooling in the United States), but as a deliberate rejection of the rigid, stifling, and conformity-inducing educational practices of contemporary educational institutions. In Skellig by David Almond (1998), Stargirl by Jerry Spinelli (2000), Surviving the Applewhites by Stephanie S. Tolan (2002), and Ida B by Katherine Hannigan (2004), we see an almost startling development of central themes in Rousseau. These texts from the last dozen years show children reared according to nature, reveling in their freedom to learn and develop as they choose, and exhibiting a passionate connection to the natural world. While I make no claim that these authors would trace their stories in any way to a reading of Rousseau's Émile, I present these books for our consideration as evidence of Rousseau's legacy on the field of children's literature, which endures even in the absence of an explicit homage to his philosophical oeuvre.

The last quarter-century has seen an explosion in the rates of homeschooling in the United States, where over two million children are now educated at home (West 7); the vast majority of parents who choose homeschooling for their children do so for religious reasons, most self-identifying as evangelical or fundamentalist Protestants (West 7). But this is not the landscape of homeschooling in recent children's literature. Perhaps reflecting the near-absence of any mention of religion in mainstream children's book publishing, the homeschooling families of notable recent children's literature have far more in common with Émile than with Jesus Camp. The children in these books, like Rousseau's Émile, are not subjected to any form of rote learning or standardized curriculum; they do not fill out worksheets and indeed, in some cases (Skellig), mock the dull assignments dutifully completed by non-homeschooled friends. The children in these books follow their own natural interests and curiosity, often focusing their "studies" on the natural world. Unlike Émile, however, they are not subjected to supervision by an omnipotent, omniscient tutor, but are more self-schooled than his protégé. And unlike Émile, homeschooled children in recent children's literature are often enthusiastically engaged with the arts, an activity for which Rousseau famously expressed disdain. In his *First Discourse*, the *Discourse on the Sciences and the Arts*, he answered the question posed by the Academy of Dijon—"Whether the restoration of the Sciences and Arts has contributed to the purification of morals"—resoundingly in the negative, even as he himself went on to write and publish the best-selling novel of the eighteenth century (*Julie, or The New Heloise*) and wrote both score and libretto for an opera that was the toast of Paris (*Le Devin du Village—The Village Soothsayer*). So the homeschooling projects of these recent books do not map neatly onto Rousseau's template. But it is nonetheless compelling to see clear echoes of Rousseau in any portrait of child learning that removes children from a rule-bound, institutional setting and allows them to follow their own interests and passions in harmony with their own unfolding nature.

Skellig is a haunting, fantastic story of two children, Michael and Mina, who encounter a strange creature in Michael's decrepit garage: part man, part angel, part bird. Their encounter with this individual, who calls himself Skellig, helps Michael cope with his infant sister's critical heart condition and subsequent surgery. Michael himself attends a neighborhood school (though he is absent from school much of the time, excused to help with household projects); his next-door neighbor Mina is homeschooled. "My mother educates me," she explains to Michael. "We believe that schools inhibit the natural curiosity, creativity, and intelligence of children. The mind needs to be opened out into the world, not shuttered down inside a gloomy classroom" (49). She invokes William Blake as the source of her family's educational philosophy, frequently quoting his verses expressing opposition to traditional schooling. On the wall by Mina's bed hangs the family motto, "How can a bird that is born for joy / Sit in a cage and sing?" (50). Just as chicks don't need a formal classroom to make them fly, neither does Mina need a traditional schoolroom to help her learn (50). Later, she quotes Blake again,

But to go to school in a summer morn,
O! it drives all joy away;

Under a cruel eye outworn,
The little ones spend the day
In sighing and dismay. (59)

Although Mina takes Blake as her only reference point, she could equally well have quoted Wordsworth's "Intimations of Immortality from Recollections of Early Childhood," where the child "trailing clouds of glory" soon faces the dreariness of formal education: "Shades of the prison house begin to close / Upon the growing boy," the lad who upon entering society will soon make his "whole vocation" "endless imitation." Or, for that matter, she could have quoted Rousseau himself, who describes traditional education in this way: "Goodbye, joy! Goodbye, frolicsome games! A severe and angry man takes him by the hand, says to him gravely, 'Let us go, sir,' and takes him away. In the room into which they go I catch a glimpse of books. Books! What sad furnishings for his age! The poor child lets himself be pulled along, turns a regretful eye on all that surrounds him, becomes silent, and leaves, his eyes swollen with tears he does not dare to shed, and his heart great with sighs he does not dare to breathe" (*Émile* 159). Rousseau would replace this regime of constraint and coercion with its opposite: "All the instruments [for successful education of children] have been tried save one, the only one precisely that can succeed: well-regulated freedom" (92).

Mina clearly spends her days engaged in freedom, well regulated or not: climbing trees, painting and drawing, and observing nature. In response to Michael's question, "You're doing science?" she laughs: "See how school shutters you. . . . I'm drawing, painting, reading, looking. I'm feeling the sun and the air on my skin. I'm listening to the blackbird's song. I'm opening my mind. Ha! School!" (58). Like Émile, Mina learns through drawing: "I would want my child to cultivate this art, not precisely for the art itself but for making his eye exact and his hand flexible . . . my intention is that he be able not so much to imitate objects as to know them" (144–45). Her minute observation of nature reflects Rousseau's similar preoccupation and fascination with the detail of the natural world; in late life he was an ardent botanist. In the abandoned house that Mina has inherited lives a family of baby owls; the two children spend considerable time observing the fledglings and celebrating their growing ability to survive, as the owl chicks bring home "A dead mouse, a tiny dead baby bird. Blood was still trickling through the ripped fur, through the young feathers" (173).

Mina describes the baby owls she and Michael are observing several times as "savages"—as "wonderful" savages (51) and "beautiful tender savages" (173). When Michael comments, "They think we're something like them," Mina replies, "Perhaps we are" (173). Although he never actually used the phrase that has become so identified with his thought— "the noble savage"—Rousseau's extended portrait of "savage man" in his *Second Discourse*, the *Discourse on the Origin and Foundation of Inequality among Men*, is the portrait of a state of radical innocence from which man is gradually corrupted, first through the development of *amour-propre* (the problematic, essentially comparative, form of self-love, possible only after a certain state in the development of human society) and even more through the institution of private property. Rousseau retains this contrast between savage man and civilized man, offered to the advantage of the former, in *Émile*. In Book IV of *Émile* he writes, "It is not philosophers who know men best. They see them only through the prejudices of philosophy, and I know of no station where one has so many. A savage has a healthier judgment of us than a philosopher does" (243). The philosopher judges men as wicked; the savage judges them, more accurately, as mad. Rousseau concludes: "My pupil is that savage" (243). But Émile is a savage who must live among civilized men: "He is a savage made to inhabit cities. He has to know how to find his necessities in them, to take advantage of their inhabitants, and to live, if not like them, at least with them" (205).

Even as *Skellig* points backward to what we have in common with more primitive and "savage" forms of life, it also points forward to an evolutionary future that may bring us closer to angels, our shoulder blades the site where emergent wings might develop: "There's no end to evolution," Mina tells Michael. "We have to be ready to move forward. . . . Maybe this is not how we are meant to be forever" (99). Mina and Michael are both fascinated with the scientific study of evolution. Mina learns about evolution through her observation of hollow bird bones—"This too is the result of evolution. . . . The bone is light but strong. It is adapted so that the bird can fly. Over millions of years, the bird has developed an anatomy that enables it to fly" (61). Michael learns about evolution through the school worksheets that Mina mocks: "It is thought that Man is d_____ from the apes";

"This is the Theory of E_____"; This theory was developed by Charles D_____."
(89). The mystery man, Skellig, seems to be proof of the possibilities of
further human evolution, with his folded angel wings and ability to fly
away from Michael and Mina at the end of the book.

Rousseau, too, is associated with an evolutionary view of human nature, though one that is redemptive rather than Darwinian. Thus, in *Skellig* we see Rousseau's twin, seemingly contradictory, themes of both the
corruption and redemption made possible by evolution: the corruption
of man from a more innocent savage state, as in the *Second Discourse*, and
the subsequent redemption of man in *Of the Social Contract*: "his faculties
are exercised and developed, his ideas enlarged, his sentiments ennobled,
his entire soul is elevated to such an extent, that if the abuses of this new
condition did not often degrade him to beneath the condition he has left,
he should ceaselessly bless the happy moment which wrested him from it
forever and out of a stupid and bounded animal made an intelligent being
and a man" (53). Robert Wokler comments on the influence that Rousseau's reflections on "orang-utans" in the *Second Discourse* had upon "the
early history of physical anthropology and evolutionary biology" (46).
Wokler writes, "No one in the eighteenth century envisaged human nature
as more subject to change in the course of its development. No one supposed savage man so much more like an animal than like civilized man.
No one before Rousseau came closer to conceiving human history as mankind's descent from an ape" (46–47). And human beings, unlike apes, in
Rousseau's view have the possibility of evolving still further, of "making
themselves progressively more perfect as moral agents" (Wokler 44)—or
of abusing that possibility.

A parallel fascination with evolution—in particular, in this case, its
attendant losses—animates *Stargirl* by Jerry Spinelli. The self-named girl
of the book's title, previously homeschooled, astonishes and confounds
her classmates when she enters public school for the first time in eleventh
grade. Spinelli's novel gives no explanation of her family's reasons for
rejecting traditional schooling up to this point, but it is certainly not to
shield Stargirl (Susan) from secular influences and to immerse her in religious fundamentalism. A philosophy of homeschooling is laid out more
directly in the book's presentation of the informal "school" that retired
paleontologist Archie holds in his home for his self-selected "students."

Narrator Leo describes Archie's school as "No tests, no grades, no attendance record. Just the best school most of us had ever gone to" (31). Archie's "curriculum," like Rousseau's, focuses on the natural world—"He covered everything from toothpaste to tapeworms and somehow made it all fit together" (31)—and kids are welcome to talk to Archie anytime: "My school . . . is everywhere and always in session" (31). Students in Archie's "school" learn whatever they learn only according to the natural curiosity that impels them to come to him in the first place.

Living in harmony with her natural proclivities is at the core of Stargirl's character: she follows her own natural predilections in ways that defy her classmates' expectations at every turn (serenading people on their birthdays, accompanied by her ukulele, dressing in an outlandish way, carrying around a pet rat, cheering for both teams during school basketball games). Like Skellig's Mina, Stargirl carefully observes the natural world, including the puzzling and bizarre world of human beings. Leo says, reflecting on his growing closeness with Stargirl: "She taught me to revel. She taught me to wonder" (107). Her repeated instruction is "Look!" (107). And "What she saw, she felt. Her eyes went straight to her heart" (108).

Of the homeschooled characters in the four books I have considered here, Stargirl is the one whose admirable moral qualities are most salient. Almost saintly in her concern for others, Stargirl devotes herself to reading newspaper "fillers" that can allow her to choose just the right cards and gifts for complete strangers; yet she is also almost completely clueless about the social structures of a contemporary high school and how to engage with her classmates there. Leo notes of Stargirl that her most remarkable feature was that, while she cared about the bad things that befell others, "bad things falling on her—unkind words, nasty stares, foot blisters—she seemed unaware of. I never saw her look in a mirror, never heard her complain. All of her feelings, all of her attentions flowed outward. She had no ego" (52–53).

Here we see another striking similarity with Rousseau's Émile, who is raised to be indifferent to extremes of heat and cold, to tolerate loud noises and minor illnesses without even seeming to notice them. He is also raised to know little or nothing of egotistical self-appraisal: "Self-love, which regards only ourselves, is contented when our true needs are satisfied. But amour-propre, which makes comparisons, is never content and never could be, because this sentiment, preferring ourselves to others, also demands others to prefer us to themselves, which is impossible. This is how the gentle and affectionate passions are born of self-love, and how the hateful and irascible passions are born of *amour-propre*" (213–14). Young Émile is a stranger to this dangerous passion: "*Amour-propre* . . . is still hardly aroused in him" (208). Having no ego, Stargirl likewise knows nothing of *amour-propre* until she is corrupted by her exposure to society, that is to say, by her exposure to high school, and comes to care for the first time about what her classmates think of her. Leo accuses her: "You don't seem to care what everybody thinks. You don't even seem to *know* what everybody thinks" (135). He chides her, "We aren't alone, are we? We live in a world of them, like it or not" (138). Stargirl then "vanishes" and becomes Susan again, the girl who wants to do whatever "Evelyn Everybody" would do (142).

As a paleontologist, Archie is positioned to situate Stargirl not as a more evolved creature than her classmates, but as one who is marvelously less evolved: "And I think every once in a while someone comes along who is a little more primitive than the rest of us, a little closer to our beginnings, a little more in touch with the stuff we're made of" (177). She is "who we really are. Or were" (32). Stargirl thus has connections of her own with Rousseau's savage man. In Rousseau's words in the *Second Discourse*: "The example of the Savages . . . seems to confirm that Mankind was made always to remain in [this state]; that this state is the genuine youth of the World, and that all subsequent progress has been so many steps in appearance toward the perfection of the individual, and in effect toward the decrepitude of the species" (167). Stargirl represents the genuine youth of the world, the genuine "earthling" as Archie calls her (33), the only one who is truly in touch with the earth, and with herself.

Stephanie S. Tolan's Newbery Honor book, *Surviving the Applewhites*, features a juvenile delinquent who is sent to the Creative Academy homeschool run by the nonconformist Applewhite family, in lieu of being sent to Juvenile Hall. The educational philosophy of the Creative Academy could have come straight from the pages of Rousseau: "the Applewhites didn't believe in telling students what to study and when. The Creative Academy wasn't so much a homeschool as an *unschool*. Its students were supposed to follow their own interests and create their own educational plans. Separately. Individually. Creatively" (19).

The Creative Academy is Jake Semple's last chance to avoid criminal penalties for his past transgressions; we might say, then, that in being forcibly placed into the educational freedom of the Applewhites, Jake is being "forced to be free," in unconscious echo of Rousseau's famous dictum that those who transgress against the laws of civil society must be "forced to be free" (*Of the Social Contract* 53), that is to say, constrained to follow the laws that provide the conditions under which they, and others, can be most truly free. Despite his criminal past—Jake was expelled from every public school in the state of Rhode Island for having set his previous school on fire (2)—Lucille Applewhite, who "can't ever believe a bad thing about anybody" (4), pronounces Jake to be "a radiant light being, that's what you are. A radiant light being" (23). If one ignores its New Age overtones, this could be a restatement of Rousseau's faith in the basic goodness of the child. Lucille's statement that "Human beings are almost infinitely adaptable" (40) could be a gloss on Rousseau's belief in human perfectability: "In his original condition each person must have had the capacity not only to change his essential qualities but also to improve them" (Wokler 44).

In the course of his time with the Applewhites, Jake develops an especially close relationship with four-year-old Destiny, a fellow free spirit. When Destiny tells Jake that "he could spend the day in pajamas if he wanted to and sometimes he did," Jake sighs and thinks to himself, "It wouldn't be possible for Destiny to grow up to be a delinquent—there didn't seem to be any rules for him to break" (74). This isn't strictly true, however, as Destiny is not allowed to do anything seriously dangerous, such as play with matches (45). While Jake may mean here only that if delinquency by definition requires rule-breaking, it literally cannot exist in the absence of any rules, his comment connects with one of Rousseau's central insights in *Émile*. Rousseau's tutor is committed to raising Émile without rules: "one ought to demand nothing of children through obedience" (116). Indeed, it is by imposing duties on children that one instead inculcates vices: "duties . . . are never prescribed to children except in such a way as to make them not only hateful but impracticable. Appearing to preach virtue to children, one makes them love all the vices. The vices are given to them by forbidding them to have them" (103). In his central example of this phenomenon, Rousseau argues that it is by insisting on obedience that we produce in the child the necessity of lying about his disobedience (101). So it is indeed, according to Rousseau, the very presence of rules which ends up producing the inevitability of delinquency.

The central story line of Tolan's novel focuses on the entire Applewhite family's involvement in a new staging of *The Sound of Music*—antithetical to Rousseau's stated disdain for the theater. But Jake's connection with this production immerses him fully and deeply in the Applewhite community, aligning him with the Applewhites in a common project, which leads to his sharing, if you will, in their "general will." As rehearsals progress, Jake begins to realize that "He'd become impossibly entangled with the Applewhites" (139), and that all of the Applewhites have become impossibly entangled with the show: "All of them, even the invisible Hal, had put their whole *selves* into this show by now. . . . It didn't matter anymore that it was Randolph's show, that it was a project nobody else had wanted anything to do with. Everybody was involved in it now" (173). This is precisely the kind of transformative identification with a community that is the basis of Rousseau's political freedom: "Freedom, Rousseau insists, requires participation in a particular community, rather than existence in an amorphous society. Indeed, we may say that freedom and identification with the particular community are one" (Gauthier 64). Jake finds himself when he identifies with something larger than himself, just as Rousseau's denatured no-longer-savages redeem their lost natural freedom by finding civic and moral freedom within the bounds of community.

In the fourth novel to be examined here, *Ida B*, spirited Ida B finds the constraint of kindergarten intolerable, with its enforced boredom and rules for the sake of rules. At school, she loses not only her connection with the natural world outside the school windows—"I swear I could hear the brook calling to me, over that distance and through those closed-up windows" (45)—and her inborn joy, as she gets "so droopy and forlorn looking" (54). She even loses her identity: her teacher refuses to call her "Ida B," insisting that her proper name is only "Ida." After a dreary two weeks and three days of kindergarten, Ida B's parents decide to remove her from school and educate her at home: "Ida B is free, Ida B is free. Come fly with me, Ida B" (56). But when the action of the book begins, four years later, Ida B's mother's cancer necessitates Ida B's reenrollment in public school, in the face of Ida B's angry decision to "hate school and anything that goes with it. And I completely expect that being a student in this class will suck the life out of me before the end of this week" (105). This time, however, Ida B is placed in the classroom of a kindly, understanding teacher who encourages Ida B's love of reading.

As with the other homeschooled children discussed above, Ida B's years of homeschooling have given her a deep and abiding love of the natural world, here, an almost mystical communion with trees. For Ida B, each tree has a name and a distinct personality; she talks to them and hears them speak to her. The novel takes this in the direction of an environmental message, that we are caretakers of the earth, even as the earth is our caretaker as well. While it would be anachronistic to read this kind of message into Rousseau, the freedom that Ida B experiences only in communion with nature strikes a familiar chord to readers of Rousseau: "Instead of letting him stagnate in the stale air of a room, let him be taken daily to the middle of a field. There let him run and frisk about" (*Émile* 78). It resonates with the love of natural beauty exhibited on almost every page of Rousseau's late-life *Reveries of the Solitary Walker*.

Ida B's unexpectedly successful return to school helps blur the sharp dichotomy between homeschooling and traditional schooling, indeed between solitude and society. The latter is the central tension at the heart of all Rousseau's writings, the problem that the social contract is intended to solve, by taking distinct, separate, and isolated individuals and forming them into one whole, yet without sacrificing their essential liberty. Rousseau states the central problem of politics in this way: "To find a form of association that will defend and protect the person and goods of each associate with the full common force, and by means of which each, uniting with all, nevertheless obey only himself and remain as free as before. This is the fundamental problem to which the social contract provides the solution" (*Of the Social Contract* 49–50). Rousseau intends Émile's education apart from other men to fit him for ultimate integration into society, to allow him to become a savage who can not only live with civilized men but be a leader among them: "be their benefactor and their model. Your example will serve them better than all our books" (474).

Stargirl highlights the challenges of such a project, as Stargirl is alternately shunned, celebrated, and then shunned again by her classmates; she ultimately disappears never to be seen again. Delinquent Jake of *Surviving the Applewhites* is likely to remain in many ways a social misfit, although a social misfit who can contribute to society through his gifts for theatrical performance and who no longer needs to strive deliberately for social alienation and antagonism. Michael in *Skellig* is able to engage both with homeschooled Mina and with his sporty chums at school and learns to go back and forth comfortably between their two divergent worlds. And by the end of her story, Ida B is able to find happiness both at home and at school, to keep her connection with her beloved trees even as she forms a friendship with a new neighbor (and classmate) whose arrival in the neighborhood occasions the destruction of some of the trees. Thus, these recent children's texts show how we continue to struggle with the fundamental questions Rousseau posed two and a half centuries ago. Does our integration into society corrupt our fundamental nature or help us to realize it? Under what conditions are we most truly ourselves? And they show that Rousseau continues to provide the framework within which children's literature offers answers to these questions, answers lying in educating children to live freely in harmony with their essential nature.

WORKS CITED

Almond, David. *Skellig*. New York: Delacorte, 1998.

Damrosch, Leo. *Jean-Jacques Rousseau: Restless Genius*. Boston and New York: Houghton Mifflin, 2005.

Gauthier, David. *Rousseau: The Sentiment of Existence*. Cambridge and New York: Cambridge UP, 2006.

Hannigan, Katherine. *Ida B . . . and Her Plans to Maximize Fun, Avoid Disaster, and (Possibly) Save the World*. New York: Greenwillow, 2004.

Patterson, Sylvia W. *Rousseau's Émile and Early Children's Literature*. Metuchen, NJ: Scarecrow, 1971.

Rousseau, Jean-Jacques. *Émile, or On Education*. Trans. and ed. Allan Bloom. New York: Basic Books, 1979.

———. *Reveries of the Solitary Walker*. Trans. Peter France. London and New York: Penguin, 1979.

———. *The Discourses and Other Early Political Writings*. Trans. and ed. Victor Gourevitch. New York and Cambridge: Cambridge UP, 1997.

———. *The Social Contract and Other Later Political Writings*. Trans. and ed. Victor Gourevitch. New York and Cambridge: Cambridge UP, 1997.

Spinelli, Jerry. *Stargirl*. New York: Alfred A. Knopf, 2000.

Stevenson, Deborah. "History of Children's and Young Adult Literature." In *Handbook on Research in Children's and Young Adult Literature*. Ed. Shelby A. Wolf, et al. New York and London: Routledge, 2011. 179–92.

Tolan, Stephanie S. *Surviving the Applewhites*. New York: Harper Collins, 2002.

Townsend, John Rowe. *Written for Children: An Outline of English-Language Children's Literature*. Lanham, MD, and London: Scarecrow, 1996.

West, Robin. "The Harms of Homeschooling." *Philosophy and Public Policy Quarterly*. Vol. 29, nos. 3/4 (Summer/Fall 2009): 7–12.

Wokler, Robert. *Rousseau*. Oxford and New York: Oxford UP, 1995.

JAN SUSINA

⤳ Teletubbies and the Conflict of the Romantic Concept of Childhood and the Realities of Postmodern Parenting

Teletubbies is the popular but controversial television program, developed by the BBC specifically for very young children, which ran from 1997 to 2001, first in England. The program was subsequently introduced a year later on PBS in the United States. This children's television program both reintroduced and questioned some of the basic Romantic notions of childhood in the era of postmodern parenting. While the program has ceased production, *Teletubbies* has achieved an influential and lasting impact on children's television and other forms of children's screen media that are currently being created for very young children. Developed by Anne Wood and Andrew Davenport, *Teletubbies* completed production after 365 episodes in 2001 and was viewed in more than fifty countries. While *Teletubbies* is no longer in production, the children's television program continues to be shown on various cable television channels in the United States, and many of the episodes are available on DVDs or videos.

Designed specifically for toddlers and infants aged two and younger, *Teletubbies* created a firestorm of controversy when it first appeared on PBS in the United States in 1998. In 1999, the Committee of Public Education of the American Academy of Pediatrics issued "Media Education," a policy statement that included the recommendation urging "parents to avoid television viewing for children under the age of 2 years" (341). While

Teletubbies was not explicitly mentioned in the American Academy of Pediatrics policy statement, which was developed by its Committee on Public Education, it is clear that the popularity of the program, as the first and best-known television program to be designed specifically for very young children to be broadcast in the United States, was one of the chief motivations for the creation of the media education guidelines. Despite the widely publicized American Academy of Pediatrics media guidelines, the success of *Teletubbies* encouraged the development of more, rather than less, television programming for very young viewers and opened media development for other television programs, such as *Blue's Clues*, *Dora the Explorer*, and *Bear in the Big Blue House*, which are all intended for the same demographic. Another well-publicized criticism of *Teletubbies* was raised when Jerry Falwell, then the spokesperson for the conservative Moral Majority, denounced the program in February 1999; he suggested that Tinky Winky, the largest of the Teletubby characters, was a homosexual role model for young children (Samburg).

Despite criticisms from both progressive and conservative perspectives, *Teletubbies* became the first of an increasing number of television programs, DVDs, videos, computer games, and software apps created for very young children. In the Kaiser Family Foundation report *Zero to Six: Electronic Media in the Lives of Infants, Toddlers and Preschoolers* (2003), Victoria Rideout, Elizabeth Vandewater, and Ellen Wartella acknowledged "an explosion in electronic media marketed directly at the very youngest children of our society" that includes "a booming market of videotapes and DVDs aimed at infants one to 18 months, the launching of the first TV show specifically targeting children as young as 12 months" and "computer games and even special keyboard toppers for children as young as nine months old" (2). *Teletubbies* was both a groundbreaking and deeply troubling children's program for many adults since it celebrated a Romantic concept of an innocent childhood while it simultaneously embraced the technological changes of childhood in the late twentieth and early twenty-first centuries.

As the pioneering television program intended for very young children, *Teletubbies* influenced children's electronic media immensely. *Zero to Six*, which was released two years after the final regular airing of *Teletubbies*, observed that very young children, aged six months to six years, grow up in a world immersed in media. This study, based on random interviews of

1,000 parents and children, reports that according to parents, their children "spend an average of two hours a day with screen media, mostly TV and videos" (Rideout, Vandewater, and Wartella 12). American children spend about the same amount of time watching screen media (one hour and fifty-eight minutes) as do they spend playing outside (two hours and one minute), and three times as much time with screen media as they do reading or being read to (thirty-nine minutes) (Rideout, Vandewater, and Wartella 4). The American Academy of Pediatrics followed up its 1999 "Media Education" guidelines with "Children, Adolescents, and Television" guidelines in 2001 that still included the recommendation discouraging children two years old or younger from watching any television, and added that total media time for children older than two should be limited to one to two hours of quality programming per day (423). In contrast, *Zero to Six* reported what is actually occurring is that "68% of all children under two use screen media (59% watch TV, 42% watch a video or DVD, 5% use a computer and 3% play video games) and these youngsters will spend an average of two hours and five minutes in front of a screen" (Rideout, Vandewater, and Wartella 5). Despite its pastoral appearance and educational content, *Teletubbies* acknowledges a troubling reality about contemporary children's immersion in media.

There is much to admire and enjoy in *Teletubbies*. Teletubbyland is a comforting pastoral landscape full of scurrying rabbits and talking flowers presided over by a laughing baby sun. The program is positively Wordsworthian in spirit with the innocent Teletubbies playing endlessly in an idealized garden. The opening line of the program, spoken by the unseen adult narrator, announces, "Over the hills and far away, Teletubbies come to play," which evokes the idealized world of William Blake's children joyfully playing in gardens. The vibrant and somewhat psychedelic use of color brings to mind Blake's illuminated books. Iona and Peter Opie, in their introduction to *The Oxford Dictionary of Nursery Rhymes* (1951), note that G. K. Chesterton "observed that so simple a line from the nursery as 'Over the hills and far away' is one of the most beautiful in all English poetry," and then adds, "as if in confirmation, Gay, Swift, Burns, Tennyson, Stevenson, and Henley thought well enough of the line to make it their own" (2). The *Teletubbies* creators very consciously established the program within this Romantic tradition. The *Teletubbies* setting of the unspoiled, idyllic English countryside is reminiscent of the Hundred Acre Wood of A. A. Milne's *Pooh* books.

The actual filming of *Teletubbies* took place outside of Stratford, England, so it was perhaps closer in feeling to Shakespeare's Forest of Arden. The magic of the fairies has been replaced by the magic and power of television. Set in a landscape of gently rolling hills, the Teletubbies live in a safe, green world of friendly animals and talking flowers. The program makes a striking contrast to the urban setting of PBS's *Sesame Street*. It is generally spring and summer in Teletubbyland. Sunny weather is the norm; however, in a few episodes there is just enough rain to create puddles for the Teletubbies to jump in, or on rare occasions, a light dusting of snow to the delight of the characters. Despite its pastoral landscape, the program is rich in technology. The Teletubbies are four multicolored and multicultural creatures that seem to be a fusion of characters from *Barney & Friends* and *Pee-Wee's Playhouse*.

The four Teletubbies are creatures that resemble life-size stuffed animals but with television sets fixed in their stomachs. Anne Wood has suggested that the Teletubbies were intended to combine the friendliness of a stuffed animal and the technology of a television ("Nine Ways" 4). In contemporary childhood, the television has become the new constant companion that Pooh and the other stuffed animals once were for Christopher Robin. According to *Zero to Six*, nearly all American children (ninety-nine percent) live in a home with a TV set (Rideout, Vandewater, and Wartella 4). Forty-two percent of the parents of children aged six or younger believe that television "mostly helps" children learn (Rideout, Vandewater, and Wartella 8).

Tinky Winky is the largest and the most gentle of the group. He is purple and resembles a younger and friendlier version of Barney, the dinosaur, the central character from *Barney & Friends*, with a triangle antenna affixed to the top of his head. His purple triangle and the magic bag that he frequently carries, which Jerry Falwell called a purse, are the reasons that Tinky Winky was considered a gay character by several commentators. Dipsy is the green Teletubby who often wears his favorite black-and-white top hat. Dipsy also has darker facial features than the other Teletubbies. Laa-Laa is the yellow Teletubby and the most social of the group. She is concerned to know where the others are and is frequently seen playing with her orange ball. The smallest Teletubby is Po, whose name references Milne's Pooh. Po is red and is the most popular character with young audience members. She is the most independent of the Teletubbies and spends a great deal of time riding around Teletubbyland on her scooter.

A typical episode of *Teletubbies* begins with the bright yellow sun, which features the laughing infant in its center, rising over the lush, green landscape. The laughing baby sun appears to be the benevolent ruler of Teletubbyland and occasionally shows his appreciation and delight at the actions of the Teletubbies by laughing in approval. The camera follows the gently rolling hills full of brightly colored flowers and rabbits as the narrator announces, "Over the hills and far away, Teletubbies come to play." The four cuddly Teletubbies pop out of their futuristic home, the Tubbytronic Superdome, which appears to be part space station and part mother's womb covered in synthetic grass. The Teletubbies cheerfully emerge from a hole in the center of the roof where they dance to the program's theme song, "Teletubbies Say 'Eh-oh!'" "Eh-oh" is Tubby speak for Hello, and the program's theme song introduces the four characters by name, multiple times, as the Teletubbies laugh, dance, and happily bump into one another. The song ends with a big group hug as the four creatures embrace each other, an action that is frequently repeated during the thirty-minute program. The announcer regularly reminds viewers that "The Teletubbies love each other very much." By the theme song's conclusion, the Teletubbies have disappeared into the landscape in a game of hide and seek as the voice trumpets emerge from the ground and ask the viewer, "Where have the Teletubbies gone?" Throughout the program the announcer and the Teletubbies directly address the viewer, encouraging young children to make television an active rather than passive activity. This is followed by a short episode in which the Teletubbies learn through play. The Teletubbies spend a great deal of time in many of the episodes playing with their favorite objects or exploring their environment. The group activity is interrupted when the magic windmill begins to turn and mysteriously summons the Teletubbies to the top of a hill. Then they wait expectantly until one of the characters receives a television transmission that appears on the screen that is implanted in each of their tummies. The other Teletubbies crowd around to watch the "Here and Now" segment of the program that features a child or children participating in a simple activity such as picking oranges, playing in a wading pool, or helping a parent set up a bicycle. The Teletubbies are so delighted with watching this short television episode that they insist that it be repeated. They shout, "Again, Again," and their request is granted. The live action "Here and Now" segment is then followed by another Teletubby play activity that imitates a portion of the actions that they have just observed being performed by the children in the "Here and Now" segment. There is usually another group dance and a big hug in the second half of the program. At the end of the program, the Teletubbies are reluctant to leave and delay their departure by playing hide and seek with the viewers. But they eventually say their farewells to the viewer and cheerfully return to the Tubbytronic Superdome as the laughing baby sun sets behind the hills of Teletubbyland.

Wood created the Teletubbies to be a combination of the traditional soft toy that a child might cling to for emotional support and the new electronic technology that is a part of their daily environment. Wood explains that by "taking a television—the most magical piece of technology for a child—and putting it on the tummy of a soft toy. We developed the characters from that, creating technological babies, the Teletubbies" ("Nine Ways" 4). So Winnie-the-Pooh + television = Po, or the postmodern Pooh. Frederick Crews has poked fun at the excesses of recent literary theory in his *Postmodern Pooh* (2001), but it turns out Crews wasn't being as ironic as he assumed.

The costumes of the Teletubbies are reminiscent of the psychedelic creatures that populated Sid and Marty Krofft's *H. R. Pufnstuf* and *The Bugaloos*, children's television programs created in the late 1960s and early 1970s. While the Teletubbies live in a rural pastoral landscape, their home is the Tubbytronic Superdome, a futuristic space station in this brave new/old world of children's television. The Teletubbies eat Tubby Custard and Tubby Toast, which they make themselves. Their chief companion is Noo-Noo, an overeager vacuum cleaner.

The popularity of the *Teletubbies* has only increased its role in the long-running debate about the quality and amount of television that children ought to watch. John Hersey's influential essay "Why Do Students Bog Down on the First R?: A Local Committee Sheds Light on A National Problem: Reading," published in the May 24, 1954, issue of *Life* magazine, criticized the "pallid primers" that were used to teach reading in schools and is widely credited for encouraging Dr. Seuss to compose *The Cat in the Hat* (1957). But immediately after Hersey made his recommendation that one way to improve reading instruction in schools was to have the "insipid illustrations" found in many basic readers replaced by the more lively drawings "of the wonderfully imaginative geniuses among children's illustrators, Tenniel, Howard Pyle, Dr. Seuss, Walt Disney," he addressed another and perhaps greater concern: "Television, the enemy" (148). Hersey realized as early as 1954 that children's reading was increasingly competing with other visual media including comics, magazines, radio, and film, but "Above, all, with television" (147). Hersey discovered in 1954 that only fifteen out of 230 fourth grade children in Fairfield, Connecticut, reported not having a television in their homes (147). As noted previously, the number of homes that report owning at least one television in the United States is now ninety-nine percent. Hersey and his committee were appalled to discover that in 1954 children self-reported that they watched on average three hours, eight minutes, twenty-four seconds of television per day (150). So as early as 1954 children were exceeding the amount of television viewing that the American Academy of Pediatrics media guidelines proposed in 2001. Victoria Rideout, Ulla Foehr, and Donald Roberts's *Generation M²: Media in the Lives of 8- to 18-Year Olds*, published by the Kaiser Family Foundation in 2010, reports that media time for American children has increased to seven and a half hours a day, seven days a week (1). Hersey's concern with television may account for the absence of a television set in Seuss's *The Cat in the Hat*. But the lack of a television set would have already been an anomaly in 1957 in the affluent community of Fairfield, Connecticut, and its absence makes the reading of *The Cat in the Hat* by contemporary children confusing. For children that grow up from birth in environments surrounded by a host of electronic entertainment including televisions, VCR/DVD players, computers, xBoxes, Wii, and various handheld computer games, the premise of Sally and her brother spending a rainy afternoon staring forlornly out the window makes Seuss's picture book almost impossible to comprehend. *Generation M²* is a follow-up report to those published by the Kaiser Family Foundation in 1999 and 2004, which track media use by American children; and its 2010 report noted that the amount of time that children spend with media has increased in every category—television, music, computer, video games, movies—with one exception:

reading. While the amount of time that children watch television per day has increased by thirty-eight minutes to four hours and twenty-nine minutes, the amount of time reading has been reduced to from forty-three to thirty-eight minutes a day (Rideout, Foeher, and Roberts 2). While *The Cat in the Hat* is a beloved picture book for older generations of readers, the text embodies an idealized version of 1950s childhood that doesn't mesh with the world of contemporary childhood. Most of the toys that the children own in *The Cat in the Hat*, such as a bicycle, a tennis racket, and balls of various sizes, are intended for outdoor activities. According to *Zero to Six*, contemporary children aged six and younger spend as much time with screen media as they do playing outside (Rideout, Vandewater, and Wartella 4). *The Cat in the Hat* evokes a simpler time in American culture—a sort of picture book equivalent of the popular television program *Leave It to Beaver*, which debuted in 1957, the same year that Seuss's picture book was published—representing childhood before television, telephones, radios, concerns about stranger danger, and, apparently, even before the use of babysitters when mother is away for the day.

One of the chief reasons that Wood and Davenport created *Teletubbies* was their realization that children—including infants, toddlers, and preschool children—live in a rich technological environment, a situation that is confirmed by the Kaiser Family Foundation reports. They recognized that very young children were watching television, but until *Teletubbies* there was little programming created specifically for them. Davenport explained that the function of *Teletubbies* is "to encourage children to become screen literate; it's going to be a world of screens rather than pages when they grow up" (BBC "Teletubbies FAQ" 4). The Kaiser Family Foundation reports on children's media use, *Zero to Six* and *Generation M²*, only confirm Davenport's prediction. According to *Generation M²*, "Eight- to eighteen-year-olds spend more time with media than in any other activity besides (maybe) sleeping—an average of more than 7 1/2 hours a day" (Rideout, Vanderwater, and Wartella). Given that children were already watching television, Wood and Davenport concluded it would be more appropriate to have them viewing quality programs that were specifically created for them.

PBS children's television programs—such as *Sesame Street*, first aired in 1969 and *Barney and Friends*, first aired in 1992—were created for slightly older children than was *Teletubbies*, but it is certainly true that some toddlers and infants have watched these PBS programs. These popular children's television programs were constructed to be faster paced in a style that psychologists suggest is inappropriate and confusing for very young children. Virginia Heffernan reported in "Sweeping the Clouds Away," in an 18 November 2007 *New York Times Magazine* article, that while the earliest episodes of *Sesame Street* are now available on DVD, Volumes 1 and 2 of *Sesame Street: Old School* (2007) now include the warning: "These early *Sesame Street* episodes are intended for grown-ups, and may not suit the needs of today's preschool child" (63). The closest counterpart for *Teletubbies* was *Blue's Clues*, which was in active production from 1996–2006, although it can still be seen in the United States on Nickelodeon. This children's television program is much slower paced and more repetitive than PBS's *Sesame Street*. Both *Blue's Clues* and *Teletubbies* were created based on research of young children and their television watching behavior that had developed since the début of *Sesame Street* in 1969. Malcolm Gladwell has contrasted the different educational theories and media designs of *Blue's Clues* and *Sesame Street* in *Tipping Point: How Little Things Can Make a Big Difference* (2000). Gladwell explains the effectiveness of the "stickiness factor" of these programs and how they improve the retention of educational content with very young viewers (91–93). One only has to consider the calm, highly repetitive pacing of *Teletubbies* in contrast to the more frenetic pace of *Sesame Street*, which took its inspiration from television commercials, to realize that these programs were intended for different ages of children. It is the slow pacing and constant use of repetition of *Teletubbies* that makes the program accessible to infants and toddlers but tends to irritate older viewers, especially adults. After viewing the live-action "Come and See" segment that appears on the television sets that are embedded in their stomachs, the Teletubbies request to see it, "Again, Again," and this segment is repeated. Much of the dialogue among the Teletubbies simply repeats the information that has been provided to the viewer by the narrator. With the success of *Teletubbies* and *Blue's Clues* and the acknowledgement that viewership of the program includes very young children, *Sesame Street* has also modified and slowed down some of its pacing so that it resembles the more deliberate pacing of some of these other children's programs.

Within months of its première, *Blue's Clues* became the highest rated show for preschoolers on commercial television (Gladwell 111). Given that *Sesame Street* was aired on PBS and available to anyone owning a television while *Blue's Clues* was aired on Nickelodeon, a cable station with a more limited audience, this success is even more impressive. It does seem as if PBS was searching for a preschool program that could become the PBS equivalent of Nickelodeon's *Blue's Clues*, when they found BBC's *Teletubbies*. The "Educational Philosophy" for *Teletubbies* on the PBSKids.org website suggests to parents that "Teletubbies provides a new generation of television viewers—the youngest and most impressionable—with the opportunity to feel safe in and enjoy the ever-changing world" (4).

Teletubbyland is an adult-free zone where the Teletubbies interact with their viewers, in much the same way that Steve or Joe, the calm narrators of *Blue's Clues*, speak directly to the viewer. But in *Teletubbies*, it is a child figure speaking directly to a child viewer, as is the case with *Dora the Explorer*. Building on the research involving young children and their television-watching behavior, these programs strive to make television watching a highly interactive experience. The language that the Teletubbies use to converse with one another and address the viewer is a sort of toddler talk, so that Po's scooter is often pronounced "cooter." Davenport, a linguist, developed the scripts for the program and created the Tubby language to duplicate the speaking efforts of a one-year-old—designed to aid children's speech development. Despite the concerns of some parents that the program's language might encourage young viewers to mispronounce words, only fifteen percent of the dialogue is presented in Tubby speak, while the majority of the program is spoken in standard English by way of voiceovers and the "Come and See" segments.

But the process of watching television is at the heart, or more accurately, at the tummy of *Teletubbies*, which is the center of any infant's universe. As the title of the television program makes explicit, each of the Teletubbies has a television screen implanted in its stomach. Watching television has become as natural as eating and sleeping for children. The aspect most difficult for adults to stomach is that in each episode of the program the Teletubbies gather as a group at the top of a hill and wait expectantly for one of them to receive a television transmission to be played on one of their screens. In a self-referential move, the child viewer watches the Teletubbies, as the characters watch television. The Teletubbies model television-watching behavior, which clearly brings them great pleasure, and becomes the prompt for their subsequent play. The Teletubbies view live-action "Come and See" segments narrated by young children. Judith Williamson has argued that *Teletubbies* celebrates and denaturalizes the conventions of television for children, enabling even toddlers to experience themselves as viewers (Margaronis 34). While one of the key elements of *Barney and Friends* is singing, the most important elements of *Teletubbies* are simple physical actions and movements as the characters learn through play. Much of the program is focused on walking and exploring as the Teletubbies learn to navigate their magical world.

Wood, who had previously produced other successful BBC preschool children's programs including *Tots TV* and *Rosie and Jim*, explains that "The Teletubbies live in the land where television comes from, in the land of childhood, in the land of nursery rhymes" ("Nine Ways" 5). *Teletubbies* bridges the traditional concept of childhood, where a parent might lull an infant to sleep with a lullaby or where children entertain themselves with a jump rope rhyme, to the postmodern world, where children entertain themselves by watching television. Television has become such an integral part of postmodern childhood that it is now on equal footing with picture books and stuffed animals. The PBS *Teletubbies* website features a "PBS Parents FAQ" and its first question is, "Don't the television sets in the Teletubbies tummies promote television viewing?" The PBS response is, "Television is part of our daily culture, and serves as a window to the world for many families and young children" and add that ninety-nine percent of U.S. homes have a television set ("PBS Parents FAQ" 1). Given this media-rich environment, Wood maintains that very young children, even infants, are shaped by this media revolution that is symptomatic of postmodern culture. Gil Scott-Heron famously announced, "The revolution will not be televised," in the song of the same name on his 1970 album *Small Talk at 125th and Lenox* (Scott-Heron). But when it comes to children's culture, the revolution is television. According to *Zero to Six*, "59% of all children under two watch TV every day" (Rideout, Vandewater, and Wartella 5). The same study reports that seventy-four percent of all infants and toddlers have watched TV before the age of two (Rideout, Vandewater, and Wartella 5).

So the least fantastical aspect of *Teletubbies* turns out to be when the characters watch television. Just as the Romantic Era experienced the increasing transformation of children's culture from oral to print, postmodern culture is beginning to experience the gradual transformation of children's print culture to screen culture.

Teletubbies is the literal embodiment of Marshall McLuhan's famous aphorism in *Understanding Media: The Extensions of Man* (1964) that, "the medium is the message" (7). The primary message of this educational children's television program is that the watching of television has become so internalized that it has become a natural function akin to eating, speaking, or sleeping for toddlers. Technology is rapidly transforming American childhood. *Teletubbies* more accurately reflects the lives of most American children than the television-free world of *The Cat in the Hat*. Television has become an essential aspect of postmodern childhood along with playing with stuffed animals or reading picture books. The various Kaiser Family Foundation reports suggest that television and other screen media are beginning to play a far more significant role in postmodern childhood than reading print texts. While this may be unsettling for adults who came of age in a primarily print culture, it also argues for the increased development of carefully designed educational television programs for young children, such as *Teletubbies*.

Douglas Rushkoff in *Playing the Future: How Kids' Culture Can Teach Us to Thrive in an Age of Chaos* (1996) goes one step further and argues that adults who wish to adapt to the contemporary cyberculture would do well to take their cues from children's television programs and video games. *Teletubbies* was one of the first children's programs to prominently feature the program's website, which was intended for both children and adults, at the conclusion of each episode. It is increasingly common for children's television programs, children's authors, and individual children's books to feature a website. Rushkoff argues that both children and adults need to accept technological change as a constant and that adults need to model themselves after contemporary "screenagers," those children "born into culture mediated by television and computers" (3). Perhaps a good first step for very young children to help them and their parents enter into this world of new media might be watching *Teletubbies*. Maria Margaronis in *The Nation* has noted that *Teletubbies* is "indeed radically child-centered" in that it "neither patronizes children like *Barney & Friends* nor tries to amuse their parents like *Sesame Street*" and that "there is no didactic, adult bottom line" (3).

Yet the creation of a television program whose primary audience is composed of children two years old and younger is deeply troubling to many adults, especially parents. Rather than mandating no television for very young children, perhaps it would be more realistic to recommend limited viewing to age-appropriate or content-appropriate television programs. The American Academy of Pediatrics media guidelines recommend avoiding the use of any screen media, including television, as an electronic babysitter, and the co-viewing by an adult and discussing the content of children's television programs with the child ("Media Education" 341). Laudable concepts, but difficult to achieve in the context of postmodern parenting. The recommendation that parents should limit the amount of television viewing by children to two hours a day of quality programming is even less than the amount reported by John Hersey in 1954. The American Academy of Pediatrics media guidelines reflect an elitist bias since many contemporary families lack a stay-at-home parent or do not employ a full-time daycare provider to monitor television usage of children. Television as a form of an electronic babysitter is an extremely tempting option for many busy parents. Given the rise of dual working-parent and single-parent families, this appeal has only increased since the initial airing of *Teletubbies* in 1998.

Gina Kolata has reported in "Muddling Fact and Fiction and Policy," in the 8 August 1999 issue of the *New York Times*, that neuroscientists have dismissed the American Academy of Pediatrics position that television should be discouraged. However, there seems to be no research to support the American Academy of Pediatrics claims. Dr. Marjorie Hogan, the chief author of the American Academy of Pediatrics report, acknowledged that there are "no studies with young children showing actual brain changes occurring with television viewing," and that the American Academy of Pediatrics "extrapolated" from other research to "infer that children's brains are harmed when they spend their time gazing at television screens instead of interacting with humans" (Kolata 5). A similar misguided extrapolation is the so-called "Mozart Effect," a test done on college students, which showed that they performed slightly better on tests after listening to ten minutes of Mozart. John Bruer, in *The Myth of the First Three Years: A New Understanding of Early Brain Development and Lifelong Learning* (1998), has shown that the "Mozart Effect" evolved into the popular but mistaken notion that playing Mozart, and by extension any sort of classical music, will make young children smarter (200–01). Pediatricians are not trained as media specialists, although the American Academy of Pediatrics recommends that "pediatricians should begin incorporating questions about media use into their routine" ("Media Education" 341). The American Academy of Pediatrics guidelines seem to promote a more Romantic concept of childhood than the one that is being articulated on *Teletubbies*. The very young children who are not supposed to watch any television at all are actually exceeding the daily recommendation of television viewing proposed for older children. PBS officials argue that since children under two are watching television, it is better to have them watch quality programming, like *Teletubbies*, created specifically to encourage these very young children to learn. Yet organizations such as the American Academy of Pediatrics insist:

> Although certain television programs may be promoted to this age group, research on early brain development shows that babies and toddlers have critical need for direct interaction with parents and other significant care givers (eg, child care providers) for healthy brain growth and the developments of appropriate social, emotional, and cognitive skills. Therefore, exposing such young children to television programs should be discouraged. ("Media Education" 341)

So which side of this ongoing debate promotes the Romantic concept of children? *Teletubbies* seems to offer a utopian world of childhood that encourages cooperation, independence, individuality, and creativity for very young children. Under the protective eyes of the laughing baby sun, *Teletubbies* celebrates the innocence of young children joyfully playing in an idealistic postmodern garden. Critics insist that television is the dangerous serpent that lurks in the garden. Leo Marx has noted in *The Machine in the Garden: Technology and the Pastoral Ideal in America* (1964) that American writers have long recognized "the contradiction between the rural myth and the technological fact" (354). While *Teletubbies* has the appearance of a pastoral landscape, it is a carefully designed television program intended to introduce very young viewers to the world of technology within this world of unspoiled nature. Children's television and its growing brood of vipers of other forms of screen media have made a permanent home in the contemporary garden of childhood, and to many adults these seem to threaten the health and safety of children. Others view television programs such as *Teletubbies* and other screen media as simply a new form of technology that can effectively be used to entertain and educate even very young children. Clearly *Teletubbies* has begun the process of creating screen media for very young children, and how such media will influence young children is still very open to debate. This groundbreaking program, and subsequent television programs created for toddlers and infants that it has inspired, have destabilized previous notions of children and childhood and reconfirm that childhood is very much a social construct that is profoundly influenced by changes in technology. Parents and children are encouraged to enter this ambiguous postmodern garden of childhood at their own risk.

WORKS CITED

BBC. "Nine Ways to Learn with the Teletubbies." *BBC: Teletubbies.* 1–6. Web. 5 June 1999.

———. "Teletubbies FAQ (Frequently Asked Questions)." *BBC: Teletubbies.* 1–7. Web. 5 June 1999.

Bruer, John T. *The Myth of the First Three Years: A New Understanding of Early Brain Development and Lifelong Learning.* New York: Free Press, 1999. Print.

Committee on Public Education. "American Academy of Pediatrics: Children, Adolescents, and Television." *Pediatrics* 107:2 (2 Feb. 2001): 423–26. Print.

———. "American Academy of Pediatrics: Media Education." *Pediatrics* 104.2 (2 Aug. 1999): 341–43. Print.

Gladwell, Malcolm. "The Stickiness Factor: *Sesame Street, Blue's Clues* and the Educational Virus." *The Tipping Point: How Little Things Can Make a Big Difference.* Boston: Little Brown, 2000. 89–132. Print.

Heffernan, Virginia. "Sweeping the Clouds Away." *New York Times Magazine* (18 Nov. 2007): 63–64. Print.

Hersey, John. "Why Do Students Bog Down on the First R?: A Local Committee Sheds Light on a National Problem: Reading." *Life* (24 May 1954): 136–50. Print.

Kolata, Gina. "Muddling Fact and Fiction and Policy." *New York Times* (8 Aug. 1999): Week in Review. 5. Print.

Margaronis, Maria. "Teletubbies." *Nation* (16 March 1998): 32. Print.

Marx, Leo. *The Machine in the Garden: Technology and the Pastoral Ideal in America.* New York: Oxford UP, 1964. Print.

McLuhan, Marshall. *Understanding Media: The Extensions of Man.* New York: New American Library, 1964. Print.

Opie, Iona, and Peter Opie, eds. Introduction. *The Oxford Dictionary of Nursery Rhymes.* Oxford: Clarendon Press, 1951. 1–43. Print.

PBS. "Educational Philosophy." *Teletubbies: PBSKids.org.* 1–2. Web. 1 Jan 2011.

———. "PBS Parents: FAQ." *Teletubbies: PBSKids.org.* 1. Web. 1 Jan. 2011.

Rideout, Victoria J., Elizabeth A. Vandewater, and Ellen A. Wartella. *Zero to Six: Electronic Media in the Lives of Infants, Toddlers and Preschoolers.* Menlo Park, CA: Kaiser Family Foundation Report 3378. 2003. Print.

Rideout, Victoria J., Ulla G. Foehr, and Donald F. Roberts. *Generation M²: Media in the Lives of 8- to 18-Year Olds.* Menlo Park, CA: Kaiser Family Foundation Report 8010. 2010. Print.

Rushkoff, Douglas. *Playing the Future: How Kids' Culture Can Teach Us to Thrive in an Age of Chaos.* New York: Harper Collins, 1996. Print.

Samburg, Bridget. "Notebook: Tinky Winky Trouble." *Brill's Content.com.* May 1999. Web. 1 January 2011.

RODERICK MCGILLIS

⤜ The Sustaining Paradox

Romanticism and Alan Moore's Promethea Novels

"The apocalypse has already happened, and it will happen again."
—Lex van der Raadt

In 1957, Frank Kermode published *Romantic Image* and put paid to the half century of resistance to the lure of Romanticism expressed by writers as diverse as T. S. Eliot, F. L. Lucas, F. R. Leavis, and T. E. Hulme. Since then, the continuing influence of Romanticism right up to our own day is pretty much a given. In 1985, Jerome McGann published *The Romantic Ideology*, and perhaps we thought we had shucked the Romantic ideology in favor of a postmodernist relativism. But for diehard utopians, Romanticism offers a healthy dose of skeptical idealism. Alan Moore is a diehard skeptical idealist, and his debt to William Blake specifically and Romanticism generally is clear. Moore offers overt references to Blake, Shelley, and others in *Watchmen* (1986–1987), *V for Vendetta* (1982–1985), *From Hell* (1991–1996), and *Promethea* (1999–2004). Each of these graphic novels (each first appeared serially and then came out in one volume or in the case of *Promethea*, in five volumes) explores Moore's fascination with the convergence of popular culture with myth and magic. Both *V for Vendetta* and *From Hell* offer anamorphic versions of history, the former playing with the Guy Fawkes story and the latter recreating the Jack the Ripper saga. Both *Watchmen* and *Promethea* revision the superhero comic of mid-twentieth-century

America, the former chronicling the exploits of a group of superheroes in the 1980s, and the latter positing a mythic female version of the Greek titan Prometheus. My interest is in what McGann identified as Romantic ideology and its continuing relevance for any comprehensive approach to the problem of "being." If I focus on Alan Moore, I do so for convenience rather than for specificity. Despite his distinctive vision, Moore reflects the inescapability of the Romantic ideology, and I propose to explore this ideology as it percolates in both the form and content of Moore's work.

Moore scripts graphic novels and he works closely with the artists who provide the graphics. His scripts are famously lengthy, with detailed instructions concerning the visual aspect of the comic book page as well as the dialogue and narrative blocks that propel the story. His work is, in other words, a form of what Jean Hagstrum termed "composite art." We can locate the source for this kind of graphic narrative far back on cave walls or on the tombs of Egyptian pharaohs. We can do this, but really a more immediate source for the graphic novel is in the mid to late eighteenth century with the work of William Hogarth and more obviously William Blake. I will take Blake as ground zero for my analysis of Moore. Moore commented on Blake for the *Observer* newspaper (22 October 2000), saying,

> I read Blake at O level, but studied him seriously when I was researching *From Hell*, my book about Jack the Ripper, which has lots of references to Blake; him seeing a spectre at his house in Hercules Road, for example. Blake represents the visionary heroism of the imagination. He was living in a London which was not much more than a squalid horse toilet, on which he superimposed a magnificent four-fold city and populated it with angels, and philosophers of the past. Art at its best has the power to insist on a different reality. (Spencer)

Both artists are furiously independent, and they both tackle tradition with an eye to preserving and at the same time transforming tradition. Opposition is true friendship, and for these artists paradox is all we know and all we need to know. Both men are visionaries who tackle the mysteries of apocalypse. Whereas for Blake, apocalypse reveals an eternal and ongoing struggle for the perfectibility of humanity, for Moore, apocalypse reveals a darker side. The future from the perspective of the late twentieth and early twenty-first centuries is ambiguous at best. The Romantic position that situates humanity uneasily in nature is evident from the outset of Moore's major work.

SWAMP THING AND "THE SLEEP OF REASON"

Early in his career, Moore evokes the Romantic ethos when he recreates the DC Comics character, Swamp Thing, a character created by Len Wein and Berni Wrightson in 1971. Moore's work for *Swamp Thing* begins with issue 20 (January 1984). By the 25th episode Moore has firmly stamped *Swamp Thing* with his writerly vision. As it happens, the final page of issue 24 shows the swamp creature in a pose remarkably reminiscent of William Blake's "Glad Day." (Another visual echo is probably unintended, but nevertheless I cannot resist noting the similarity between Swamp Thing and Blake's Ghost of a Flea, an image that turns up later in Moore's *From Hell*.) Beneath the illustration is the advance notice for issue 25, "The Sleep of Reason." "The Sleep of Reason" issue invokes the famous drawing of the sleeping painter with the horrors of his imagination evident above his slumped body. The image is Plate 43 of Francisco Goya's series of etchings, *Los Caprichos* (1797). Moore's invocation of this image, apparent on page 2 of the comic book and again more clearly as the final panel on the last page (23), directs the reader to Romantic notions of reason and imagination. Both in Goya's image with its inscription, "El sueño de la razón produce monstruos" (the sleep of reason produces monsters), and in Moore's *Swamp Thing* the mind at rest is open to monstrous dreams that might suggest that the human imagination is a dangerous thing when uncontrolled by reason. Such a suggestion, however, is hasty. Moore's interest in magic, an interest that will gain full expression in his later work *Promethea*, is evident in *Swamp Thing* here in issue 25 when the Devil purchases Goya's etching from the comic/magic shop and later in issue 41, "Southern Change," which deals with the murky world of Southern Gothic and conjuring. In fact, *Swamp Thing* is as Gothic as they come. It deals cleverly with matters of incest (issue 29), devilry, vampirism (issues 38 and 39), lycanthropy (issue 40); mental instability (pretty much in every issue), and the amorphousness of evil.

Indeed, *Swamp Thing* is a handbook for Romanticists. First, we have the ecological or green vision of a future when human and vegetable cohabit lovingly. I refer to the Creature and Abigail, who form an affectionate bond. But the ecological theme turns up forcefully in the Floronic Man episode in issue 21 and later in "The Nukeface Papers" (issues 35 and 36). This green vision chronicles the troubled relationship between humans and their environment. By "troubled," I mean simply humanity's penchant for exploiting and even devastating nature. Then we have the focus on dreams and the irrational as forces more powerful than reason and judgment. For Moore, the sleep of reason that produces monsters is a failure of reason. When reason works for humanity it is reason in her most exalted mood; in other words, reason at its best is a form of imaginative activity. Moore's play with Alec Holland's identity also reminds us of Romantic self-consciousness. Holland's struggle is to come to terms with his realization that he is no longer the person he thought he was; in fact, he is no longer a person at all. He is now a new life form, a sentient plant, a truly sensitive plant. The creature Holland has become reminds us of that most famous of Romantic creatures, Frankenstein's monster. Created by a science gone wild, the Swamp Thing represents Romanticism's revenge on the Enlightenment. Moore returns to this theme in the monstrous activities of the Royal physician Sir William Gull in *From Hell*. Gull is a Freemason who allows his mystical training to excuse and explore his psychic perversions. He is a trained physician who lives out the sleep of reason. He is, in other words, the obverse of Alec Holland, who tries frantically to maintain reason in the face of a hideously irrational reality.

This hideously irrational reality brings me to the final connection to Romanticism: apocalypse. Romanticism is an end time state of mind. It takes an interest in apocalyptic vision, but a particular kind of apocalyptic vision. Perhaps Coleridge gives us as good an explanation as we could wish for when he writes in "Dejection : An Ode": "Joy, Lady! is the spirit and the power, / Which wedding Nature to us gives in dower, / A new Earth and new Heaven." The Romantic apocalypse delivers a vision of a renewed earth, a marriage of Heaven and Hell, a release of Promethean energies in an epithalamion such as we have in act 4 of Shelley's *Prometheus Unbound*. This apocalypse unites the various facets of the Romantic vision: self-consciousness, ecological harmony, and dream and reality. Our life is no dream, but it ought and may become one. Romantic apocalypse envisages a unified earth; it is a secular vision of what happens in the final book of the Bible. But another side of this vision exists, a dark Romantic apocalypse seen in a poem such as Byron's "Prometheus" or in Mary Shelley's novel, *The Last Man*. This secular vision is less optimistic than the work touched by the euphoria of July 14, 1789; it reflects the pessimism rising from the failure of that revolution. This inverted apocalypse informs our contemporary sense of end times, and Moore's work shares more with this vision than it does with the ecstatic visions of the Romantic renovated earth. By the time Moore began his career, he had lived to see and reflect on the flower-power, age-of-Aquarius 1960s, as well as the Cold War with its fear of nuclear annihilation and the Vietnam War with its nonsensical sense of a never-ending conflict that takes place in a surreal setting. Both the Cold War and the Vietnam War introduce us to what we now think of as the posthuman, although we might locate the first suggestions of the posthuman at least as early as Romantic works such as E. T. A. Hoffmann's "Sandman" or Mary Shelley's *Frankenstein*. In "Sandman," the posthuman is evident in the automaton Olympia, a character familiar to those who know Offenbach's opera, *Tales of Hoffmann*; in *Frankenstein*, of course, the posthuman is the monster, a creation formed from various human remains. In any case, *Swamp Thing*, and especially Alan Moore's *Swamp Thing*, presents an apocalyptic vision that includes the posthuman. Moore's Alec Holland is clearly a new life form, neither biologically human nor fully botanical. He is the creation of a science gone out of whack. As a posthuman entity, he participates in human desire, the desire to love and be loved. Alec Holland engages in what Morse Peckham identified as the fundamental Romantic exercise: the intellectual struggle to locate meaning in a world that has dislocated meaning.

DESIRE AND FORM

I begin with one example, a double-page spread from Book 3 of *Promethea* (2002). Before I look at this double-page spread, I notice the protagonist of this book—Promethea. Romanticism took an intense interest in Prometheus, the messianic hero who helps humans despite Zeus's strictures against Prometheus's philanthropic endeavors. Prometheus is one manifestation of the Romantic hero: strong, self-sacrificing, self-conscious, and fiercely independent. Prometheus is the high mimetic hero who represents a masculine ideal. He is, arguably, the liberal humanist vision of the great man. We see him as representative of victorious humanity in Shelley's *Prometheus Unbound*. In this great visionary work, Prometheus is the human form divine. What Alan Moore and his collaborators, J. H. Williams III and Mick Gray, perform is a masterstroke of updating, making Prometheus female and undifferentiated. In *Promethea*, the title character appears at first glance to be a version of Wonder Woman; however, this Amazon is quite unlike Promethea. Promethea is not one but several women who take their place in various times. The implication is that Promethea is not an individual, but rather she is a function, or better yet, a state of mind. In his study of the comic book, *Reading Comics*, Douglas Wolk notes that the latest incarnation of Promethea, Sophie Bangs, can invoke the physical presence of the mythical heroine "by acts of imagination and creativity" (246).

"Imagination and creativity" invoke Romanticism in all its anti-Enlightenment glory. But as the formal symmetries of Moore's work make clear, his Romanticism is not simply atavistic, but rather it is, in good Coleridgean fashion, esemplastic. Take a look at this double-page spread from chapter 15.

Here is a visual and verbal field that has no beginning and no end, a Moebius strip that allows the reader to begin anywhere and follow a loop that demands a topsy-turvy reading, literally since the reader has to turn the book upside down if she wishes to read all the speech balloons. At the same time, this visual and verbal field does have a beginning and an end. The reader begins by turning to the previous page and ends by turning to the following page. The Moebius strip is both self-contained and set in a context that asks that we read beyond the strip. In other words, the Moebius strip is an embodiment of paradox, and paradox nicely combines both imagination and reason. As we look at the double-page spread, we see the clash of Romantic and Enlightenment imagery. The strip represents the infinite possibility of Romantic desire, whereas the pyramidal shapes in the distance remind us of the geometry of Newtonian science. A sort of alchemy brings together disparate images and the strip itself begins to look like a mask through which we see the world. This mask is also a fallen number eight resting on infinity or at least on the openness of galaxies unexplored. At work in the visual field is a dialectic of frames and broken frames. The strip crosses the borders between the five panels, and the

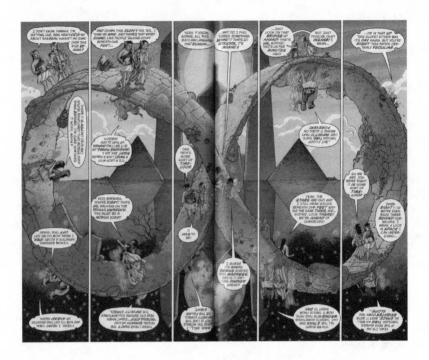

A double-page spread from book 3 of Alan Moore's *Promethea* (2002), showing a Moebius strip (no start, no finish), allowing the reader to begin anywhere. Copyright © DC Comics, used by permission of DC Comics.

speech balloons serve as both a frame at that top and bottom, and as a sign of randomness as they are scattered through the middle of the panels. The viewer sees here a fearful symmetry.

Alan Moore's work, then, rests on the foundations of what he might call "magic," the latter-day Romanticism of the Golden Dawn and Aleister Crowley. But it does so in the way Yeats's poetry rests on secret or kabbalistic material or Blake's work rests on a personal mythology. Alan Moore's work updates its source material in what we might call a postmodern dance of selves. Even a book like *Watchmen* tests the notion of the individuated self. The lone figure, like the marooned sailor in *The Black Freighter* (the interpolated comic book in *Watchman*) or like Adrian Veidt, lives a horror of isolation and missteps; the contemporary figure is a collective figure, a combination of caped searchers after meaning and clarity and common humanity with its desires and weaknesses. The Romantic enterprise is always utopian, but its utopianism comes with a necessary knowledge that utopia, like the individual, is never finished. One of the chapters in *Promethea* has the title "Metaphore." Metaphor contains the essential paradox; the vehicle in any metaphor both is and is not the tenor. Once again, what we have here is a fearful symmetry.

FEARFUL SYMMETRY AND *WATCHMEN*

Watchmen confronts Romantic and Enlightenment ideas self-consciously, and it does so in the two characters, Dr. Manhattan and Adrian Veidt. Manhattan, like Alec Holland before him, represents science gone wild, although unlike Holland, Manhattan represents the end product of science working, ostensibly at least, to advance the post human condition. Manhattan is virtually the human being developed to its godly potential. Neither time nor space restricts Manhattan. He is invulnerable to everything but desire. But this magical being perceives reality as the Enlightenment watchmaker. In Manhattan we have the deist's god: the watchmaker who designs an intricate machine with its escapements and cogs, winds this machine to start it running, and then steps back to watch the machine work. Manhattan's world is a world that runs according to the machinery, but that machinery can malfunction and produce the threat of nuclear disaster as well as brutal events such as the Vietnam War (a war that in this book comes to an end because of the presence of Manhattan). Because Manhattan concludes (more for emotional than for scientific reasons) that humanity is not worth his efforts, he plans to create a new world and set it going. In Manhattan, we have the Enlightenment project taken to its ultimate possibility, but the apocalyptic result of Manhattan's activities does not appear attractive. In this vision we have loneliness, full predictability, selfishness, and individuation without community.

Contrasting Manhattan, we have Adrian Veidt. Moore calls Veidt "an enlightened human." He goes on to say that he "is fiercely intelligent, and he believes that—he's a lot like a Nietzschean character—it's the individual man taking responsibility for his circumstances that can change the world. Unfortunately, he perhaps believes in taking that kind of belief to its extreme and you end up with an arrogance that borders on delusions of godhead" (Khoury 113). Veidt takes for his superhero identity the name Ozymandias, invoking not only the Egyptian ruler Ramesses the Great, but also Percy Shelley's sonnet "Ozymandias." Like his namesake in Shelley's poem, Veidt is a Romantic overreacher. He has a plan to create chaos by bringing a nuclear disaster to America in order to force humanity to stop fighting and live peacefully. In other words, he believes the end will justify the means even though the means will cause countless deaths. Whereas Manhattan sees order and balanced design as necessity, Veidt sees the means to order in disorder. Perhaps this is why Moore names a central chapter devoted to Veidt "Fearful Symmetry." The invocation of William Blake's "The Tyger" suits Veidt, who is both well meaning and frightfully maniacal. On what wings dares Veidt aspire? In what furnace burns his brain? We have Veidt's Romantic sublime contrasted with Manhattan's cool Brobdingnagian menace.

Fearful symmetry nicely captures the sensibility at work in *Watchmen*, and in Moore's work generally. It contains paradox. What does it mean for symmetry to be fearful? First, that which is symmetrical may be sinister in its perfection. This is symmetry serving to keep things in place. This is classicism in all its conservative and political regularity. Second, symmetry is fearful when it somehow breaks the very order that it creates. For Blake, the tyger represents such symmetry; it is both a consummate creation and a frightful force. The symmetry of the tyger presents us with a mystery. Blake's depiction of the tyger appears anything but frightful in the illustration, serving to contrast the fearful creature in the poem. The symmetry Blake offers his reader is fearful because it is mysterious and hence uncontrollable, unknowable.

The phrase "fearful symmetry" serves as the title to chapter 5, which contains a variety of symmetrical patterns both visually and verbally, culminating in the unconventional wordless double-page spread at the center of this chapter.

Just as there are six stanzas in Blake's "Tyger," we have six panels running down pages 14 and 15. These panels frame a central elongated picture of Adrian Veidt clonking his attacker. These outer panels dare frame that central symmetry. These panels deliver a mirror effect, and mirroring is an insistent motif here. In the elongated central panel the water serves as mirror, but the two figures of the standing Veidt and the falling attacker mirror

The "fearful symmetry" of the unconventional wordless double-page spread, showing a triumphant Ozymandias, in *Watchmen*. Copyright © DC Comics, used by permission of DC Comics.

also each other. On the horizontal plane, the decorative head of Ramesses mirrors the head of the falling attacker in an irony we might call Romantic. Indeed, the entire page is replete with competing ironies. Just prior to this page, Veidt and his secretary have entered the huge foyer of Veidt's building. They have been talking about morbidity and death, Veidt arguing that the ancient Egyptians saw death "as launching on a voyage of spiritual discovery" and his secretary countering these words with her interest in a pay raise, in Gloria Vanderbilt, or in MTV. To her, thinking of these things is comforting (13). Then we turn the page and view the silent encounter of the attacker and his victims.

The central panel here with its large yellow V behind Veidt reminds us of his narcissism. But it also looks forward to *V for Vendetta*, the book Moore would complete the year after he published the complete *Watchmen*. Here the vendetta is as much internal as it is external, Veidt battling his inner demons as he sets out to force humanity to be better than it is. He and his would-be murderer are mirror images of each other. What is fearful about this symmetry is the attraction of this very repulsive character, Adrian Veidt. He represents both the best in human potential and the perversion of this best. We notice the yellow flower he wears, his boutonnière. Yellow is a main color motif in the book, associated most insistently with the smiley button that first appears on the front cover and then throughout the text until its final appearance in the book's final panel. Both this final panel and the cover (which shows an extreme close-up of this button as it appears in the final panel) present the smiley button with a smear of red across the right eye. Similarly, in the final panel on page 15, we see Adrian Veidt's yellow boutonnière with a smear of red across it. The symmetry is apparent, yet not quite exact. Adrian is a good guy, but an uneasy, even dangerous good guy. The flower reminds us of the smiley face, but in reminding us it also lets us know the importance of difference. When is a smiley face not a smiley face? When it is a flower.

Such ambiguity works throughout this book, perhaps most compellingly in the character of Rorschach. Rorschach, with his constantly mobile mask, is an emblem of fearful symmetry. His mask is a moving Rorschach test. The pattern on the mask continually changes its symmetrical patterns; and as the patterns change the symmetry is broken, and then reassembled (Zach Snyder's film version of *Watchmen* captures this effect well). Rorschach is as clear-sighted as a person can be. He claims to know right from wrong; he claims moral laws are unbreakable and without ambiguity. For him, good and bad are absolute terms. What is fearful about such clarity, such insistence on a symmetrical approach to morality, is its result in moral failure. If I could find a Romantic equivalent to Rorschach, it would be Robert Wringham in James Hogg's *The Private Memoirs and Confessions of a Justified Sinner* (1824). Like Wringham, Rorschach justifies horrendous acts for their justifiable ends, and like Wringham, he suffers acute mental instability from the effort it takes to sustain such a morally stringent position.

Chapter 5 ends with Rorschach leaping from Moloch's apartment only to find a gaggle of policemen waiting for him. As the police pummel Rorschach, he mumbles to himself: "Must get up. Been framed." The police remove Rorschach's mask and discover what they refer to as "This ugly little zero" who has been "the terror of the underworld." Now they intend to lock him up with his enemies, and one policeman notes that "It's karma, man. Everything evens out eventually. Everything balances" (28). References to framing and balancing remind us of this chapter's obsessive use of fearful symmetry. Like Blake's tyger (and the chapter ends with the first verse of that poem), Rorschach is both fearful and insignificant. He is a character driven by desire, as are all the characters in this work. This desire, ultimately, is for a return to that which never was. In Lacanian terms, Rorschach and the others desire a time and a place when subject and object had not been ruptured. If I turn to Adrian Veidt again, I notice that his desire for a period of peace and unity depends on the chaos of the Real, that amorphous state in which the self is lost amid the swirl of unmeaning. This goes some way to explaining one of the Veidt corporation's products: the perfume Nostalgia.

NOSTALGIA FOR THE REAL

Nostalgia defines Romanticism, but in a richly ambiguous manner. What one knows about Romanticism is its interest in the child, and perhaps the best-known expression of Romantic childhood appears in Wordsworth's "Ode on the Intimations of Immortality" (1802–1804). Here the child is a sage and seer blest, coming into the world trailing clouds of glory. The time of childhood is the time of splendor in the grass. The desire for childhood expressed in this poem is a longing for the past, a wish that we could go home again. Nostalgia of this kind looks behind and seeks the security of the way things were. Such nostalgia is doomed to frustration because the way things were is always the way we imagined things were, and such imagining is always an imagining of that which we desire rather than that which actually existed or could exist again. But this nostalgia is only one possibility for that longing for home we call nostalgia. Wordsworth's poem ends with the lines, "To me the meanest flower that blows can give / Thoughts that do often lie too deep for tears" (http://www .bartleby.com/101/536.html). The poet feels that he has received abundant recompense for growing up and leaving behind the pastoral virtues of childhood. In short, those thoughts that lie too deep for tears remind us of the freshness of each day; they look forward as much as they look back. In other words, nostalgia can look forward when it sees the past as formative for the future. In *Watchmen*, the play of nostalgia is evident in the transition from the Veidt company's perfume called Nostalgia to its new product called Millennium.

Throughout *Watchmen* we see advertisements for the perfume Nostalgia. The label is a cue for the book's look back at the superhero tradition in American comics. Moore has made no secret that the early idea for *Watchmen* was to "come up with a new treatment for the Charlton characters" (Khoury 109). Charlton Comics was an American comic book publisher from 1946 to 1985; it had a range of superhero characters that included Captain Atom, Mercury Man, Son of Vulcan, and Peter Cannon, Thunderbolt. The prose sections at the end of all but the final chapter of *Watchmen* draw heavily on the history of not only the Charlton line of superheroes, but the superhero comic in general. *Watchmen* offers a nostalgic look back at the superhero tradition in American comics. Clearly, Moore's characters fondly recreate the worlds of Metropolis and Gotham City and the other settings for superhero action. Nite Owl invokes DC's Batman, Rorschach invokes Charlton's The Question, the Comedian perversely invokes Captain America, and so on. This nostalgia for the early age of American superhero comics reflects a reactionary desire to return to a more innocent time before the terrors of Vietnam and the Cold War.

Return is, however, not an option. As Adrian Veidt unleashes a disaster of huge proportions on the city of New York, any nostalgia seems sorely out of joint. After the city begins its recovery from the disaster, the Veidt company comes out with a new cologne called Millennium. Millennium replaces Nostalgia, but not really. Millennium is just another word for nostalgia, although this is a forward-looking nostalgia with apocalyptic proportions, if nostalgia may be said to have proportions. After he causes the great deaths in New York, Adrian asks Manhattan if he did the right thing, saying that "it all worked out in the end." Manhattan's response is:

"In the end? Nothing ends, Adrian. Nothing ever ends" (chapter XII, 27). The apocalypse has already happened and it will happen again. Millennium refers to that thousand year period when Satan is bound and Christ reigns; in other words, the millennium is a period of peace and harmony, but it is time bound, fated to end, or at least to change into something else when the thousand years come round. The longing for a better world is, then, a Romantic nostalgia that looks forward knowing that utopia is, truly, nowhere.

THE SUSTAINING PARADOX

This is the paradox: the longing and hope for a better world must continue even in the knowledge that such a better world can never come to pass. Without contraries no progression is possible. Perhaps the point appears in one of Moore's lesser works, *Judgment Day* (1997). The title is apt, if somewhat misleading. The judgment in the story involves a trial in which the murderer of a female superhero is discovered. But Moore is aware of the apocalyptic implications of his title. One of his characters says the court case is "full of revelations. Revelations as in Apocalypse. Revelations as in Judgment Day" (n.p.). Here, as in all of Moore's work, we have the working of paradox. This is paradox as the Romantic ideology conceives it: the blending of the possible and the impossible. This is a vision at once both idealist and skeptical. Another way of articulating Moore's Romantic sense of paradox is available in an article by Roger Whitson. Whitson argues that a defining feature of both William Blake's work and Alan Moore's is the notion of "parallax." "Parallax" is a term Whitson picks up from Kojin Karatani and Slavoj Žižek, and it means "a mechanism of capitalism fixing the subject in a loop of interpellation and transgression favoring a growing, elastic market that can accomodate [sic] both" (Whitson, paragraph 1). For Whitson, both Blake and Moore struggle to find themselves an independent place from which to disseminate their personal and transgressive visions while maintaining at the same time a position in the capitalist marketplace. They position themselves paradoxically in their artistic, political, and spiritual work. In Blakean terms, they combine the energies of both the prolific and the devourer, Orc and Urizen.

NOTE

My thanks to Lex van der Raadt, a graduate student at the University of Calgary, for providing the epigraph to this essay. Lex has also shared with me his interest in and knowledge of comics and popular culture.

WORKS CITED

Coleridge, S. T. "Dejection: An Ode," Accessed online, Bartleby.com, April 28, 2011. http://www.bartleby.com/41/421.html

Hagstrom, Jean H. *William Blake. Poet and Painter. An Introduction to the Illuminated Verse.* Chicago: U of Chicago P. 1964.

Kermode, Frank. *Romantic Image.* London: Routledge and Kegan Paul, 1957.

Khoury, George, and friends. *The Extraordinary Works of Alan Moore.* Raleigh, NC: TwoMorrows Publishing, 2008.

McGann, Jerome J. *The Romantic Ideology: A Critical Investigation.* Chicago: U of Chicago P, 1983.

Moore, Alan, and Eddie Campbell. *From Hell.* Marietta, GA: Top Shelf Productions, 2009.

Moore, Alan, Rob Liefelf, and Gill Kane. *Judgment Day.* Miamisburg, OH: Checker Book Publishing Group, 2003.

Moore, Alan, J. H. Williams III, and Mick Gray. *Promethea.* Book One. La Jolla, CA: America's Best Comics, 1999–2000.

———. *Promethea.* Book Two. La Jolla, CA: WildStorm Productions, 2001.

———. *Promethea.* Book Three. La Jolla, CA: America's Best Comics, 2002.

———. *Promethea.* Book Four. La Jolla, CA: America's Best Comics, 2003.

———. *Promethea.* Book Five. La Jolla, CA: America's Best Comics, 2005.

Moore, Alan, Stephen Bissette, and John Totleben. *The Saga of the Swamp Thing.* Book One. New York: DC Comics, 2009.

———. *The Saga of the Swamp Thing.* Book Two. New York: DC Comics, 2009.

———. *The Saga of the Swamp Thing.* Book Three. New York: DC Comics, 2010.

Moore, Alan, and David Lloyd. *V for Vendetta.* New York: DC Comics, 2005.

Moore, Alan, and Dave Gibbons. *Watchmen.* New York: DC Comics, 1986, 1987.

Peckham, Morse. *Beyond the Tragic Vision: The Quest for Identity in the Nineteenth Century.* New York: George Braziller, 1962.

Spencer, Neil. "Into the Mystic: Visions of Paradise to Words of Wisdom . . . An Homage to the Written Word of William Blake." *The Observer*, October 22, 2000. Accessed online, April 28, 2011. http://www.guardian.co.uk/books/2000/oct/22/classics.williamblake

Whitson, Roger. "Panelling Parallax: The Fearful Symmetry of William Blake and Alan Moore," *ImageTexT: Interdisciplinary Comics Studies*, Volume 3, Issue 2 (2006). Accessed online April 10, 2011. http://www.engl...hitson/index.shtml

Wolk, Douglas. *Reading Comics: How Graphic Novels Work and What They Mean*. Cambridge, MA: De Capo Press, 2007.

Wordsworth, William. "Ode on Intimations of Immortality." Accessed online, Bartleby.com, April 28, 2011. http://www.bartleby.com/101/536.html

Notes on Contributors

JENNIFER SMITH DANIEL received her M.A. in English at the University of North Carolina, Charlotte. She currently teaches in the English composition program and the Core Program in the Liberal Arts at Queens University of Charlotte.

ELIZABETH A. DOLAN is associate professor of English at Lehigh University. Her publications include *Seeing Suffering in Women's Literature of the Romantic Era* (2008); Vol. 12 of *The Collected Works of Charlotte Smith*, which she edited (2007); and *Anna Seward's Life of Erasmus Darwin*, coedited with Philip K. Wilson and Malcolm Dick (2010). She serves as book review editor of the *Keats-Shelley Journal*.

RICHARD FLYNN, professor of Literature at Georgia Southern University, edited the *Children's Literature Association Quarterly* from 2004 to 2009. Recent essays include "The Fear of Poetry" in the *Cambridge Companion to Children's Literature* (2009) and "Randall Jarrell's *The Bat-Poet*: Poets, Children, and Readers in an Age of Prose" in *The Oxford Handbook of Children's Literature* (2011). He has delivered presentations on Bob Dylan and is conducting a series of interviews for Joni Mitchell's official website: http://jonimitchell.com.

ELIZABETH GARGANO is associate professor of English at the University of North Carolina, Charlotte. She has published *Reading Victorian Schoolrooms: Childhood and Education in Nineteenth-Century Fiction* (2008). Her essays have appeared in *Children's Literature*, *Children's Literature Association Quarterly*, *Eighteenth-Century Fiction*, *Women's Studies: An Interdisciplinary Journal*, *Texas Studies in Literature and Language*, and other journals.

MARY ELLIS GIBSON is Elizabeth Rosenthal Professor of English and Women's and Gender Studies at the University of North Carolina, Greensboro. Her most recent books are *Anglophone Poetry in Colonial India*,

1780–1913: A Critical Anthology (2011) and *Indian Angles: English Verse in Colonial India from Jones to Tagore* (2011).

DOROTHY H. MCGAVRAN is professor of English at Queens University of Charlotte. In 1998 she was the inaugural recipient of the Hunter Hamilton Award for Teaching Excellence. For eight years she directed the Core Program in the Liberal Arts at Queens. This is her third published essay on Elizabeth Gaskell.

JAMES HOLT MCGAVRAN, JR., is professor of English at the University of North Carolina–Charlotte. In 2006 he was the recipient of the Bank of America Award for Teaching Excellence. He has published in *European Romantic Review, Children's Literature, Women's Writing*, and other journals. His latest book is *In the Shadow of the Bear: A Michigan Memoir* (2010).

RODERICK MCGILLIS is professor emeritus at the University of Calgary, Canada. He has published *He Was Some Kind of a Man: Masculinities in the B Western* (2009). With John Pennington he coedited *Behind the Back of the North Wind* (2011) and George MacDonald's *At the Back of the North Wind* (2011).

CLAUDIA MILLS is associate professor of philosophy at the University of Colorado, Boulder. She publishes frequently on ethical and philosophical themes in children's literature. She is the author of over forty books for young readers, including most recently *One Square Inch* (2010) and *Mason Dixon: Pet Disasters* (2011).

JOCHEN PETZOLD is professor of British Literature and Cultural Studies at the University of Regensburg, Germany. He has published *Reimagining White Identity by Exploring the Past: History in South African Novels of the 1990s* (2002). He has written on South African children's literature after Apartheid for the *Children's Literature Association Quarterly* (2005) and on the militarization of cricket in Victorian boys' magazines for the *Journal for the Study of British Culture* (2011).

MALINI ROY, an independent scholar, has worked at the Sussex Centre for Folklore, Fairy Tales and Fantasy (University of Chichester, UK). Her doctoral thesis (Oxford 2008) explores representations of the child as a trope of political resistance in the writings and political philosophy of

Mary Wollstonecraft, William Godwin, and Mary and Percy Bysshe Shelley. She is coediting an essay anthology entitled *Space and Place in Children's Literature*.

ANDREW J. SMYTH is associate professor of English at Southern Connecticut University. His research includes studies in Maria Edgeworth, Renaissance literature, and English education. Doing in-country research in Kenya, he has begun a comparative study of secondary teacher training in the English language arts in the light of reform movements in the U.S. and Kenya.

JAN SUSINA is professor of English at Illinois State University, where he teaches courses in children's literature, Victorian studies, and visual culture. He is a former editor of *The Lion and the Unicorn*. He analyzed the Arthur Hughes illustrations for Roderick McGillis and John Pennington's edition of George McDonald's *At the Back of the North Wind* (2011). His *The Place of Lewis Carroll in Children's Literature* (2010) has recently been released in paperback.

Index

Bateman, Richard (Wordsworth character), 8–9, 10
Batten, Guinn, 6
Baumrind, Dianna, 15n5
Beachy Head and Other Poems (Smith), 56
Benjamin, Walter, 28, 32
Bentham, Jeremy, 44
Bhabha, Homi, xx
"The Bird Robbers" (anonymous), 132
"The Bird World" (Gardiner), 144
bird-nesting, 128–45; as adventure, xxi, 137–40, 145; as cruel, 131–37, 142–43, 144, 145, 146n5; morality of, 129–31, 135–37; in periodicals, 131, 146n1, 146n4; prevalence of, 128; as science, 140–44, 145
"Bird-Nesting" (anonymous), 133, 136
"Birds' Eggs and Egg Collecting" (Wood), 142
"The Bird's Nest" (Taylor), 132–33
"Birds'-nesting in Earnest" (Cousin William), 137
Bissette, Stephen, 202–3, 204
blackmail, 102
Blake, William: and Alan Moore, 201; and child slave characters, 69n6; on education, 173–74; "Glad Day," 202; "The Little Black Boy," 69n6; paradoxical position of, 213; and personal mythology, 206; and religious/political themes, 122–23; and Romantic childhood, 32; *Songs of Innocence and Experience*, 32, 122; and *Teletubbies*, 186; "The Tyger," 208, 211
"Blowin' in the Wind" (Dylan), 157, 159–60, 166n6
Blue's Clues, 192, 193
Boggs, Colleen Glenney, 47

Bonaparte, Felicia, 90
Bonca, Teddi Chichester, 31
The Borrowers (Norton), 74
Boulukos, George, 57
bourgeois domesticity, 107
"Boy of Windermere" (Wordsworth), xviii–xix
Boym, Svetlana, 165n2
Boys of Empire, 116
The Boy's Own Magazine, 108, 124n7, 141
The Boy's Own Paper, 138, 142, 143–44
Bracy, Bard, 14n1
British and Foreign Bible Society, 111
Brothers Grimm, 82
"The Brown Bull of Norrowa" (Laski), 78–79, 82, 85
Bruer, John, 197
Bull, Angela, 78
Burke, Edmund, 27
Burnett, Frances Hodgson: *Little Lord Fauntleroy*, 171; *The Little Princess*, 74; *The Secret Garden*, 74, 86n1

Cadell, Thomas, Sr., 58
Calvinism, 113, 123
Campbell, Eddie, 200, 201, 202
Cantwell, Robert, 166n5
capitalism, 6, 9, 11, 51, 119
Carlson, Julie, 14n1
Carroll, Lewis: *Alice's Adventures in Wonderland*, 73–75, 86n1; *Through the Looking-Glass*, 73–75, 86n1; and Victorian children's literature, 123
Cary, Meredith, 41
"Casabianca" (Hemans), 125n9
The Cat in the Hat (Seuss), 190–91, 195
Chad Mitchell Trio, 158
"Chapters for Young Naturalists" (Ullyett), 143

charity, 105

Charlton Comics, 212

Chatterbox, 143

"The Cherry Orchard" (Myers), 51

Chesterton, G. K., 186

"The Child" (Wordsworth), xiii

"childhood-in-crisis," xvi–xvii

Children and Childhood in Western Society Since 1500 (Cunningham), xiv

The Children of the Poor (Cunningham), 27

The Children's Friend, 107, 131, 135, 141

Children's Literature Association Quarterly, xvii

children's rights, 32

The Children's Treasury, 134

Children's World, 111

The Child's Companion, 124n7, 131, 133, 141

The Child's Own, 114

chivalry, 116

"Christabel" (Coleridge), 2–6, 8–10, 12–14, 13n1

Christian Vernacular Education Society, 111

The Chronicles of Narnia (Lewis), 74

Church Missionary Juvenile Instructor, 107, 111

Church Missionary Magazine, 123n2

Church Missionary Society (CMS), 109, 111, 123n2

Church of England, 112

"The Circle Game" (Mitchell), 154–55

"The Claims of the Needy" (Green), 105–6

Clarkson, Thomas, 9, 60, 63

class issues: and economic security of women, 91; and education, xx, 41, 43–44, 46–50; and English

economic life, 6; and gender oppression, 27, 102; and missionary literature, 106–7, 109–10; and myth of carefree childhood, xv; and oppression of women, 22; and patriarchal power, 29; and philanthropy, 27–28; and wealth inequality, xvi; and Wollstonecraft, 34n8

Clemens, Samuel, xiv–xv

Cloke, Paul, xx

coffeehouses, 160–61

Cohen, Ronald, 158, 159

Coleridge, Samuel Taylor: and apocalypticism, 203; "Christabel," 2–6, 8–10, 12–14; "Frost at Midnight," 10; and lost childhood, 2–5, 8, 10–13; *Lyrical Ballads*, xviii, 1, 3, 12, 21, 32, 138; *On the Slave Trade*, 62; "Rime of the Ancient Mariner," 12

Collings, David, 2, 3

colloquial language, 21

Colón, Susan, 93–94

colonialism, 45, 48, 50. *See also* imperialism

comedy, 80

Committee of Public Education of the American Academy of Pediatrics, 184–85

community, identification with, 180

Conrad, Joseph, 2, 13

Conversations Introducing Poetry (Smith), 57

"Conversations on the Band of Mercy" (Arachne), 144

Cooper, Anton Ashley (Lord Ashley), 106

Coral Island, 109

Coral Missionary Magazine, 123n2

education of children: Blake on,
173–74; and class issues, xx, 41,
43–44, 46–50; education policy, xiv,
xvi; in *Émile*, 169–70, 181; and gender issues, 93–95, 98, 140; in *Ida B*,
180–81; pedagogical philosophy,
40–53; and poor children, 48–49;
reforms, 41, 50–51; Rousseau's
model of, 169–71, 172–73, 174,
178; science in, 140–41; in *Skellig*,
173–76; and slavery, 60–62; in
Stargirl, 176–78; in *Surviving the
Applewhites*, 178–79; vs. training,
xvi; Wordsworth on, 174

Edwards, Bryan, 61

Eger, Elizabeth, 44

Elegiac Sonnets (Smith), 56–69

Elliot, Anne (Austen character), 13

Emergency (music club), 161, 166n9

Émile (Rousseau): Edgeworth's reaction to, 45; educational model in,
169–70, 181; and homeschooling in
literature, 172–73; *Ida B* compared
to, 181; natural-world emphasis of,
25, 137; savage ideal in, 170, 175,
181; *Skellig* compared to, 174, 175;
Stargirl compared to, 177–78; *Surviving the Applewhites* compared to, 179;
Wordsworth's opinion of, 8

Emma (Austen), 7

enchantment, 72–73

Enlightenment, 207

Ennui (Edgeworth), 41, 50–51

Enscoe, Gerald, 5

Equiano, Olaudah, 63

*Essay on the Slavery and Commerce of the
Human Species* (Clarkson), 60

*The Essential Principles of the Wealth of
Nations* (Gray), 52

ethical issues: and animal cruelty,
42–43, 131–37, 142–43, 144, 146n5;
animal rights, 40, 47; of childhood
education, 42, 68; and homeschooling, 172; and imperialism, 122; and
love, 28; and materialism, 117; and
missionary magazines, 106–13,
123n2, 124n5; of patriarchal oppression, 29; of philanthropy, 27;
of slavery, 68. *See also* morality

evangelical Christianity: and homeschooling, 172; and imperialism,
122; and materialism, 117; and missionary magazines, 106–13, 123n2,
124n5; and philanthropy, 27

Evenings at Home (Aiken), 58

Every Boy's Annual, 114

Every Boy's Magazine, 138

Every Girl's Annual, 114

Every Girl's Magazine, 116

evolution, xxi, 175–76

experiential education, 8

*Fabulous Histories Designed for the
Instruction of Children, Respecting
their Treatment of Animals* (Trimmer),
58, 136, 146n2

fairytales, 34n9, 86n8

Falwell, Jerry, 185, 187

family structure, 11, 114

fantasy literature, 74, 77

"fearful symmetry," 206–11, 209

feminism, 22, 28–29, 67, 101

Ferguson, Moira, 57, 67

Festival! (Lerner), 155–56, 157

festivals, 155–57

"A Few Thoughts about Birds,
Their Nests and Their Robbers"
(Russell), 136

Moore, Alan, (*continued*)
202; idealized characters of, 204–5;
Judgment Day, 213; and magic, 202;
and nostalgia, 211–13; paradox used
by, 213; *Promethea*, 200–1, 204–7,
206; and Romanticism, 200–1;
Swamp Thing, 202–3, 204; use of
form, 205–6, 206; *V for Vendetta*,
200, 210; *Watchmen*, 200–1, 206,
207–11, 212–13

Moorman, Mary, 9

Moral Majority, 185

morality: and bird-nesting, 129–31,
135–37; and children's moral state,
68–69; and economic conditions,
101; and fantasy, 82; and gender,
136, 145; and gossip, 100; and
magical storytelling, 72–73; moral
reasoning, 59; and slavery, 56–69.
See also ethical issues

More, Hannah, 32, 50

mortality, 81

Moss, Anita, 86n9

"mother wit," 93–94

"Mothers, Monsters, and Morals in
Victorian Fairy Tales" (Moss),
86n9

"Mozart Effect," 196–97

"Muddling Fact and Fiction and Policy"
(Kolata), 196

Murnane, Richard J., xvi

"My Heart Leaps Up" (Wordsworth),
xiii

Myers, Mitzi, 34n9, 41, 44, 47, 51

The Myth of the First Three Years (Bruer),
197

National System of Education, 50

natural freedom, xiii

A Natural History of Birds (Smith), 56,
57–58, 65

nature and natural world: in children's
literature, 172; in *Ida B*, 180, 181;
Rousseau's emphasis on, 137, 169,
171, 172, 174–75, 181; in *Skellig*,
174–75; in *Stargirl*, 177; in *Teletubbies*, 186–87

"The Negro Boy's Tale" (Opie), 69n6

Nesbit, E., 123

New Christy Minstrels, 158

Newbery, John, 130, 131

Newport Folk Festival, 155–56

News from Afar, 111

Nielsen, Aldon, 166n7

No Child Left Behind Act of 2001, xvi

Nodelman, Perry, xvii, 153, 165n1

Norton, Mary, 74

nostalgia, 152–55, 164, 165n2, 211–13

nurseries, 75

"Ode: Intimations of Immortality from
Recollections of Early Childhood"
(Wordsworth), xiii–xiv, 1, 174,
211–12

Of the Social Contract (Rousseau), xiii,
176, 179, 181

Old Manor House (Smith), 57

O'Malley, Andrew, xiv

"On the Education of the Poor"
(Edgeworth), 48–49, 53

On the Slave Trade (Coleridge), 62

"Only a Pawn in Their Game" (Dylan),
157

Opening the Nursery Door (Hilton, Styles
and Watson), 34n9

Opie, Amelia, 68–69, 69n6

Opie, Iona, 186

Opie, Peter, 186

primogeniture, 24

"The Princess and Curdie"
(MacDonald), 123

The Princess and the Goblin (MacDonald),
74, 82, 123

*The Private Memories and Confessions of a
Justified Sinner* (Hogg), 210

Prochaska, F. K., 125n8

Promethea (Moore, Williams, and Gray),
xxi, 200–1, 204–7, 206

Prometheus Unbound (Shelley), 203, 205

property rights, 24–25, 45–46, 65–67

Protestants, 111

publishing industry, 108, 130

punishment in children's literature,
171

Puritanism, xv

"The Purple Jar" (Edgeworth), 171

Quakers, 56

"The Rabbit" (Edgeworth), 40–41,
43–44, 47–48, 51

race issues, xv, 62–63. *See also* slavery

Raferty, Deirdre, 50

Ragged School Union Magazine, 105–8

Rainbow Quest (Cohen), 158

Raleigh, Walter, 113

Rambles Farther (Smith), 57–60, 65–67

Reading Comics (Wolk), 205

Rebecca of Sunnybrook Farm (Wiggin),
171

The Recluse (Wordsworth), 11

redemption themes, 75, 171

Reform Bill of 1832, 91

religion, 59, 105–23

Religious Tract Society, 111, 124n7

resentment, 20–33

resistance ideology, 25

Reveries of the Solitary Walker (Rousseau),
181

The Revolt of Islam (Shelley), 30–31

revolutionary change, 29

Reynolds, Malvina, 160

Rich, Adrienne, 91–92

Rideout, Victoria, 185, 190

"Rime of the Ancient Mariner"
(Coleridge), 12

Ritvo, Harriet, 42

A River Runs Through It (Maclean), 13

Roberts, Donald, 190

Robinson, John, 66

Robson, Catherine, 1–2

Roderick, Gordon, 140–41

Roland, 14n1

The Romantic Ideology (McGann), 200

Romantic Image (Kermode), 200

Romanticism: and apocalypse, 203–4;
and education policy, xvi, 51; and
gender oppression, 34n9; influence of, 200; and intergenerational
conflict, xx; and *Lyrical Ballads*,
21; and Moore, 200–1; and myth
of carefree childhood, xv; and
nostalgia, 211–13; and parental
responsibility, 3, 13; Romantic
childhood, 2, 20–23, 32–33; and
Swamp Thing, 202–3; and wanderer
figures, 28, 31

Romanticism and the Vocation of Childhood
(Plotz), 152–53

Rose, Jacqueline, xvii–xviii

Rousseau, Jean-Jacques: *Discourse on
the Origin and Foundation of Inequality
among Men*, 175, 176, 178; *Discourse
on the Sciences and the Arts*, 173; Edgeworth's reaction to, 45; educational
model of, 8, 169–71, 172–73, 174,

178; *Émile*, 8, 25, 45, 137, 169–70, 172–73, 174, 175, 177–78, 179, 181; emphasis on early years, xiii; on evolution, 176; and gender roles, 25–26; on goodness/innocence of children, 144, 169, 171, 179; on identification with community, 180; influence on children's literature, 170–71, 182; and modern home-schooling, xxi; and moral purity of children, 61, 68; natural-world emphasis of, 137, 169, 171, 172, 174–75, 181; *Of the Social Contract*, xiii, 176, 179, 181; on politics, 181; *Reveries of the Solitary Walker*, 181; on rules and obedience, 179–80; savage ideal of, 170, 171, 175–76, 178, 181

Rovee, Christopher Kent, 125n9

Roy, Malini, xx, 20–33

Rudd, David, xvii, 15n4

rules and obedience, 179–80

"Rumpelstiltskin" (Brothers Grimm), 82

Rural Walks (Smith), 58

Rushkoff, Douglas, 195

Russell, G., 136

Rzepka, Charles J., 11

"Sacrificial Sites, Place-Keeping, and 'Pre-History' in Wordsworth's 'Michael'" (Rzepka), 11

Saïd, Edward, xvii

"Sandman" (Hoffmann), 204

Sapiro, Virginia, 30

savage ideal, 170–71, 175–76, 178, 181

Scarr, Sandra, 15n5

Schacter, Daniel, xviii

Schor, Hilary, 95

science: bird-nesting as, 142–44, 145; in education, 140–41; popularization of, 141–42; Wordsworth on, 146n9

Scott-Heron, Gil, 194

Scottish Missionary Society, 111

"Seasons" (Flynn), 153–54

Second Discourse (Rousseau), 175, 176, 178

The Secret Garden (Burnett), 74, 86n1

secularism, 112, 113–14, 124n6

Select Magazine for the Instruction and Amusement of Young, 112

self-love, 177–78

Sesame Street, 191–93, 196

Shelley, Mary: and Coleridge's "Michael," 3; *Frankenstein*, 6, 204; *The Last Man*, 32

Shelley, Percy Bysshe: *The Defense of Poetry*, 28; *Prometheus Unbound*, 203, 205; *The Revolt of Islam*, 30–31; *Shelley's Mirrors of Love* (Bonca), 31

shipwrecks, 119

Short Residence (Wollstonecraft), 30

Simmel, Georg, 91

Sircar, Sanjay, 86n5

Skellig (Almond), 172, 173–76, 182

slavery, 9, 56–69, 69n6

"Sleeping Beauty," 82

Smith, Adam, 50–51, 57

Smith, Benjamin, 59, 67–68

Smith, Charlotte, 56–69; *Beachy Head and Other Poems*, 56; *Conversations Introducing Poetry*, 57; *Desmond*, 57; *Elegiac Sonnets*, 56–69; *Letters of a Solitary Wanderer*, 57; *A Natural History of Birds*, 56, 57–58, 65; *Old Manor House*, 57; *Rambles Farther*, 57–60, 65–67; *Rural Walks*, 58;